The Holocaust of Texts

The Holocaust of Texts

Genocide, Literature, and Personification   Amy Hungerford

The University of Chicago Press   Chicago and London

Amy Hungerford is assistant professor of English and American studies at
Yale University.

The University of Chicago Press, Chicago 60637
The University of Chicago Press, Ltd., London
© 2003 by The University of Chicago
All rights reserved. Published 2003
Printed in the United States of America
12 11 10 09 08 07 06 05 04 03   1 2 3 4 5

ISBN: 0-226-36076-8 (cloth)

An earlier version of chapter 3 appeared as "Surviving Rego Park: Holocaust
Theory from Art Spiegelman to Berel Lang," in *The Americanization of the
Holocaust,* edited by Hilene Flanzbaum (Baltimore: Johns Hopkins University
Press, 1999), 102–24, © 1999; it is reprinted here by permission of the Johns
Hopkins University Press. A portion of chapter 4 appeared in "Memorizing
Memory," *Yale Journal of Criticism* 14.1 (2001).

Figures 1 and 3 (see pages 74 and 89) are reprinted from *Maus I: A
Survivor's Tale / My Father Bleeds History,* by Art Spiegelman, © 1973, 1980,
1981, 1982, 1984, 1985, 1986 by Art Spiegelman. Used by permission of
Pantheon Books, a division of Random House, Inc. Figures 2, 4, and 5 (see
pages 86, 90, and 94) are reprinted from *Maus II: A Survivor's Tale / And
Here My Trouble Began,* by Art Spiegelman, © 1986, 1989, 1990, 1991 by
Art Spiegelman. Used by permission of Pantheon Books, a division of
Random House, Inc.

Library of Congress Cataloging-in-Publication Data

Hungerford, Amy.
    The holocaust of texts : genocide, literature, and personification / Amy
Hungerford.
        p. cm.
    Includes bibliographical references and index.
    ISBN: 0-226-36076-8 (alk. paper)
    1. American literature—20th century—History and criticism. 2. War in
literature. 3. World War, 1939–1945—United States—Literature and the
war. 4. Holocaust, Jewish (1939–1945), in literature. 5. Identity (Psychology) in literature. 6. Nuclear warfare in literature. 7. Personification in
literature. 8. Plath, Sylvia—Views on war. 9. Bellow, Saul—Views on
war. 10. Roth, Philip—Views on war. 11. Group identity in literature.
12. Genocide in literature. 13. Jews in literature. I. Title.

PS228. W37 H86 2003
810.9′358—dc21   2002006716

For P

Contents

Acknowledgments

This book could not have been written without the support, guidance—and even resistance—of many people. First among them are Walter Benn Michaels and Allen Grossman, who guided the project in its early stages, and Ruth Leys, who has been indispensable to my thinking on psychoanalysis. The questions they taught me to ask will remain with me for a long time. I also wish to thank the faculty and graduate students of the Johns Hopkins English department. During my time there as a student, they created an atmosphere in which my thinking was both challenged and encouraged with unmatched rigor and intensity. I am grateful that such a place exists and that I was lucky enough to learn there. Since then, I have benefited from the intelligence, generosity, and kindness of my colleagues at Yale University, especially Bill Deresiewicz, Elizabeth Dillon, Mary Floyd-Wilson, Laura Frost, Langdon Hammer, Michael Trask, Laura Wexler, and Sarah Winter. Each has read pieces of this book or discussed related issues with me and each has strengthened my thinking. Rebecca Boggs's careful reading of the manuscript at a late stage saved me from many technical errors and infelicities. And I am grateful for the kindness of strangers, as well—for the anonymous readers who reviewed the manuscript and whose detailed reports helped me to improve it. Several groups with whom I have shared parts of this work contributed significantly to its development. These include the Holocaust Working Group at Yale's Whitney Humanities Center, the New York Americanists' Group, and the scholars who gathered in May 2001 at the Center for Advanced Holocaust Studies at the U.S. Holocaust Memorial Museum for the museum's first literature symposium, "The Holocaust: Literature and Representation." For financial support for the publication of this study, I thank the Frederick W. Hilles Publication Fund of Yale University.

Jack Kerkering and Pericles Lewis deserve special acknowledgment. Each gave unstintingly of their time, their ideas, and their friendship as I worked on this project. Their willingness to discuss even the messiest and earliest versions of these pages made their help especially invaluable. Their intellectual companionship made the work a pleasure even at its most difficult moments.

Finally, I am grateful to my family: to my mother and sisters, for unflagging moral support; to Peter Chemery, for reminding me what was important in the world and for making so very many good dinners; to Clare Chemery, for arriving just as I was finishing this book and reminding me, if I needed it, that there is a great and joyful difference between a book and a baby.

On January 13, 1954, the American Jewish writer Meyer Levin placed an open letter on the theater page of the *New York Post*. Angry that his stage adaptation of Anne Frank's *The Diary of a Young Girl* had been rejected by the Broadway elite in favor of a rival script, he challenged the play's producer, Kermit Bloomgarden, with a pointed question: "Is it right for you to kill a play that others find deeply moving, and are eager to produce?" Levin's plea to the public, that they pressure Otto Frank and Bloomgarden to allow his adaptation a public hearing, closed by urging readers to "write or send this ad to Otto Frank . . . as a vote for a fair hearing before my play is killed."[1] The disagreement with Bloomgarden and Otto Frank that became so public in Levin's letter centered around the question of Jewishness, more specifically, the Jewishness of Anne Frank as depicted on the stage. In Levin's adaptation, Anne's Jewish identity was an important part of the story, highlighted in various parts of the play but most obviously in Anne's speech—taken almost verbatim from the diary—about the history of Jewish suffering. The family's capture by the Nazis, depicted at the close of the last act, drove home the terrible reality of that history. But in the play that was eventually produced, written by the husband and wife team of Frances Goodrich and Albert Hackett, Anne's Jewishness was muted, there was no explicit depiction of the Nazi raid on the Annex, and the play as a whole stressed the universal appeal of the young Anne's musings upon adolescence, family, and love and her optimism in the face of suffering.[2] For Levin, the difference between such a universalist adaptation and his particularistic one raised a moral issue, to be cast in the galvanizing terms of life and death, of killing and letting live. In private letters to Otto Frank, Levin spelled out the analogy implied by the language of killing we see in the *New York Post* letter, explicitly comparing his play to Anne herself and arguing that, like Anne, it was "created out of love" and deserved "a normal life and a normal death." Just as the Nazis had killed Anne, "their equivalent," he warned Anne's father, were about to kill his play.[3]

I recount this incident not because I wish to reevaluate the conflict between Levin and Broadway. Two books on the subject, Lawrence Graver's *An Obsession with Anne Frank* and Ralph Melnick's *The Stolen Legacy of Anne Frank*, have already told this story in all its details.[4] Rather, I am interested in Levin's notion, apparent in both the public letter and his private correspondence, that his play could be killed. For most, this has seemed a case of inappropriate emotional hyperbole. Otto Frank took issue with Levin's comparison between the play and Anne herself, and indeed, the extreme language of the *New York Post* ad and Levin's many later pleas won him few allies. Levin's rhetoric, apparently used for its shock value, became the sign of his obsession with the diary and his emotional instability. But what if we were to take Levin's claim seriously—and not simply as an uncomfortable choice of hyperbole? If we do, we can see that it suggests a complex set of beliefs about the relation between persons and the texts they produce, a set of beliefs that, I will argue over the course of this book, have been accepted more easily and more widely than the resistance to Levin's rhetoric would suggest.

Levin here imagines Anne Frank's diary as the equivalent of the living Anne Frank, whose death is in turn imagined not as the final event of her life but as an event that can be repeated, as a "murder" that can continue in 1950s America. And imagining Anne Frank's murder as repeated makes the second murder Levin invokes—the murder of his play—into something more, into a repetition and, indeed, an expansion of the Holocaust. What Levin imagines, then, is both the destruction and the creation of identity through the conflation of person and text: when the Jewishness of the diary is destroyed, producing the repeated murder of Anne Frank, Levin can create for himself what he seems to see as a newly authentic Jewishness by making him and his play, like Anne, victims of the Holocaust. The fact that Meyer Levin identified closely with the Holocaust is widely known, and the psychological power of that identification was admitted by Levin himself on and off throughout his life.[5] He was one of the first journalists to report on the opening of the concentration camps in Europe, and from that time on he devoted himself to telling the story directly or through his decades-long (and, he admitted in his own memoir, "obsessive") involvement with the dramatic adaptation of Anne Frank's *Diary*.[6] Levin is thus an early example of what has since become much more common. He was an American Jew who grew up ambivalent about his Jewishness and largely without religious training, who nevertheless found a powerful call to Jewish identity and solidarity in images of the Holocaust. The extreme identification we see in his claims about his murdered play was evidently the culmination of a much broader identificatory response.

By the 1970s, this kind of identification was commonplace enough for the novelist Philip Roth to make comic use of it. In *The Ghost Writer* (1979) the young writer Nathan Zuckerman, at odds with his family over a story they find anti-Semitic, writes a new story, inspired in part by the urging of his family and the local Jewish bigwig to prove his commitment to the Jewish community by going to see *The Diary of Anne Frank* on Broadway. In a new story (contained in the "Femme Fatale" chapter of Roth's novel), Nathan goes them one better. He imagines the fetching female protégée of his mentor E. I. Lonoff as a secretly surviving Anne Frank and proceeds to imagine himself married to her and to fantasize about his parents' consequent repentance. "Anne, . . . *the* Anne?" Nathan imagines his father saying with delight at his son's nuptial news; "How I have misunderstood my son."[7] Identifying with Anne through marriage and through their shared writerly vocation, Nathan becomes—in his fantasy at least—just as authentically Jewish as Meyer Levin, the man who, in the world outside Roth's novel, was responsible for the *Diary*'s American publication in the first place. Roth's parody suggests his discomfort with the notions of authenticity and the coerciveness entailed by this kind of identification, and I will argue in chapter 5 that *The Ghost Writer*, even in the fantasy about Anne Frank, ultimately works to resist such coercion by making Anne more importantly a writer than a survivor. For now it is enough to note that both Roth and Levin represent (in fiction and in life, respectively) public statements of Jewishness that rest upon identification with the Holocaust.

One need not commit to the extreme version of identification Levin lived out and Roth parodies in order to employ the logic of Levin's claim about the murdered diary. However one might come down on the appropriateness of equating the anti-Semitism of the Holocaust with the anti-Semitism of Broadway, and whatever the facts might be behind the rejection of Levin's adaptation of Anne Frank's *Diary*—positions and facts well documented and debated in Melnick's and Graver's accounts of Levin's story—his hyperbolic assertion and its implications exemplify what I will argue is a persistent set of beliefs about persons and texts in the postwar period. Thirty years later Art Spiegelman's graphic novel *Maus I: My Father Bleeds History,* concludes with the main character, Art, making a similar claim. Upon discovering that his mother's Holocaust diaries had been burned by his father, Vladek, Art calls Vladek a murderer. And we see such conflation between the life of the person and representation of this particular kind—representation that is taken to denote or contain one's identity—in discourse ranging from the poetry of Sylvia Plath to the "Silence = Death" slogan used by AIDS activists in the 1980s and 1990s.[8]

Postwar criticism and literary theory has shared this tendency to imagine the literary text as if it bore significant characteristics of persons, despite the effort made in two of the most powerful twentieth-century critical movements, New Criticism and deconstruction, to limit and critique the relationship between persons and texts.[9] Steven Knapp has pointed out how W. K. Wimsatt, in *The Verbal Icon* (a seminal work of New Criticism), imagines the literary text as embodied and self-conscious. Knapp argues, for example, that Wimsatt presents us with a version of the concrete universal that treats "a symbol as if it could itself have—or perhaps as if it could *be*—an experience, which would amount to treating it as if it could have or be a body."[10] Indeed, in one of the best-known lines in Wimsatt and Monroe Beardsley's classic essay, "The Intentional Fallacy," the authors use the figure of personification to advance their argument against referring to the author's intentions or the critic's historical knowledge as the basis for interpreting the text: "The poem is not the critic's own and not the author's (it is detached from the author at birth and goes about the world beyond his power to intend about it or control it)."[11] Wimsatt and Beardsley go on to say that the poem is a public possession that is most importantly "about the human being," but we can see in the metaphor of birth that the difference between being "about" and simply "being" a human being has already begun to erode. The implication of this slippage, for Knapp reading Wimsatt four decades later, is that the things New Critics claim are characteristic of the literary become "trivially ordinary"; the literary character's "concrete universality comes to seem indistinguishable from the concrete universality already built into our perception of actual persons."[12] For Knapp this kind of personification renders literature "trivially ordinary" because it fails to make its case for the distinctiveness and value of the literary in comparison to any other kind of discourse. It fails, that is, to answer the question Knapp struggles with in *Literary Interest*, about why we are interested in literature at all. In the context of my readings, what for Knapp is trivial suggests a culturally and philosophically significant tendency in New Criticism, extended and elaborated in its theoretical and literary descendants: a tendency to personify the literary text.

For deconstruction, a most influential formalist descendant of New Criticism, the personified text has always served a special function. This is not only because Paul de Man declared that personification was the "master trope" of literary language, an idea developed most fully by J. Hillis Miller in his *Versions of Pygmalion*.[13] Personification represented for deconstructive critics the very fantasy about language that they were trying to deconstruct, the fantasy of referentiality and human presence. But I will show in the chapters that follow that personification plays a more important role in deconstructive thought when it is not the explicit subject of such writing—a role that becomes most evident in the work of later psychoanalytic critics such as Jacqueline Rose and Shoshana Felman who deploy deconstructive methods. In trying to produce a critique of personification, critics like de Man, Miller, and Jacques Derrida finally allow personification to become all the more powerful in the work of this later generation of critics. In arguing for the independence of language from persons and their intentions and for the impossibility of finding anything but the sign of the lack of human presence in language described as above all mechanical (or playful), deconstructive critics imagined a text that was radically autonomous, even active. And in this regard they were following the lead, or perhaps I should say extending the lead, of the New Criticism, which, as we have seen, imagined texts as going about the world unhindered by the merely contingent biography or unrecoverable intentions of the author. Instances of the personified text like those I mentioned at the start preserve this postwar theoretical emphasis on language as in some sense independent of persons and their intentions—an emphasis apparent not only in literary criticism but also long-noted in the experimental fiction of writers such as William Burroughs, John Barth, Thomas Pynchon, and Don DeLillo. At the same time, because of its very autonomy, language imagined in this way provides a site where one can locate the ethnic or racial identities we ordinarily describe as belonging to persons. It is telling, for example, that such identities are described, in discussions of multiculturalism, as "life-scripts," and that Judith Butler, in *Bodies That Matter*, theorizes the body as inextricable from the discourse of gender identities.[14]

The text that can bear cultural identity, and more specifically, the text that can then, in this capacity, be murdered, is thus, I will argue, important to the history of criticism in the second half of the twentieth century. And while this alone might explain why we should take Meyer Levin's hyperbole seriously and find Wimsatt's version of the concrete universal more than trivial, there are yet broader implications that arise from the personified text. In the chapters that follow, I will show how such conflations of text and person have come to structure postwar discourse about destruction of human life on the massive scale that World War II—with the Nazi genocide of the Jews on one hand and the United States' use of atomic weapons on the other—suddenly made imaginable. While it would be a mistake to claim that the conflation of life and self-expression, of death and the destruction or blockage of representation, or more generally, of person and text is always made in conjunction with claims about genocide, the various instances of the personified text that I take up over the course of this analysis suggest that the conflation of texts and persons has nevertheless been crucial to postmodern understandings of both nuclear holocaust and ethnic holocaust.

This is not just because, as Alvin Rosenfeld pointed out some time ago in *A Double Dying*, writing about the Holocaust by Jewish authors sometimes dramatizes the relationship between the Jewish people and their textual tradition and links the destruction of Jewish libraries with the destruction of the Jewish people themselves.[15] The identification of person and text, that is, appears not only in the writing of those who take the Holocaust as their subject but also appears in the writing of critics interested in what they take to be the theoretical problems raised by the Holocaust. George Steiner, for instance, in thinking through the relation between author and text, criticizes Sylvia Plath for having created poetic speakers who identify with Holocaust victims when she herself was not Jewish, suggesting that Plath herself and her representations *should* correspond to one another in this respect. Even in discourse that does not take genocide as its subject in a literal or theoretical way, we see a connection between the impulse to personify texts and notions of holocaust. Sylvia Plath, for whom personification of the poem was central to her desire for and her efforts to produce literary fame, has gained at least an element of that fame (or infamy) by employing the Holocaust imagery with which Steiner takes issue. Equally, some AIDS activists have claimed not only that "Silence = Death" but also that the epidemic could be thought of as the "gay holocaust."[16] This book thus focuses not simply or primarily on personification *in* poems or novels but on the personification *of* poems and novels, and of texts in general, because, as I shall argue, the idea of personification is required in order to make sense of what would otherwise be the incomprehensible notion of a murdered text. And it is that notion that lies at the heart of our contemporary understanding of genocide.

The idea of the murdered text can be found at the very origin of the post–World War II legal and political discourse about genocide. If genocide is, as Senator Jacob Javits remarked in 1977, "murder and more," we were challenged after World War II to specify and codify what that "more" might be. While Hannah Arendt gave one answer to the question in *Eichmann in Jerusalem* (1963)—arguing that genocide is a "crime against the human status"— a more common answer can be found in the position that Arendt described Israel taking when its leaders argued that they must try Eichmann in a Jewish court because his crimes were against the Jewish people. According to this argument, genocide threatens not the "human status," but the particularity of a culture. Therefore, the argument goes, representatives of the particular culture or nation must administer justice. While the Israeli court went to some lengths to find Eichmann guilty of an actual act of murder in addition to acts of destroying whole Jewish communities (not directly by murder but through deportation to the site of murder), the question of what exactly one must be guilty of to be guilty of genocide haunted the trial throughout and preoccupies Arendt's analysis of it. Did Eichmann need to be sadistic, to have taken life with his own hands and with pleasure, in order to be guilty of genocide? While the premise of the Israeli trial suggests not, suggests instead that cultural destruction defined the crime and thus justified a Jewish trial, the prosecutor's and many witnesses' effort to cast Eichmann as a sadist indicates otherwise. Somehow, it seemed, Eichmann must be guilty of the kinds of acts we have always called murderous in order to be guilty of genocide.[17]

This tension, evident in the trial itself and in Arendt's reflections, is intrinsic to the notion of genocide as such. Though legal definitions of genocide grounded in the U.N. Genocide Convention of 1948 in most cases require the actual destruction of persons or their physical harm, what we might call cultural genocide has nevertheless always been thought of as part of the crime. Raphael Lemkin, the Polish jurist who coined the term "genocide" in 1944, did so by combining two kinds of crimes he had articulated earlier, in the 1930s: barbarity—"oppressive and destructive actions directed against individuals as members of a national, religious, or racial group"—and vandalism—"malicious destruction of works of art and culture" that "represent the specific creation of the genius of such groups."[18] The concept of genocide was to encompass both the personal destruction of "barbarity" and the cultural destruction of "vandalism." The language of the first resolution regarding genocide passed by the United Nations General Assembly united these ideas but maintained the language and the rubric of classically defined murder: the opening lines of Resolution 96 (I) (1946) declared that "genocide is the denial of the right of existence of entire human groups, as homicide is the denial of the right to live of individual human beings."[19] The U.N. Genocide Convention that followed from Resolution 96 (I), by including as genocidal crimes acts like the forced adoption outside the group of children of the group or the infliction of mental harm, continued to suggest that the death of persons was not required in the crime of genocide. And that possibility became the sticking point for opponents of ratification in the United States, where conservatives feared that school segregation and Southern racism against blacks—not to mention lynching—might be cast as genocidal.[20]

Genocide as described in the convention clearly applied not just to state policies like the Nazi extermination of the Jews; after the threat of nuclear war was made apparent at Hiroshima and the Cold War set in, the ideas expressed in the convention seemed to describe also the outcome of this new kind of war. This sense increased as nuclear weapons became more sophisticated and more deadly and their distinction from conventional weapons began to be debated, for if a few such weapons could wipe out all the major cities of a given country, would this not be an example of genocide on a par with—or perhaps even exceeding—the destruction of Jewish people during World War II? In this more universalist vision of genocide, we can see the same distinction between the destruction of persons and the destruction of culture, as well as the conflation of the two, that is evident in the particularist version. In discourse about nuclear war, genocide is cast as the destruction either of the West (this view was more prevalent in the 1950s and 1960s) or of the human race in its entirety (a view that became more widespread as weapons increased in power and number). The nuclear arms protest slogan "Better red than dead," encapsulates the problem succinctly. In asking which fate was worse, death or the destruction of Western capitalist democracy, people also asked a question about what nuclear war destroys. Is its primary victim—in moral terms—a national culture and its political system, or biological life? (I take up part of the history of this question in chapter 2.) When we begin to think about the destruction of persons on a massive scale, we thus also begin to think about the relative value of persons and of the culture they create. And further, we begin to think about whether we can separate the concept of the person from the concept of a culturally defined personal identity.

The chapters that follow together make clear how the point of intersection I have identified between literary discourse and discourse about genocide—the personified text—plays a historically specific role in shaping our thinking on particular postwar political and cultural issues. This is not to say, though, that the personified text was invented in the postwar period, for previous instances of such personification suggest that it has not only existed but has also been put to some of the same uses (if not with the same outcomes) as we see after World War II.

In religious tradition, both Jewish and Christian, the words of God have long been personified. In Jewish practice, for example, the Torah scroll is adorned like a bride, swaddled like a baby, and greeted in procession by the congregation.[21] In the Gospel of John, Christ is described as "the Word made flesh" that comes to dwell among us. In the Western literary tradition, the personified text can be found early and often, and some of the most famous examples reveal the ways that religious belief continues to underwrite the image. In Cervantes, a priest conducts an inquisition of Don Quixote's library, calling the offending books by name and burning many for their failures of orthodoxy. The scene is a parody of the idea that the person is the text they write, that punishing the text could be equivalent to punishing the author. In Milton's "Areopagitica" books are also imagined as the equivalent of persons vulnerable to law. Arguing against restrictive licensing codes, Milton suggests that "unless wariness be used, as good almost kill a man as kill a good book: who kills a man kills a reasonable creature, God's image; but he who destroys a good book, kills reason itself, kills the image of God, as it were, in the eye."[22] In poetic and (later) novelistic *envoi,* starting at least as early as Chaucer, books are admonished as well- or ill-formed children to go out into the world to do their work, suggesting that we did not need to wait for Wimsatt and Beardsley to declare the book's human independence. In Wordsworth, landscape is persistently personified, giving us the pathetic fallacy, and one might argue that since landscape is a figure also for the poetic text (one thinks here of the inscribed Salisbury Plain, for example) that Wordsworth is animating not just landscape but language, imbuing all things in the poet's world with the poet's affect.[23]

Without developing detailed readings of each of these instances, it may yet be useful to outline the structure and purposes of the examples I have mentioned as a way of noting both the continuities and the discontinuities of this tradition with the personified texts mobilized in the postwar period. In the scene from *Don Quixote,* books take on the spiritual disposition of persons and can therefore be condemned for religious crimes such as heresy that would seem to apply only to beings that possess both minds and souls. The parody of inquisition that ensues allows Cervantes to critique the Church's prosecutorial excesses, and the scene succeeds as a parody and a critique only if we agree that it is absurd to treat books like persons, to grant them a spiritual status. For Milton, the spiritual status of the book is, on the contrary, to be taken seriously. The book takes on the aspect of personhood that defines the human being in Genesis—the image of God, defined by subsequent theology and philosophy as reason. In a way, Milton may be understood to be employing personification in the way we see it used from Spenser on through the eighteenth century, where it makes an abstraction such as virtue or chastity into a character (usually called Virtue or Chastity). Milton makes both persons and books the personifications of reason. The person and the book both embody that abstraction, albeit in different ways, and make it an agent in the world. (He thus avoids the sense of absurdity so apparent in Cervantes's comical scene, since books and persons are not being treated as alike in a material sense.) By personifying books in this way, as embodying the element of persons marked as most divine, Milton makes it difficult for opponents to argue, among other things, that Christian morality could be the basis for licensing laws. Finally, Wordsworth's personifications come a step closer to the postwar instances I examine in that they serve to expand and exalt not only poetic power in general but also Wordsworth's own subjectivity, as contained in the details of his particular life. In this sense the *Prelude,* which is replete with both personification and autobiographical detail, suggests that the very proximity of the writer and the text blurs the boundary between them (that proximity is figured both in the biographical detail and the immersion of the speaker in a landscape that is imagined as the poetic text itself). That kind of blurring is evident in some of the examples I mentioned briefly at the beginning: in Plath's personified and autobiographical poems and in the personification of diaries in Levin and Spiegelman.

What many of these earlier examples have in common with postwar personification of texts is the effort to articulate the value of writing, especially when it is perceived to be threatened. Writers turn to personification when they need to assert the importance of a literary project vis-à-vis other kinds of projects and demands. The divinity associated with the word in the religious examples constitutes the highest value one can confer; when that divinity is transferred to all persons, and then, through personification, to all texts (as it is in *Areopagitica*), all texts become sacred in the way persons are sacred. While the postwar examples I examine are largely secular themselves and arise in a largely secular culture, the highest cultural or moral value remains attached if not to God then to the person. Advocates of multiculturalism in the 1980s take this logic a step further. Recognizing first that Western traditions of valuing the person do not value all persons equally, multiculturalism suggests a way to compensate for this by building up the cultural and political value of particular kinds of persons. As the culture wars of the 1980s and 1990s demonstrated, this revaluation was often fought for on the syllabi of English courses, testifying to how the value of persons remains bound up with the value of texts. In ways that will become clear in the individual chapters of this book, the highest cultural value is assigned not simply to persons in the humanistic sense but to persons as embodying cultural identities (hence the ways identity is entwined with personification in the examples of Levin and Roth). Personification of texts both mobilizes that cultural value for the text and mirrors the structure of the valuation itself, for what are cultural identities if not a kind of text imagined as embodied in particular persons?

The culture wars that solidified the importance of such identities in American public life coincided with a historical shift in the character and uses of personification that will become evident across and between the chapters of this book. During the Cold War, a liberal humanism prevailed that emphasized the importance of democracy, freedom, and equality at the expense of recognizing the institutional and cultural differences that kept women and people of color from having equal access to those very goods. As Peter Novick has explained, discourse about the Holocaust during this time followed suit, focusing less on the specificity of Jewish suffering and the dangers of state-sponsored racism than on the suffering of the individual under a totalitarian state. Novick argues that this emphasis shifted in response to changes in Cold War political dynamics, eventually resulting, after 1989, in the full-fledged embrace of the Holocaust as a defining element of Jewish identity within the context of multiculturalism.[24] Earlier postwar examples of personified texts and those throughout the period that are associated with worries about nuclear war—such as those we encounter in Ray Bradbury's *Fahrenheit 451* or in Jonathan Schell's antinuclear writing—tend to take a liberal humanist view of the personhood conferred upon the text. Later examples, generally speaking, confer multiculturalism's particularistic identities.

It is this particularism that distinguishes postwar personification from the examples from other centuries that I discussed above, though we can see the seeds of both particularism and the idea of genocide as early as Cervantes. The Inquisition certainly persecuted Jews in a way that suggested their vulnerability as a people and not simply as a religious group, since it was instituted in part to determine which of the so-called New Christians were in fact crypto-Jews, relying on "pure blood" laws in addition to tests of belief or daily practices to draw the distinction. As Jerome Friedman has argued, the very success of earlier waves of forced and voluntary conversion—which produced a great number of sincere Christians among the descendants of *conversos* and among *conversos* themselves—gave rise to the anxiety that somehow Jewish blood might be impervious to baptism. Sixteenth-century Spain marks a time and place where the idea that one could convert to save oneself from death began to transform into the idea that ancestry and blood, rather than belief, makes one Christian or Jew. Remaining interest in belief, combined with the newly racial understanding of New Christians, marks the Inquisition as both distinct from and an early version of the twentieth-century examples of genocide I focus on (indeed, Sancho Panza exhibits this prejudice against converted Jews).[25] No Jew could avoid death under Nazi rule by converting, because the kind of prejudice we see against New Christians had, by the twentieth century, become reified and codified by nineteenth-century racial science. This racial or ethnic particularism defines the twentieth-century discourse about genocide and is reflected in the moments of personification that accompany it, despite what I have said about liberal humanist understandings of the crime. Even liberal humanist writers produce early versions of the particularistic logic of multiculturalism whenever personification of texts appears. For instance, the discussion in chapter 2 reveals that Bradbury's humanist vision of the personified text is built upon imagery that suggests personified texts are more like the Jewish people in particular than humanity in general. Jacques Derrida, trying to articulate a theoretical understanding of the universal nuclear threat turns, for a model of that threat, to the experience of specific identity groups. The very idea of genocide as described in the Genocide Convention and formulated in countless discussions of nuclear and ethnic holocaust puts in place a dual logic about representations and persons: personhood consists most importantly in circumscribed cultural identities; therefore, destroying particular cultures (or their cultural products) is equivalent to destroying persons.

I am making the claim, then, that understandings of literature and understandings of holocaust are connected by certain beliefs about the nature of representation and its relation to persons in the second half of the twentieth century. Thus, while I demonstrate the importance of the personified text for our understanding of genocide, I am also arguing that the connection we find between literature and holocaust produces the convergence of two of the dominant forces shaping the study of literature since the Second World War: the theoretical phenomena of New Criticism and deconstruction and the social and political phenomenon of multiculturalism. They converge because the contemporary conception of genocide—the murder not simply of persons but of a people and its culture—relies on and gives a special urgency to the claims that multiculturalism makes about the centrality of racial and ethnic identity to human subjectivity and to the claims about literature that follow in turn.

~~~~~~~~~~~

Undertaken in these terms, such an analysis constitutes a revision of three specific bodies of scholarly work: general critical accounts of post-1945 American literature, more specific studies that have sought to detail the importance of trauma and crisis in literature of this period, and the branch of what we have come to call Holocaust Studies that deals with literary representations of the Holocaust.

General accounts of post-1945 American literature have tended to bracket the question of the Holocaust or nuclear genocide, even when the history of the Cold War is mapped onto the literary history being given. In a collection of essays on post-1945 American literature, entitled *Traditions, Voices, and Dreams* (1995), for example, the Holocaust is mentioned only in passing, in an essay on Jewish writers. A separate essay on Philip Roth and Cynthia Ozick (who has come to be closely associated with writing about the Holocaust both because of her novella *The Shawl* and because of her writing on the subject in venues like the *New Yorker*) does not mention the Holocaust at all. The fact that nuclear threat dominated significant parts of this period is even less apparent in these essays. Wendy Steiner, in her discussion of American fiction from the 1960s through the 1990s in volume 7 of the *Cambridge History of American Literature* (1999) assigns the Holocaust and the Cold War greater importance, going so far as to claim that the Holocaust is central to postmodern fiction, but her chapters do little more than raise interesting questions about how that is so. On the other hand, Kalí Tal, in *Worlds of Hurt* (1996), asserts the centrality of the Holocaust (as well as the trauma of the Vietnam War and the abuse of women and children) by structuring her readings of post–World War II American literature and culture around these specific instances of trauma.[26] Likewise, Kirby Farrell, in *Post-traumatic Culture: Injury and Interpretation in the Nineties* (1998), analyzes thematic instances of trauma in American literature and culture, choosing to focus not only on the trauma of the Holocaust, Vietnam, and sexual abuse, all very much present in public discourse of the 1990s, but also on thematic instances of violence and trauma in literature from the 1890s.[27]

By contrast with the work of Tal and Farrell and those who study the literary representation of the Holocaust in novels, poetry, and survivor memoirs, I seek in the present analysis less to understand how traumatic events are imagined in this period than to understand how the idea of such events has structured, and is structured by, our beliefs about representation and persons. Holocaust Studies, despite its narrower focus on the writing of survivors and on literature that takes the Holocaust as its theme or setting, has opened up the possibility that genocide has an impact on our beliefs about representation, an idea I want to take in a new direction.

Scholars in Holocaust Studies have opened up this possibility by persistently taking up the question of representability (frequently, the question of whether the Holocaust is representable at all). Both historians and literary critics who write about the Holocaust, for example, have found in deconstruction's emphasis on absence and unspeakability a way of understanding language that seems to mirror the absence of the millions murdered in the Nazi genocide. This is especially apparent in Shoshana Felman's readings of Paul Celan in *Testimony*. Sara Horowitz, though she is not espousing a strictly deconstructionist view of language, centers her study *Voicing the Void* on the trope of unspeakability in Holocaust fiction, casting this trope as the outstanding contribution that fiction, and literature more generally, can make to our understanding of the Holocaust. Even critics who, like Lawrence Langer, resist the application of literary theory to accounts of the Holocaust continue to refer to suffering that stands outside of language, a concept that brings in the questions literary theory raises even though the critic does not turn to theory for answers. And deconstruction is not the only theory relating to language that Holocaust Studies has incorporated. The theoretical interest in narrative and how it determines meaning—an interest related to deconstruction but not equivalent to it, developed in the work of Michel Foucault, Hayden White, and many feminist critics—also informs scholars' attempts to decide whether the Holocaust could or should ever be thought of as recoverable through the making of meaning. Some scholars, such as Michael Rothberg in his *Traumatic Realism,* move out from claims about Holocaust literature to claims about postwar literature as such; others, like Horowitz, speak more to those interested in how the Holocaust itself, as a historical event or set of events, may be understood (one of her goals, for example, is to demonstrate why and how Holocaust literature can lead us to insights about the Holocaust that history-writing alone cannot reveal). In either case, the work of Holocaust Studies scholars who think specifically about literature or the literary aspects of survivor testimony, when taken together, makes an implicit claim about the importance of genocide to our understanding of the literary in this period.[28]

The value and the influence of this work is evident in Wendy Steiner's essay in the *Cambridge History*. That essay is a precursor for the kind of account I am constructing, despite the fact that she does not fully develop her argument about the importance of the Holocaust to literature in this period. Her argument is nevertheless worth looking at closely, for it reveals, first of all, how assumptions developed in Holocaust Studies have come to hold a place in literary-critical discourse. Steiner writes that "the job of assimilating this nightmare [the Holocaust] had barely begun in 1960s fiction, and even with D. M. Thomas's *The White Hotel* (1981) and William Styron's *Sophie's Choice* (1979), and other harrowing novels of recent years, the Holocaust is still an 'unspeakable' reality." She goes on to cite George Steiner's assertion that the aftermath of the war was characterized by "the shrinking of the sphere of the verbal . . . , the unspeakable thought of Auschwitz, and hence the expansion of the domain of silence."[29] This kind of claim about silence and the limitations of language after the Holocaust is commonplace among those who write about the Nazi genocide of the Jews, as I have suggested; I want to point out first, then, how that assumption (here attributed to George Steiner, though there are many writers Wendy Steiner could have invoked, starting with Theodor Adorno and Celan) underlies not only a local claim about how the Holocaust has been dealt with in the American novel since the 1960s, but also a much more general claim about the character of fiction in this period. This claim is made clear when Steiner goes on, in the next sentence, to argue that the Vietnam War brought home the tension between fact and fiction, between representation and the unspeakable, that the Holocaust had engendered. "As the reportage of that war increased," Steiner writes, "Americans felt themselves implicated in events of equal horror to the Holocaust, surpassing the ugliness of any fictional imaginings." She suggests that the Holocaust was the "most important 'proof' of the merging of fact and fiction"—a merging undeniably important to postmodernism—because "in Nazi Germany the unimaginable became real."[30]

This claim about unspeakability and the unimaginable condenses a number of assumptions that I find difficult to sort out. If fact and fiction merged in the Holocaust and in Vietnam, would it not be because what Steiner calls here "unimaginable" had indeed been imagined in our darkest fictions (Kafka comes to mind), but had never, on a large scale, been lived out? I take this condensation and its attendant difficulty as testimony to the way assumptions about the unspeakability of the Holocaust have been assimilated and then extended by critical discourse about the literary, for this not-fully-explained moment comes as an anomaly in Steiner's chapters on postmodern fictions, which are both analytically brilliant and lucidly argued. But my point about the swift acceptance of concepts like unspeakability reveals only half the story about how the work of scholars such as George Steiner who are concerned specifically with the Holocaust has played a role in the way we think about literary history in this period—for despite the difficulty in understanding precisely what Wendy Steiner means by the reference to the "unspeakable" or the "unimaginable," her claim about the relations between the Holocaust, the Vietnam War, and the blurring of fact and fiction in postmodern writing takes seriously the idea that literary history must take the fact of genocide into account. And this idea, as I have indicated, owes much to the work of scholars such as Lawrence Langer, Alvin Rosenfeld, Geoffrey Hartman, Marianne Hirsch, Michael Rothberg, James Young, Sidra Ezrahi, and Sara Horowitz whose effort is not, like Steiner's, to account for the sweep of post-war American literary history, but to interrogate representation of the Holocaust specifically.

Indeed, by taking the Holocaust seriously within such a survey, Steiner begins to posit the kind of connection I seek to construct in these pages between the idea of holocaust and literary history since 1945. Steiner starts off in the vein of Tal and Farrell, by suggesting that the "assimilation" of the Holocaust in the literary realm has something to do with thematic reflections upon those events—with novels on the model of *The White Hotel* or *Sophie's Choice*. She goes on to suggest, as Tal and Farrell do, that the questions raised by the Holocaust are in fact raised as well by other historical contingencies of the period. Steiner departs from these two critics, however, by suggesting that the implications of such events center not so much on our understanding of trauma or of politically motivated violence as on our understanding of the relation between fact and fiction in postmodern writing. What Steiner suggests, then, is that the impact of the Holocaust and the Vietnam War can be seen in novels that ostensibly have nothing to do with either event.

Though Steiner does not connect this position, as I do, with the phenomenon of the personified text, she does nevertheless mark fetishization (the psychoanalytical equivalent of personification) as a central characteristic of the novels in this period. She notes as well, as I will, that the divide between the experimental fiction of writers like John Hawkes and John Barth—what she describes as the conservative avant-garde—and the writing of women and people of color—what she sees as a radical traditionalism—is in fact a false one. She demonstrates, for instance, how Thomas Pynchon, usually categorized with the high-prestige experimentalists, takes up questions about feminine subjectivity in *The Crying of Lot 49*. Equally, she shows how writers like Philip Roth, Louise Erdrich, and Annie Proulx, generally assigned to the lower-prestige, radical traditionalist category, engage questions of reading and self-reflexivity that have been thought the property of the experimentalists and of literary theory. Steiner's emphasis on fetishization and her effort to undo the false dichotomy between experimentalists and women and writers of color (writers whose work is often taken up with questions of identity) lays some of the foundation for my own work. The personified texts I describe in these chapters reveal how the larger currents that Steiner sets out do not simply share space in this period, but are specifically, necessarily, and philosophically bound up with one another.

~~~~~~~~~

Because I have not organized this book chronologically, because the kinds of texts I deal with in each chapter may seem odd bedfellows, and because I advance a critique of the personified text that some may find difficult to accept, I want briefly to lay out the argument and structure of each chapter, in hopes that having once seen the overall structure of the book, readers will find its turns easier to follow. I will demonstrate as I go along how the chapters excavate a common logic of personification, how they together constitute a historical narrative of sorts, and how they raise recurring larger questions of literary, ethical, and political importance. I will also outline the critique of the personified text that I advance in the later chapters and suggest in conclusion both the implications of that critique and the ways it may be misunderstood.

Each of the chapters in this study takes up a different set of instances in which we see personified texts. It will quickly become apparent that by *personification* I do not mean just one thing. Rather, personification as I understand it in this analysis represents a set of strategies by which something ordinarily thought to be particular to conscious (or, in some cases, merely living) beings comes to be assigned to a text. That might mean, for example, that the text is imagined as having a body, as being aware of its own mortality, as having a psyche, as having the capacity to have or embody experience, or as bearing the highest moral value relative to other objects in the world. These differences allow personification of texts to serve various purposes in discourse about genocide, in discourse about literature, and in discourse that takes up questions of identity and of cultural value.

In chapter 1, I show how criticism of Sylvia Plath's poetry, in focusing on questions about Holocaust imagery in her work, has evolved since the 1960s from criticism that takes up Plath's biography to criticism that, in eschewing the biographical, transforms Plath's poems themselves into something like persons—specifically, autonomous psychic entities that exist in the world independent of any particular historical person. I argue that, while Plath herself imagined her poems as proxies for her person, she thought of them as very much attached to herself, for it was through that attachment that she could hope to gain the fame she so desired: the poem's fame and recognition, because the poem itself stood as her proxy, would become her own. I argue that the psychoanalytic critic Jacqueline Rose revises Plath's version of the personified poem by freeing it from Plath herself, presenting the texts instead as dynamic psyches in their own right. In the course of showing what Plath and her critics have thought about the relationship between writing and life, I seek to show that the transformation of the text into a psyche serves certain literary-critical purposes. Specifically, making claims about the relationship between the writer and her work allows Plath and her critics to make claims about the value of her work that they could not make otherwise—whether that value is in the end positive or negative. Thus, chapter 1 not only shows what several related versions of the personified text look like, and how ideas about personification are articulated by a group of critics from the 1960s through the 1990s, but also presents some of the political and cultural uses to which the personified text has been put. Two of the critics I consider, for example, use personification to make a case for the importance of Plath's identity as a woman in evaluating her work.

Chapter 2 focuses more closely on such political and cultural uses of the personified text. It takes up not a body of work by and about one writer, but a set of texts from various corners of public discourse that all engage the idea of nuclear holocaust from points of view that combine political and literary interests. As in the first chapter, these texts represent a trajectory in time, from Ray Bradbury's 1953 novel *Fahrenheit 451*, through the writings of nuclear analyst Herman Kahn in the early 1960s, to antinuclear writing by Jonathan Schell and a theoretical essay by Jacques Derrida from the 1980s. I bring these writers together not because they influence each other or are in conversation with each other, as the critics of Plath are—indeed, the later writers in this chapter may never have read the earlier ones—but because they make explicit a set of logical positions about the relationship not only between texts and persons but also between the destruction of culture and the destruction of persons. Personification in this chapter does not produce texts that are living yet disembodied psyches, as it does for Jacqueline Rose at the end of chapter 1. Rather, I show how, particularly for writers in the 1980s, it produces texts that are embodied and thus, like persons, mortal and vulnerable to extinction. The similarity between the case of Plath and the case of these nuclear writers lies in the fact that for the nuclear writers, as for Plath and her critics, personification of the text underlies claims about the value of literary enterprises or textual production more generally—be it a book on nuclear outcomes, an archive of literary texts, or a school of criticism such as deconstruction. Chapter 2 also begins to argue that deconstruction, despite its practitioners' explicit intention to mount a critique of the personified text, ends up laying the groundwork for more powerful instances of such personification. I detail those later instances in chapter 4.

The third chapter focuses not on nuclear holocaust but on what has come to be known as *the* Holocaust, the Nazi genocide of the Jews. Here again I bring together writers who may have little to do with each other institutionally or experientially—and indeed, who would seem to disagree with each other sharply about the status of literature in relation to the Holocaust. But as in the case of the writing I consider in chapter 2, the representations I examine in chapter 3 articulate a shared logic by which texts are personified. Taking up the work of Art Spiegelman, historian and philosopher Berel Lang, Steven Spielberg's *Schindler's List,* and the United States Holocaust Memorial Museum, I argue that these representations of and about the Holocaust produce a conflation of texts and things that are not texts—including persons, historical events, and experience itself. In doing so, these representations attempt to make the Holocaust transmissible to a generation of people (both Jews and non-Jews) who could not have experienced it. This chapter shifts the historical focus of the discussion more exclusively to the 1980s and 1990s, where it will remain through chapter 4, and begins to reveal my own critique of the personified text. The analysis in this chapter allows us to ask questions that will return throughout the chapters that follow: Why must we "remember" the Holocaust rather than "learn" about it? Why should any particular culture survive? Why do we want to imagine that the experience of trauma and suffering is transmissible, from father to son, from history to the historian, from the dead to the living? What are the consequences of making identification the privileged model for how we understand things outside ourselves and our experience?

Chapter 4, in focusing on the literary-critical (as distinct from the clinical) version of trauma theory that became influential in the early 1990s, shows how such questions are answered by critics trained in and committed to the theoretical positions of Paul de Man, Jacques Derrida, J. Hillis Miller, and others. The later generation of critics combines deconstructive theory with concern about the trauma of the Holocaust and of genocide in general to produce the most extreme form of the personified text. In this chapter I show how the trauma theory of Shoshana Felman and Cathy Caruth imagines texts as traumatic experience itself, thus transmissible from person to person through reading. I show how these critics' theoretical positions share the logic about texts and persons that underwrites the fake Holocaust memoir of Binjamin Wilkomirski, whose *Fragments* (1996) both embodies and thematizes the relationship between language and experience that is posited by trauma theory, and in strikingly similar terms. As I extend the critique of personification that I began to make more explicit in the previous chapter, I raise questions about the ethics of understanding both trauma and texts in this way. The case of Wilkomirski—who many suspect fabricated his Holocaust past in order to make his life seem more significant—brings those ethical questions to the fore.

The final chapter returns to the wider historical trajectory that characterizes the first two chapters of the book, as I describe an alternative understanding of the relation between persons and texts as articulated in the work of Saul Bellow and Philip Roth. I argue that these writers present us with a relationship between persons and texts that avoids the pitfalls of the kind of personification I critique in chapters 3 and 4. Bellow and Roth represent ways of thinking about that relationship, and about the relationship between ethnic and racial identities and the persons who inhabit them, that do not conflate persons with representations. This is not to say that these two writers do not posit an intimate relation between persons and texts; indeed, they insist upon such intimacy. But I argue that, by maintaining the distinction between these two things, they make room for personal and artistic freedoms that are foreclosed by those committed to the various versions of the personified text I take up in the first four chapters. Such freedom includes, for each writer, the freedom from being determined by history and by experiences one did not have—a freedom denied by a writer like Art Spiegelman, who frequently defines his own identity (and that of his children) by the fact of his parents' experience in the concentration camps.

In the conclusion, I outline in more polemical terms the problems that come from conflating texts and persons and the benefits of keeping the two in a dynamic relation. The problems arise in two arenas, the political and the literary-critical. With regard to political discourse, I argue that cultural destruction is a kind of destruction that requires a more complex understanding and a more nuanced set of moral terms than the rhetoric of the murdered text allows. As I will show, this rhetoric means that cultural change of many kinds—not only those brought on by coercion, persecution, and violence— can too easily be equated with murder, mobilizing a moral outrage that may shut down productive discussion about the changes to which it points. I also argue that social justice requires us to be able to recognize the otherness of other persons, an otherness that is belied by an understanding of literature based on the mechanisms of identification. To put the point more simply, if we imagine that we can actually have another's experience by reading about it, it may short-circuit more substantive efforts at understanding and entering into relationship with those who are culturally or otherwise unlike us. Finally, I argue that the conflation of texts and persons impoverishes our ideas not only of art (as I show in chapter 5) but also of persons, since it renders the fact of embodiment irrelevant, when embodiment is exactly what situates us in history and makes us vulnerable to oppression.

Before finally embarking upon the analysis I have outlined above, I want to attempt to forestall, or at the very least, to acknowledge and attempt to answer, a kind of misunderstanding of this work that I have encountered as I have presented parts of it to my colleagues in various venues. I wish to make it clear that, while I am often engaging writing that itself engages the events of the Nazis' attempted genocide of the Jewish people, I am not, in reading these texts, producing a reading of those historical events. I am not a historian, and I defer to those who are for any such reading. I am interested, rather, in thinking about how writers have thought about, and have made use of, the idea of what we have come to call the Holocaust, an idea that has generated an enormous outpouring of scholarly and popular work that examines every- thing from what the Holocaust teaches us about evolutionary survival to what it teaches us about God.[31] Equally, while my subject is discourse about geno- cide of various kinds, my subject is not the discourse of those who experienced the Holocaust. Indeed, the only memoir of Holocaust experience I cite (apart from a passing citation of Primo Levi) is, by most accounts, a false one— Binjamin Wilkomirski's *Fragments.* How people mourn for their loved ones, how people explain their losses to themselves and to others, how people re- spond, spiritually and psychologically, to violence done to them and their families and their friends, is far beyond the bounds of my subject. I do not produce an analysis, much less a critique, of such things. I am analyzing poems, novels, literary criticism, and literary theory, which, though they are certainly not divorced from things like mourning, psychology, and spirituality, nevertheless make a claim to be something beyond, or at least different from, those things—to be art, or the explication of art.

Because of the implications I draw out from the phenomenon of the personified text, my critique of that phenomenon may be read by some as a critique of a certain version of Jewish identity that centers on the memory of the Holocaust and that relies on a conception of the personified text. Those invested in a version of Jewishness that makes the Holocaust central to that identity may be offended by this critique; in fact, anyone invested in an identity that relies on the idea that traumas of the past, endured by other people, continue to be experienced in the present may well take issue with my argument's implications. The critique of Holocaust-centered Jewish identity is not a central point of my study. Or to put it another way, it is only a central point of my study insofar as it constitutes an example of ways of thinking about the relationship between persons and texts, between lived experience and cultural identity, that I want to question.

If I set my own analysis in relation to an analysis for which such a critique of specifically Jewish identity is a central aim—the historian Peter Novick's controversial and fiercely criticized book *The Holocaust in American Life* (1999)—then my point might be clearer. In *The Holocaust in American Life*, Novick gives a history of how the Holocaust has been talked about in America by a few, largely secular, Jewish organizations and argues that the changes in public discussion of this topic (such as the long silence about it on the part of survivors immediately after the war and the subsequent outpouring of testimony in the 1980s and 1990s) had more to do with the exigencies of Cold War politics, identity politics, and American foreign policy toward Israel than they did with the intrinsically traumatic nature of the Holocaust itself. He questions two fundamental assumptions of what he calls "Holocaust professionals," the assumption that the Holocaust requires us to rethink many aspects of our philosophical, political, and aesthetic traditions and the assumption that it has something to teach us about these traditions. Novick argues instead that there is nothing to be learned from the Holocaust, and he goes on to make an explicit critique—addressing his Jewish readers directly—of what he sees as the continuing effort on the part of secular Jews in America to center their identity on the memory of the Holocaust and to focus their energies on acts of memorialization. He issues, finally, a call for change in the Jewish community.

Much of the research Novick has produced in this book I find quite useful.

Discourse about the Holocaust in our culture needs to be understood not just in psychological or literary contexts, but also in political and historical contexts. And it makes sense also to reflect from this point of view upon some methods and assumptions of Holocaust Studies, such as applying the notion of traumatic delay to large-scale sociological phenomena like the absence among survivors of an immediate and public postwar discourse about the Holocaust. Unlike Novick, however, I do think that the Holocaust has an effect on our philosophical and aesthetic traditions. If for no other reason, one could make that claim because so many have now argued that it does and have worked to reformulate those traditions in response.

Perhaps more importantly, I do not set out to critique, and to change, the Jewish community, for it is not the Jewish community that perpetuates the idea of the personified text with which I take issue. It is worth remembering that the positions vis-à-vis the personified text that I ascribe to some writers who are especially interested in the issue of Jewish identity—most obviously Meyer Levin, George Steiner, and Art Spiegelman—are by no means held only by writers who engage that issue or by all writers who engage that issue. Berel Lang, for example, suggests a version of Jewish identity that is importantly tied to the Holocaust in religious ways and through a traditional religious understanding of how one can experience the past vicariously by reading a text (although, as I argue in chapter 3, his notion of how we must write history reproduces, without the benefit of religious grounding, that version of the personified text).[32] Sidra Ezrahi also engages the relation between representation of the Holocaust and Jewish identity, and turns, like Lang, to Jewish religious tradition as a way of understanding that relation (though not to religious personification).[33] As I show in chapter 5, Philip Roth and Saul Bellow, both interested in Jewish identity, work explicitly against personification of texts. The chapters here, taken together, make clear that positions like those we see in Levin, Steiner, and Spiegelman are held also by writers as different as Sylvia Plath, Jacqueline Rose, Walter Miller, Ray Bradbury, and Cathy Caruth, writers who are not themselves Jewish, or who, if they are, do not focus on that identity in their writing. It is this very variety and dispersion of the belief in personified texts that caused me in the first place to examine that belief and its implications for a broad range of contemporary literary and political discourse.

1

Plath and Her Critics, "Writing" and Life

The Writer   In the introduction to *The Haunting of Sylvia Plath*, a study of Plath's writing and its critical reception, the psychoanalytic critic Jacqueline Rose situates her work in opposition to the biographical criticism that has dominated Plath studies in the past and that continues to preoccupy popular discussions of Plath. In doing so, Rose draws what appears to be a clear distinction between Plath and her poetry. Reminding the reader that "what we are dealing with is, obviously enough, not Plath herself but her representations," Rose goes on to attack those critics who read Plath's representations for information about her life.[1] And although Rose's reminder may seem unnecessary to theorists trained since the New Criticism to distinguish between the poem and the biography, in this case the reminder is made relevant by those many critics whose interest in Plath's poetry seems sometimes to be motivated almost entirely by a fascination with her life, and, indeed, with the lives of her husband, Ted Hughes, his sister, Olwyn Hughes, and Sylvia's mother, Aurelia Plath. It is these critics, more interested in who Sylvia Plath was than in the poems she wrote, interested, in effect, in Plath instead of her poems, whom Rose means to criticize.

But there is another group of critics for whom the question of who Plath was has also mattered, though these critics are uninterested in reading the poetry as evidence about Plath's or anyone else's life. While biographical critics are interested in her poems as an avenue to her person, the critics I focus on here are interested in her person as a way of assessing the value of her poems. George Steiner was both one of the first to make a pronouncement about her work's value—in 1965 he praises "Daddy" as the *Guernica* of modern poetry—and the first to doubt his own assessment by later raising a question about Plath as a person.[2] Writing in 1969 of Plath's late poems and their powerful Holocaust imagery, he questions whether "any writer, . . . any human being other than an actual survivor, [has] the right to put on this death-rig."[3] The problem is that Plath appears to claim—or at least her lyric speakers claim—an identification with the victims of the Holocaust on the grounds of shared experience, when it is clear that Plath herself was a product of Smith and Cambridge, not Dachau and Belsen.[4] Steiner reminds his readers that "Sylvia Plath was not a Jew . . . she had no personal connections with the holocaust . . . she was a child, plump and golden in America, when the trains actually went."[5] Thus, while it matters for Steiner who Plath was, his interest is not wholly in her biography, that is, in the specific experiences and events that made up her life. More importantly, he is interested in her identity.

It is not entirely clear, in Steiner's brief essay, what precisely he means when he says Plath "was not a Jew," for he could be speaking of Jewish identity as racial, cultural, or religious, or as a mixture of all three. We can only say that he is speaking of a kind of identity (any one of these options would do) that would associate Plath with the Jewish victims of the Holocaust. Thus, no matter which of these versions of Jewishness he means to invoke, the problem of Plath's identity comes down to a problem about experience—in particular, about what constitutes a shared experience that might produce legitimate claims of identification between persons—for it is not really the case that Steiner thinks that only an "actual survivor" has the "right to put on this death rig." His comment about Plath's lack of Jewishness and of "personal connections" suggests, rather, that those who are Jewish or closely acquainted with someone who experienced the camps might legitimately identify with the "actual survivor." At issue, then, is what counts as one's experience. For Steiner, experience can be shared through shared race, through membership in a particular ethnic community, or through simple social proximity (through relatives or through friends), which is to say that what counts as your experience is not only what we usually think of—what happens to you—but also what happens to the people you know and are related to. The specific content of experience, or how the facts of one person's biography compare to those of another, is secondary to how the person herself relates to the other.

By mounting his critique in the context of evaluating Plath's poetic achievement, Steiner suggests not only that common ethnic or racial identity can be sufficient grounds for claims to shared experience, but also that the claims made by poetic speakers about themselves must also be applicable to the poet, at least when the poet is talking about something as important as the Holocaust. Steiner thus makes the assumption that drives biographical criticism—that the work is about the life—into a normative criterion for poetry: poems may or may not correspond to the author's life, but under particular conditions they *should*. According to Steiner, Plath's failure to meet this criterion has both moral and artistic consequences, the moral consequences in fact producing the artistic ones. Steiner suggests that it is immoral for Plath to use images of the Holocaust, because the suffering endured at Auschwitz is a scarce and valuable commodity belonging to one only by virtue of experience—experience understood as race or "personal connection." "What extraterritorial right had Sylvia Plath," Steiner demands, "to draw on the reserves of animate horror in the ash and the children's shoes?" Steiner imagines the "horror"—a powerful affective resource, in other words—as if it were money, as if Plath's use of it could use it up. Not even her own death, Steiner argues, is horrible enough to have "balanced the account," to pay back what she owed to the Holocaust.[6] To put the point simply, then, it matters to Steiner who Plath was, because he is interested not in her biography but in finding a moral justification for the poetry. In Steiner's view, because Plath "is not a Jew" she cannot justify her use of Holocaust imagery.

The failure of justification then compromises the value of the art, so that when Steiner comes to consider Plath's status as a poet—"Will Sylvia Plath come to occupy a place, say, after Lowell and well ahead of W. D. Snodgrass or Anne Sexton?"—the power of her late poems must be discounted somehow, since Steiner questions whether their emotional power is due to the poet's talent or to her illegitimate use of the Holocaust's horror (248). Her literary greatness is compromised insofar as the Holocaust produces emotion in the reader that Plath could not produce from a poetic account of her own suffering: Steiner asserts that "without the assumption of a doomed persona," a persona he claims she had no right to assume, "the final poems, the work through which Sylvia Plath now matters, could not have been done" (248). In other words, without taking on the persona of a Jewishness that would have doomed her in the real world of the Third Reich, Plath could not have mobilized the imagery or the fateful violence that characterizes and empowers a poem like "Daddy." The then newly discovered early poems suggest, Steiner implies, the limits of what Plath could achieve without the Holocaust and that "doomed persona": he finds the poems derivative of Ted Hughes, William Butler Yeats, and John Crowe Ransom and sees only a hint of what was to appear in *Ariel*. Steiner thus encourages the reader to be skeptical about what Plath could have accomplished without having to "draw on" the Holocaust's horror.

The subsequent popularity of the logic and the moral affect—if not the precise stakes—of Steiner's critique may obscure the fact that in 1964, a year before the late poems were published in *Ariel*, it seemed less controversial to claim that experience could be shared without the kind of "personal connection" demanded by Steiner. For example, in his essay "Literature of the Holocaust," published in *Commentary* in November 1964, A. Alvarez takes the idea of personal connection beyond Steiner's restrictions of race and social proximity so that it encompasses anyone alive in the latter half of the twentieth century and ceases, in its generality, to be "personal" (in Steiner's sense) at all. He argues that images of the camps "keep such a tight hold on our imaginations . . . [because] we see in them a small-scale trial run for a nuclear war"; in minutes, he reminds his readers, a bomb could destroy as many people as the Nazis destroyed in five years. For Alvarez, the camps thus serve as a synecdoche for the problems of modernity. He argues that the century has "provided us with multitudinous, sophisticated, and . . . unprecedented means of annihilation" and calls the concentration camps "a proof of that, and a working model. In them the language of our sickness was created." Alvarez does not anticipate an objection to his claims about their universality, noting with confidence instead that this view is "more or less cliché, more or less accepted." What he wants to add to the conversation is a reflection on the extent to which "the acceptance implies understanding, and the understanding affects our behavior."[7]

To put Alvarez's argument in the terms I have been using so far, we might say that because nuclear threat is ubiquitous all people share a particular biography of suffering: we all suffer the threat of sudden annihilation. Thus, Alvarez can wonder whether shared experience *helps*, because the question of whether the experience of suffering is shared has already been decided. That we do share that experience, and that images of the camps represent it most truly for us regardless of the things Steiner refers to as "personal connection," is "more or less cliché, more or less accepted." Thus, anyone alive now is justified in turning to the Holocaust as a figure for suffering.

We can see the contrast between this view and those that follow Steiner's model most forcefully when Alvarez specifically addresses the use of the Holocaust in literature. "In his fumbling way," he writes, "I imagine Arthur Miller was after something like this [the idea that the camps are symbols of our "inturned nihilism"] when he thumbed an emotional lift from Dachau in *After the Fall.* Granted, he cheapened all those deaths by using them to say things which were trite, vulgar, and reeking of self-pity. But quality apart, there was a kind of sense in his maneuver: the camps have become a focus of contemporary suffering."[8] Alvarez suggests that the "cheapening" of deaths is a secondary issue, and an artistic instead of a moral one at that; he questions the "quality" of the art but finds the invocation of the Holocaust nevertheless fully justified. Given this position, it is not surprising that he found Plath's poetry and her use of Holocaust imagery laudable since Plath's universalizing gestures mirrored his own. (Alvarez, of course, quickly became and still is one of Plath's champions.) But by 1969 Steiner was already calling such universalizing into question and, as I shall show, by the 1980s such a position could be advanced only at risk of being called naive, or worse, morally outrageous. Why?

Edward Alexander's essay "Stealing the Holocaust," published in *Midstream* in 1980, provides a representative answer. Without referring specifically to Plath, he uses a variation of Steiner's critique to indict non-Jews like her (writers, but especially political activists) who use the Holocaust as a figure to call attention to some other instance of injustice. Like Steiner, Alexander suggests that non-Jews who use the Holocaust in this way actually use up something Jewish victims accumulated through their suffering. For Alexander, that will not be "horror," as it is for Steiner, but "moral capital."[9] He deplores, for example, the way the PLO used the story of Anne Frank as an analogy for their treatment at the hands of Israel and criticizes "the inflamed rhetoric of the American civil rights movement, with its . . . casual descriptions of Watts as a concentration camp, and of the ordinary black neighborhood anywhere as a ghetto" (48). The suffering of African-Americans in cities or Palestinians on the West Bank is not worth the same moral outrage, Alexander suggests, that images of the Holocaust ordinarily evoke. While the logic of Alexander's critique mimics Steiner's, it is clear that the stakes have changed: to police the use of certain resources, like moral outrage, has political, rather than literary, implications. The growth of racially motivated or identitarian politics makes it clear why Steiner's critique continued to be useful even for those uninterested in whether Plath ranks "below" or "above" W. D. Snodgrass in the pantheon of postwar poetry.[10]

But this is not to say that the literary stakes of Steiner's argument disappeared, or that they became detached from the question of who Plath was. In fact, the logic of justification Steiner used to cast doubt on the value of Plath's work later provided a rationale for the work's distinction. This came about in the two decades following Steiner's pronouncements, as popular feminism, what was called women's liberation in the 1970s, became at least as committed to the celebration of women's identity as it was to equal rights. In this changing context, identifying Plath as a *woman* could confer upon her work the kind of value that, because she was not Jewish, it failed to have in 1969. Because she was a woman, she was justified in writing poems that represent women's suffering, whether or not that suffering was figured through Holocaust imagery. Leaving aside for the moment Jacqueline Rose's analysis of Plath, the major study to exercise this logic has been Susan Van Dyne's *Revising Life*, which argues that Plath's writing is centrally about women's suffering. For Van Dyne this means not only that "Plath's goal was to rewrite her life" after abandoning, through divorce, the traditional feminine role she had sought to fulfill, but also that "in her practice . . . she . . . revised the very notion of 'woman.'"[11]

What does Van Dyne mean by the dual claim that Plath rewrote her life and that her poetic *practice* (as opposed, for example, to the content of her poems) revised the notion of woman? The answer turns on the role Van Dyne assigns to biographical materials in reading the poems. For example, she reads "In Plaster" as "a neat allegory that exposes the dualistic mechanism of gender formation. The mother, and the conventional definitions of femininity she models, is a plaster cast that both sustains and constrains the 'ugly and hairy' daughter within."[12] Two things are remarkable about this reading. First, biographical materials, rather than literary ones, determine the identities of the speaker and her cast, for the poem in fact makes no mention of either mother or daughter; in describing the cast the speaker instead proclaims "there are two of me now."[13] But what looks like the critic's failure to read the poem is far less interesting than the skill with which she *does* read the poem. Once we begin to imagine the plaster cast as the mother and the woman inside as the daughter, we instantly recognize something that, to be sure, looks remarkably like Plath's relation to her mother. The feelings the poem describes— of suffering, of revulsion from the body, of purity, of constraint—bring together and reflect upon the central issues in their relationship, a fact that Van Dyne amply illustrates by reference to Plath's journals. It is not hard to imagine students studying the poem this way in the classroom suddenly feeling that, with the real identity of the cast made plain, they finally could understand what the poem was *about*. But the clarity that Van Dyne's reading achieves in turn renders a crucial aspect of Plath's poetic work invisible. She does not ask what it means that feelings Plath certainly had about her mother turn up attached to something quite different—a plaster cast described as the speaker's double.

This failure to recognize poetic work stems from the basic assumption about revision that Van Dyne's study relies upon, for while Van Dyne is right to suggest that Plath imagined that her writing changed her, we might nevertheless ask whether revision is the right analogy to invoke. In a certain sense, Van Dyne does not imagine herself as invoking an analogy at all; her effort to read changes in Plath as being made through changes in her poems—actual revisions of written work—suggests instead that changing the text was the same thing as changing herself. This theoretical claim implies, for example, that when Plath revised "Daddy" to include more violence against the father, she was doing not poetic work but psychological work. Van Dyne suggests that the relevant question for the finished poem is thus not about the poetic function this violence serves but instead about "how long it took"—that is, how many revisions—for her "to accomplish the ritual murder that concludes the poem."[14] Though Van Dyne is not suggesting that revision was actually an act of murder, she nevertheless implies an equation between representation and the person who writes. The emphasis on poetic practice rather than poetic expression produces in the end a theoretical position from which one can hardly distinguish between changes made in Plath and changes made in the poems, between therapeutic processes and artistic ones. If Van Dyne had argued that Plath was revising the notion of woman when she revised the images of women in her poems to contradict given stereotypes, then the texts themselves would remain just that—texts that present certain ideas—but the insistence on the *practice* of revision as a way of revising the meaning of "woman" instead produces a personification of the text.[15] It is no longer what the text says, but its growth over time—what we finally have to call, in the context of Van Dyne's argument, its very life—that revises the notion of woman. By contrast to biographical critics, then, whose inquiry focuses on the life of the person instead of the poem, Van Dyne approaches the life of the poem as if it were the life of a person.

Though Van Dyne's study represents a theoretical innovation with respect to the relation between persons and texts, it nevertheless remains committed to the importance of actual persons as distinct from texts. Moreover, it continues to depend on the logic of justification, evident in Steiner's critique of Plath, that makes the identity of the actual author central to literary value. Van Dyne's answer to the question of who Sylvia Plath was—she was not Jewish but she *was* a woman—provides a rationale for the critic's claims about the generality, and hence the poetic importance, of Plath's work. If the discourse of justification is less explicit in Van Dyne's work than it is in Steiner's, it is because the logic has become so much a part of how we evaluate literature that Van Dyne does not need to *argue* that Plath's claims about women are authoritative because she is a woman. This is the very assumption upon which the analysis rests.

"WRITE"   The strain of Plath criticism I have been describing through the examples of Steiner and Van Dyne raises two questions, then, for the study of Plath's work: What is the relevance of who Plath was to our analysis of the poetry? And what is the relation between Plath and the poetry she wrote? This criticism offers us answers that resist ordinary biographical readings, while maintaining the centrality of biography. And while Steiner's version also preserves the New Critical commitment to poems as distinct from the person who wrote them, the extension of his logic in Van Dyne's analysis begins to blur that distinction in such a way that certain aspects of personhood are transferred to the poem through the mechanism of personification.

These questions and the answers Van Dyne and Steiner propose cut close to the core of Plath's poetic project, for Plath was indeed interested in transforming herself through poetry; she was interested, that is, in who she could become through poetry, though that transformation had little to do with the question of her being a woman or not being a Jew.[16] Addressing herself in her journal on April 1, 1956, trying to push through her writer's block, Plath invokes the relation between her life and her art as the art's very foundation: "Your problems are universal enough to be made meaningful—WRITE."[17] Plath is not saying here that her problems are meaningful simply because they are "universal"; rather, her problems, though potentially meaningful by dint of their universality, would nevertheless point to nothing beyond themselves unless they could be "*made* meaningful" through literary production. This version of what it means for experience to be shared, to be universal, is distinct from both Steiner's and Alvarez's. While Steiner suggests that experience is made meaningful when shared among members of a particular group, and Alvarez argues that universality is itself meaningful, Plath implies that some kinds of experience, "problems" in particular, are intrinsically universal but that universality confers no meaning at all. The meaning is made when you "WRITE."

Plath's formulation leaves us with a new question: What exactly does she refer to when she speaks of making meaning? Certainly, Plath is imagining a transformation through which the essentially insignificant facts of her life become something else, become literary representation. Their purpose there is not to represent her life so much as to contribute their special attribute— their universality—to a representation that would come to represent her as a poet. The transformation she imagines is thus not psychological; it is not a revision of the self in Van Dyne's sense. It is a revision produced external to the self, or a revision that changes not who the self is but how the self appears to the world. Plath is looking not to change the person she is but to make that person famous: literary representation holds out the promise of making her the *famous* Sylvia Plath, that is, the only Sylvia Plath whose biography might seem meaningful at all.

While Plath's desire for fame is legendary, recognized by critics as different in their understanding of Plath as Jacqueline Rose and Ted Hughes, we have yet to understand that desire's logical structure as distinct from its simple thematic presence in the poet's journals and letters. To unpack this aspect of Plath's work, it is useful to return to Steiner's critique because he raises important questions about how one's biography—and especially the private suffering that may have defined that biography—can become a public matter. Steiner suggests that "there was, even in [Plath's] death, a mimesis."[18] He is not exactly saying that Plath imitated the deaths of Holocaust victims, but rather that her death was mimetic of the deaths in her late poems, and thus her suicide was evidence not of real suffering like the Holocaust but of poetic suffering, of the representation of suffering. This invites a more nuanced understanding of Steiner's complaint against Plath and, moreover, reveals a new insight into her work: she does not lack the direct relation to the claims in her poems that Steiner requires. Rather, she possesses the right relation in the wrong order. She indeed represented her own extreme suffering but only afterward appeared to experience it. That *appearance* of suffering—its visibility to others in the world—matters not only to Steiner's analysis, but in Plath's poetry as well. While Steiner did not recognize the poetic representation of suffering as meaningful in the way real suffering is—the suffering was not real until she took her life—Plath imagined, to the contrary, that the representation of suffering in poetry produced something more meaningful than mere personal experience. It produced, in short, fame.

The production of fame requires the representation of suffering because, according to Plath, that kind of representation is uniquely capable of producing the identification between author and reader that will then confer upon the author the desired recognition. In other words, Plath imagined that her best writing, the writing that would make her famous, would encourage just the kind of universal identification between isolated sufferers that Steiner questions. She explains this rationale in a letter to her mother (who apparently had criticized the darkness of her work), dated October 21, 1962.

> I am doing a poem a morning, great things, and as soon as the nurse settles, shall try to draft this terrific second . . . novel that I'm dying to do. Don't talk to me about the world needing cheerful stuff! What the person out of Belsen—physical or psychological—wants is nobody saying the birdies still go tweet-tweet, but the full knowledge that somebody else has been there and knows the *worst,* just what it is like. It is much more help for me, for example, to know that people are divorced and go through hell, than to hear about happy marriages. Let the *Ladies' Home Journal* blither about *those.*[19]

Plath is imagining her ideal reader to be "the person out of Belsen." Because the master author (the author of "great things" and "terrific" novels) shares the survivor's experience of suffering and death, she has the power to connect persons of varied experience. Whether extreme suffering is "physical" or "psychological" ceases to matter. The claim that "Belsen" can be either one denies that significant (as opposed to simply material) differences in experience exist in the most extreme state of suffering: that state as a whole can be described as "Belsen."[20] While Plath may thus appear to accept the demand for justification, simply insisting on a universalist version of it as opposed to Steiner's particularist version, she is in the end less interested in whether her representations of suffering are justified by her own knowledge of suffering than she is in whether her representations of suffering can make her audience "want" her art. It is more likely, Plath implies, that an audience will "want" the art if she can represent suffering convincingly, and she believes it is likely that she can do that because the experience of extreme suffering is a universal experience, one she herself knows. The work of Plath's writing is to reveal— and thus make meaningful—an affinity, or more strongly, an identification between individual sufferers that Plath imagines already exists.

What Steiner calls "personal connection"—the connection of race, ethnicity, or social proximity—is irrelevant to Plath when she imagines what it means to share suffering, as an entry in her Cambridge journals makes clear. On Monday, February 20, 1956, she describes her despair: "The image of identity we must daily fight to impress on the neutral, or hostile, world, collapses inward; we feel crushed. Standing in line in the hall, waiting for a lousy dinner of hard-boiled egg in cheese-cream sauce, mashed potatoes and sallow parsnips, we overheard one girl say to another, 'Betsy is depressed today.' It seems almost an incredible relief to know that there is someone outside oneself who is not happy all the time" (*J,* 202). That the world is essentially devoid of "personal connection" appears here to be the precondition of existence and sets into motion the essential activity of life—"to impress" one's "image of identity" on the "neutral, or hostile, world." Alleviating the suffering that occurs when one fails in this task does not depend on recognizing and drawing upon an already-established "personal connection" with the world in the sense that Steiner means it. It depends on knowing that one is not alone in one's experience, as if finding someone to identify with in that suffering begins once more to accomplish the failed work of impressing one's identity on the world. There is nothing precisely personal about sharing such knowledge. Plath does not know Betsy at all; she simply knows they share the experience of depression. Perhaps the most striking evidence of Plath's belief in the power of generalizing personal suffering can be seen on the level of the pronoun: in the darkest passages of her journal, she refers to herself as "we" rather than "I," as if the act of representing personal suffering even in a private place—in a journal—can, by sheer will of word choice, counteract isolation.

To "want" Plath's literary product, then, is to want the universalizing, extending reference for one's own suffering that the "we" in Plath's journal wishes for and that Plath's poetry promises to provide. Plath imagines a liter-ary language adequate even to the experience of extreme states and, moreover, capable of serving some orthogenic function—capable of being a "help"—by revealing an identification that can alleviate the loneliness of suffering. Hence, her claim to her mother that "It is much more help for me . . . to know that people are divorced and go through hell, than to hear about happy marriages." To put the point slightly differently, Plath turns to poetic lan-guage in an effort to make private experience meaningful in a social context. Such experience is, importantly, a kind of suffering not because suffering tests the adequacy of language but because shared suffering produces its ade-quacy. The journal entry I cited earlier is appropriate here as well, though I would add a different emphasis: "your *problems* are universal enough to be made meaningful—WRITE." The experience Plath shares with other kinds of readers—readers of the *Ladies' Home Journal,* for instance, with whom she might share the experience not of "problems" but of "happy marriages"—cannot produce an identification that will serve to make language, and thus experience, "meaningful," and hence will not be helpful. Perhaps more im-portantly, the identification produced by shared knowledge of happy mar-riages does not require the "great things" Plath has to offer. To produce that, "blither" will suffice.

It is as the author of "great things" as opposed to "blither" that Plath imagines she will find the solution to her own worst suffering, the suffering of being invisible to the larger world. We can see this conviction in both positive and negative forms in her writing. "I am unrecognized," she laments on April 17, 1958; "The *New Yorker* has not replied to the ms. I sent off two and a half weeks ago. The *ARTnews* has not answered the two poems I sent them: I run for mail and get mocked by a handful of dull . . . circulars. . . . within a year or two I should be 'recognized'—as I am not at all now, though I sit on poems richer than any Adrienne Cecile Rich" (*J*, 371).[21] Successful poems mean that Plath will be "recognized" by others, that she will be known as Adrienne Rich is known. Thus, it is probably no accident that Plath describes her own poems as "richer" than Rich's poems and that she refers to Rich's poems not as poems but as Rich herself. The word *rich* becomes synonymous with the thing Plath desires—not wealth (riches) and not Adrienne Rich's poetic talent (the richness of poems) but the fame Rich possesses: Rich has made a *name* for herself, and that is what Plath most desires. These are, in fact, the terms she uses to denote the fame she anticipates while working on the *Ariel* poems: "I am a genius of a writer," she proclaims in a letter to her mother; "I am writing the best poems of my life; they will make my name."[22] The equation of name and poem hints at an equation between herself and her representations that is elaborated elsewhere in the journals: fantasizing on January 7, 1959, about the positive effects of fame, she writes, "I need to be tan, all-over brown, and then my skin clears and I am all right. I need to have written a novel, a book of poems, a *LHJ* [*Ladies' Home Journal*] or *NY* [*New Yorker*] story, and I will be poreless and radiant. My wart will be nonmalignant" (*J*, 457). Here, Plath imagines that representation—the book of poems, the published story, the novel—can transform the person into a socially desirable form of herself. The glamorous appearance she conjures embodies the effects of fame.

While Plath's journals and letters contain many such self-assurances about what literary fame will accomplish, her poetry more often revolves around the fear that representation will fail her, that she will never be "recognized" like Adrienne Rich. "The Bee Meeting," for example, reveals the logic both of the search for recognition and of the failure of that search, by detailing the dynamics of recognition between a female speaker and a group of villagers who are working together to care for some beehives (*CP*, 211–12). The female speaker of the poem arrives at the village bee meeting wearing a "sleeveless summery dress" and finds that the villagers gathered there "are all gloved and covered." "Why did nobody tell me?" she asks; "I am nude as a chicken neck, does nobody love me?" At first the difference between the speaker and the assembled group appears to be in relation to the bees—her dress gives "no protection"—but in fact she needs protection not so much from bees as from the villagers, for the threat here is not physical but social and psychological. It emerges even in the first line of the poem, where the speaker struggles to recognize those ready to meet her, asking nervously, "Who are these people at the bridge to meet me?" Though she soon reassures herself by naming them, they remain strange and threatening in their protective clothing. The woman's sleeveless dress becomes a sign of the social vulnerability she feels from the start, while the villagers' costumes announce their security within the group and a communal history from which the speaker is excluded. The power of that exclusion soon erodes the speaker's ability to discern the villagers' separate identities, which were at first so reassuringly clear: "Which is the midwife," the speaker begins to wonder; "is that her blue coat?"

By making clothing the figure for both the possibility and the impossibility of being known, Plath condenses ideas about the relation between herself and her representations and about the unreliability of those representations that we find in her discussions of fame and recognition in the journals.[23] Even when "The Bee Meeting"'s speaker is given protective clothing and begins to feel part of the community, the clothing forces her to fresh insistence on the separate subjectivity that initially made her vulnerable. To put the point in the journal's terms, while an "NY story" may make Plath "poreless and radiant," both visible and attractive, the kind of representation figured in the protective clothing makes its wearer invisible. Having been given the new clothing, the speaker at first jokes that she is now like "milkweed silk" that "the bees will not notice," but the line ends with an intense expression of threat: "They will not smell my fear, my fear, my fear." While the speaker wants to be unrecognizable to the bees, this requires that she be unrecognizable to persons as well, and so she insists that the reader see what the villagers cannot: her fear. Thus, it turns out that becoming, as the speaker puts it, "one of them," one of the villagers, is even more threatening than exclusion. It is inclusion, entailing here the erasure of self-representation, that precipitates the speaker's crisis at the center of the poem: "I could not run without having to run forever." By suggesting that the threat of being unrecognized is the very condition of existence, the poem echoes the journal's description of the "neutral, or hostile" world, but implies that something like the discovery that "Betsy is depressed today" can no longer bridge the gap that yawns between one person and another. Here one can only escape the failure of connection by escaping the condition under which such connection might be possible, that is, by escaping human community altogether, by running "forever."

In "The Bee Meeting" the hive becomes that place which is both completely outside of the human community and the closest approximation to the human community, and through it Plath imagines social recognition, or a version of fame, that is both perfect and deadly. The "new virgins," now waiting behind their "curtain of wax" outside the realm of recognition and sexual exchange know that their very birth will cause a shift in the hive's organization. The center of it will move "inevitably" from the old queen to the new, the new will be taken up by "a heaven that loves her." But the cost, of course, is the death of the old queen. Plath seems to be suggesting that perfect recognition, where the singularity of the one recognized is preserved in the act of recognition, will always come at the cost of death, for once the hive's acknowledgment shifts from the old queen she will die of the lack. Acknowledgment of the self by the other is always and everywhere too scarce to sustain life.

Though by "moving the virgins" the villagers ensure that life can be sustained on the level of the hive—"there will be no killing," the speaker assures us—Plath imagines no such cure for the social world they represent. In the final stanza the speaker remains unrecognizable, merely the outline of a person without subjectivity. When the speaker says, "I am exhausted, I am exhausted," it is subjectivity itself that is exhausted and with it the possibility of being known, for the "I" disappears, her place held by a "Pillar of white in a blackout of knives." When she returns, she is not "I" but "the magician's girl who does not flinch"—that is, a person who appears not to be a conscious subject at all. While the villagers can remove "their disguises," revert to distinct identities, and affirm their community with handshakes, the speaker cannot return. The multiple failures of self-representation leave her unrecognizable, and it is this that makes the bee meeting deadly. The speaker has lost her identity to such an extent that, while it seems clear that *she* is the one who has been killed, even that remains uncertain to the speaker herself: "Whose is that long white box in the grove," she wonders; "what have they accomplished, why am I cold."[24]

In "The Bee Meeting," Plath envisions the failure of representation to connect the self with others and thus also envisions the failure of literary fame. This poem thus pushes the content and the problem of personal suffering to a level of abstraction surpassing the various kinds of suffering we find represented consistently in Plath's poems. She examines a bee meeting— not a Holocaust, or a love gone wrong. There is no damage to the body here and no violent enemy such as the ones we find in "Daddy" or "The Rabbit Catcher."[25] This is in part why the poem is central to understanding

Plath's poetic work: the speaker's pain arises purely from the failure of self-representation and the corresponding failure of recognition.

This insight invites us to turn to the poems in which Holocaust imagery appears and see how the suffering brought about by failure of representation underwrites other accounts of pain. In "Lady Lazarus" Plath suggests that poetry itself is like suffering, or more specifically, like dying, regardless of whether the experience emanates from the historically specific site of the concentration camps. That site is present in the poem in the much-criticized image of "skin / Bright as a Nazi lampshade," but it is not necessary to the conceit of the poem in its central stanzas, where dying is imagined as an "art" at which the speaker is exceptional. The measure of her talent, the poem tells us, is found not only in the realism with which the speaker can pull it off, in her ability to make it feel "real" and "like hell," but more importantly in the "theatrical // Comeback in broad day," the public return that elicits the watching crowd's "brute / Amused" shout (*CP*, 245–46). Dying is thus an art because to do it so that it becomes part of the social world—so that it can be recognized by a crowd—one must also be able to do it "exceptionally well." Plath thus thinks of the art of dying as the same, in crucial ways, as the art of producing poems; they require the same talent at making suffering present to an audience. If in Plath's letter "the person out of Belsen" can successfully identify with her poetic speakers, while in "Lady Lazarus" the speaker's audience does the opposite, sees her as a freak, it is because not everyone possesses the knowledge of suffering that would make them ideal readers or spectators. Plath thus imagines a different version of failed representation than we see in "The Bee Meeting." It is not that the speaker cannot remain visible but rather that her audience fails to complete the process of identification. The exceptional poet and the one exceptional at dying require an equally exceptional audience.

That exceptional audience is written into the poem "Daddy" and becomes all the more powerful because it exists in contrast to another audience: Daddy himself, the addressee of the poem. We initially see the exceptional audience in the poem's Holocaust imagery, where the father's "obscene" German language has the effect of "chuffing" the speaker off to the concentration camps, having transformed her in the process into a Jew herself, into part of the crowd forced onto the trains (*CP*, 223). By using such imagery to describe the kind of pain this father causes, Plath not only places suffering in a public realm, but also invokes a context in which the speaker's experience will be immediately understood because it is shared and because suffering creates its own communal language. The speaker will "talk like a Jew," but she remains divided from the father by the unlearnable German he speaks. Thus, while the woman dying (and coming back to life) in "Lady Lazarus" is dramatically singular despite the fact that her suffering is public, the woman dying in "Daddy" is part of a persecuted community.

We must note, in light of Steiner's and others' emphasis on the fact that Plath herself was not Jewish, that the Jewishness of the audience in the poem, the audience with which the speaker identifies, is secondary to the fact that it, too, is oppressed by the father. The final stanza gives us a second version of this group that does not invoke racial, ethnic, or religious collectivities at all and highlights instead the community's authorizing function. Instead of naming a Jewish collectivity, this time the speaker calls an analogous audience, "the villagers," to be witnesses and fellow victims. The "villagers," like the people on the trains to Dachau, provide a community of sufferers that counteracts the speaker's isolation; choruslike, they legitimate her anger and her act of murder with their common (and, it appears, indisputable) prior intuition about the father's crime. Unlike the villagers in "The Bee Meeting," who evacuate the speaker's self-representation, these villagers have made self-representation possible because they recognize the speaker as a sufferer. Because the villagers "always *knew*" of the father's oppression, her private complaint gains a public and communal history.[26]

It should by now be clear that, in examining the question of how Plath imagined her relation to her representations, we arrive at a set of questions that reach beyond those raised explicitly by the criticism with which I began—for the failure of representation we see in "The Bee Meeting" seems to result from precisely what, in her journal and her letters, Plath claimed would enable a successful representation—universality. The difference suggests that, for Plath, there are degrees of universality; in some cases it may be one attribute of a particular person's experience, while in others the person herself may become universal. In the latter, the case imagined in "The Bee Meeting," the self *becomes* the other or disappears into the other, while in the former, the separate self identifies with the other but remains both separate and visible.[27] This distinction may indeed begin to explain the undeniable presence of biographical detail in Plath's writing. Such detail makes the particular person—Sylvia Plath herself—visible within the generalizing discourse of poetry. It may also suggest that what looks like a kind of naïveté on Plath's part—her apparent belief that publications like the *New Yorker* appeal universally to readers—is instead an instrumental blindness, one that resolves the tension between becoming famous and singular because your writing is universal and disappearing into that very universality—for fame requires distinction where universality erases it. The belief that the *New Yorker* is in fact universal keeps intact both the possibility of individual fame and the idea that universality grounds that fame.[28] These speculations and the broader question about how universality becomes a threat to individual identity can be related back to concerns we see in George Steiner, in Edward Alexander's argument about the stolen Holocaust, and, to refer back to the introduction, in Meyer Levin's crusade against the universalist portrayal of Anne Frank. (These same concerns will reappear, too, in later chapters.) Steiner, Alexander, and Levin all seem worried that the Jewish particularity of the Holocaust may disappear into universality, just as the speaker of "The Bee Meeting" fears that her particularity disappears when she joins the villagers in protective dress. If among these only Levin goes as far as Plath, treating this disappearance explicitly as a kind of death, it is only because Steiner and Alexander do not push the logic of their assumptions about the relation between person and text to the limit case of personification. In the discourse of Plath criticism, it takes poststructuralism's emphasis on the autonomous text to enable this strongest of claims about the relation between Plath and her poetry.

The "Writing"   For critics hostile to biography—Jacqueline Rose in particular—and for a certain strain of poststructuralism in general, any kind of interest in the person in addition to the poem looks problematic. In this critical context Plath's own equation between herself and her poems is read not as a commitment to the person who can be made famous by the representation but as a groundbreaking commitment to something like performative identity *avant la lettre*.[29] Though Rose does not make that specific claim, she nevertheless singles out as exceptional poems in which Plath's poetic speaker shifts constantly between subject positions. While I would argue that in these poems Plath imagines successful versions of the effort to impress one's image on the world, Rose reads them in the opposite way, as imagining a world in which something like the self—imagined as a bounded psychic entity—cannot exist at all.[30] Thus, "Poem for a Birthday," in which the speaker's location shifts from woman to animal to man to mythic speaker, becomes for Rose a demonstration, among other things, of how fantasies of identification reveal the folly of imagining that there is such a thing as a bounded self locatable in a particular person.

Such a reading stands to solve, then, the problem of who Plath was, for if the self is by definition not locatable in a person, we cannot make the kind of pronouncements that biographical critics have made about Plath. This is essentially the territory Jacqueline Rose stakes out by reminding her readers that (to quote more fully the passage I cited at the beginning of this chapter), "what we are dealing with is, obviously enough, not Plath herself but her . . . writing, together with all the other utterances which have come to crowd it— joining in the conversation, as one might say." But what is not obvious here is how something other than "writing," something that looks closer, if not identical, to "Plath herself" immediately makes its way back into the analysis. The phrase Rose uses to describe the critical and popular "utterances" that "crowd" Plath's texts is in fact the famous phrase Freud used in his founda- tional *Studies On Hysteria* (1895) to describe the hysterical symptom. It was Fraulein Elisabeth von R.'s "painful legs" that "began to 'join in the conversa- tion'" during Freud's sessions with his patient.[31] Rose's invocation of Freud—even if unattributed—is both specific and intentional and, moreover, it points toward what is most crucial about her study, for Rose eventually makes it clear that she is not simply proposing an analogy between the hysteri- cal symptom and literary criticism. As in Van Dyne's analogy between revision of texts and the psychological revision of persons, the two terms of the analogy merge: Rose suggests that Plath criticism *is* a psychic symptom, that it is somehow the equivalent of Fraulein Elisabeth's "painful legs." Methodologi- cally debarred from referring to the person in a way Steiner, Van Dyne, and Plath herself are not, Rose begins to find personhood in the writing itself.

If a psyche thus organizes the relation between Plath's writing and her critics', to whom does that psyche belong? From Rose's point of view, the organizing psyche does not, as it certainly does for Van Dyne, belong to Sylvia Plath. She asserts from the start that she does "not believe we can take writing as unproblematic evidence for the psychological condition or attributes of the one who writes."[32] This credo also rules out the possibility that criticism is the critic's symptom. In fact, Rose seems not to believe that we can speak of such a thing as an individual psyche at all, as she claims that the division between what is internal and external to the individual is not simply difficult to characterize or hard to locate but is in fact "false."[33] The beginnings of an answer can be found when Rose makes the relation between criticism and symptom explicit: "Plath becomes a symptom—or rather, responses to her writing become a symptom—of one part of the cultural repressed (it is not her problem, it is ours)" (6). The organizing psyche, then, is a collective one; it is "our" psyche that produced the symptom.

Rose locates this collective psyche not in one person or another, and not in a group of people, but in language as an abstract entity, language separated from any particular instance of it. Employing the technology of psychoanalysis, she thus transfers what most have come to accept as a fact of human psychological structure—the unconscious—into a generic structure, which is to say a structure that, like "language itself," transcends specific content or location. "For Freud," Rose explains, "the utterance can only ever be partial, scarred as it is by the division between conscious and unconscious. . . . It is that provisional, precarious nature of self-representation which appears so strikingly from the multiple forms in which Plath writes. What she presents us with, therefore is not only the difference of writing from the person who produces it, but also the division internal to language, the difference of writing from itself" (5). So it is not Plath's conscious and unconscious we see in her work, but the conscious and unconscious of "writing," which in turn correspond to specific genres, or "multiple forms," identified elsewhere as "high poetry" and "low prose." Thus, Rose describes past critics' mistakes: "they have transposed into a fact of her individual pathology the no less difficult problem of the contradictory, divided and incomplete nature of representation itself."[34]

Rose's interpretation of Plath provides a peculiar corrective, then, to the problem of biographical criticism. Though the kind of criticism exemplified by *The Haunting of Sylvia Plath* does not claim that poems either do or should represent their author or her life, it nevertheless preserves the central terms both of biographical criticism and, as I will show, of the kind of criticism that looks to biography to justify the poetry's value. The psyche has not disappeared from the analysis but has been relocated from the person (the author) to the text, to "representation itself." It is important to note that I am not arguing here that psychological questions, as distinct from an actual psyche, should disappear. Psychological questions are obviously part of my own analysis of Plath. But in positing a psyche in the text itself, one that displays the attributes and dynamics that we normally assign only to the actual psyche of a person, Rose invites us to see her study less as a corrective to biographical criticism than as a culmination of that criticism.[35] I want to ask, then, a new version of the now-familiar question: not "Who was Sylvia Plath?" but rather, "Who is Plath's writing?"

The writing, for one thing, is not the writing Plath alone produced, for in Rose's analysis of "Daddy," constituting the final chapter of her book, the poem comes to be filled with meanings drawn not from biographical materials but from other texts. Rose asserts, for example, that the poem's mythically huge father is in fact the same one that Julia Kristeva calls *"père imaginaire"*

or "PI," implying that Plath duplicated Kristeva's thought before Kristeva
thought it. The move makes sense if we believe that women's representations
of mythic fathers, whenever they were written and whatever the author's intentions, may plausibly mean what Kristeva means by *"père imaginaire,"* because Kristeva has fathomed something true about "our" cultural psyche. But
whether or not Kristeva can be right about this, and whether or not she is
in fact right, does not seem to matter to Rose, for it turns out that what
matters is not the meaning of Kristeva's concept of the *"père imaginaire"* but
its sound: "Say those initials out loud in French," Rose continues, "and what
you get is 'pays' (country or nation)—the concept of the exile."[36] The relevance of Kristeva's concept to Plath's poem is contained not in the content
of that concept or in its truth value, but in a pun produced by the sound of
its initials in French.[37] On the basis of the logic's origin—in the claim that
Kristeva's *"père imaginaire"* is essentially the same as Plath's "Daddy"—the
father image of the poem ends up referring to "the concept of exile." And
beyond that, it begins to refer to what people have said about Plath and her
father as exiles. Rose continues: "Much has been made of Plath as an exile.
. . . But there is another history of migration, another prehistory, which this
one overlays—that of her father."[38] Thus, when Rose does at last arrive at a
referent for Daddy, the question "Who is Sylvia Plath?" reappears in its familiar guise. Sylvia Plath is a woman whose father emigrated to the United States,
and "Daddy," we finally learn, is a poem best understood by referring to
Plath's actual father's experience of immigration.[39]

The significance of this reading of the father figure emerges when a second
set of texts enters Rose's analysis: case studies from the 1985 Hamburg Congress of the International Association of Psycho-Analysis, which focused almost exclusively on problems of Nazism and the Holocaust. What is remarkable about "Daddy" for Rose is that the speaker identifies both with the
oppressor (the father) and with the victims (the Jews), and that the speaker
admits even to desiring the violent father in the line "every woman adores a
fascist." Thus, " 'Daddy,' " Rose claims, "becomes strikingly resonant of the
case of a woman patient described at Hamburg"; further on she suggests that
the "reversals" of subject position between victim and aggressor are "not unlike those discovered in the fantasies of the patients described at Hamburg,
survivors, children of survivors, children of Nazis."[40] Working on the assumption that the psychic structures she finds in Plath's poems are "ours," Rose
nevertheless singles out a certain set of persons with whom Plath shares them:
the survivors of Nazi violence. And we might note here that including the
children of Nazis in this list does not actually, given Rose's terms, open it

up to the oppressor's side of the Holocaust, for the children of Nazis look much like Jews in the descriptions Rose gives of the Hamburg Conference. They, like the survivors, are said to identify with both victim and aggressor. We might also notice that children of Nazis, like the Jews, suffer on account of their biology and the Nazis' violence, albeit in a different sense. The children of Nazis suffer from their biology because, through no choice of their own, they are bound by the closest family ties to people whose actions were evil. They suffer from Nazi violence not by having been its objects but by enduring the conflict between deploring that violence and loving the parents who perpetrated it. Indeed, Rose does not include the only group that would actually implicate Plath's poetry with the psyche of the oppressor: Nazis themselves. This omission would seem to require an explanation if the psychic structures she describes are in fact "ours," belonging, that is, to everyone. Thus, if the reading of "Daddy" as an immigrant, an exile, hints at a kind of Jewishness for Plath's writing, the role of the Hamburg Congress in the analysis secures it. The turn to writing as a kind of psyche, one that comes to roost, as it were, in different speakers at different times, means that Plath's writing is itself the equivalent of a survivor. For the survivor psyche is the one that, according to Rose, comes to roost in Plath's poetry.

There is yet one more thing to say about the turn to writing as a psychic entity and its role in Rose's reading of "Daddy." It is not incidental that Kristeva's text as well as the Hamburg Congress becomes so importantly a part of Plath's text, for the Kristevan theory that appeared not to matter in Rose's reading does in fact matter, but not because it helps us understand Plath's father imagery. It matters because Kristeva has theorized writing as in some sense feminine: she suggests that, rather than being a symbolic system based on the phallic Law of the Father, language is as much or more a system characterized by what Kristeva calls the maternal *chora*, the prelinguistic bodily connection between the mother and the infant. Though Toril Moi has pointed out that Kristeva's conception of language is distinct from that of other French feminists in that it does not claim that the language of women is itself gendered, that language produced by women is *"écriture feminine,"* the Kristevan conception nevertheless suggests that women have a privileged access to the aspects of language unaccounted for by the Law of the Father. The implication is borne out in Kristeva's "Stabat Mater," where she demonstrates what it might look like for the maternal chora to erupt into the linear logic of the phallic order. In that essay, a traditional academic discussion about how language works is juxtaposed on the page with columns of ungrammatical, nonlinear, impressionistic writing meant to approximate what language would be like outside the patriarchal regime of the sign. These eruptions of the chora so insistently thematize the origin Kristeva assigns them—the body of the mother and the relation between her body and the body of the child— that the chora becomes not so much a nonlinear linguistic structure as a perfectly readable celebration of the mother's body. It thus appears that, even if language itself is not gendered (and hence personified) for Kristeva, she nevertheless assigns to women, by virtue of their bodies, a special kind of access to language.[41] In this she is not unlike Hélène Cixous, who implies a similar analogy between the female body and language, arguing that "feminine texts . . . are . . . very close to the flesh of language."[42]

It is such a concept of privileged access that, according to Rose, points toward the ultimate significance of Plath's poetic work; she concludes her reading of "Daddy" with the following: " 'Daddy' does allow us to ask whether the woman might not have a special relationship to fantasy—the only generalisation in the poem regarding women is, after all, that most awkward of lines: 'Every woman adores a fascist.' . . . could we not read in that line a suggestion, or even a demonstration, that it is a woman who is most likely to articulate the power . . . of fantasy as such? . . . This is for me, finally, the wager of Plath's work."[43] If the most important line of the poem—the line "Every woman adores a fascist"—is in fact a "demonstration" of women's special relationship to fantasy, then the psyche that is the writing appears to be a woman's psyche. *The Haunting of Sylvia Plath* finally argues that Plath's work is important not because Plath was a certain kind of person but rather because the poems themselves contain a certain kind of psyche. In light of the history of Plath criticism represented by Steiner and Van Dyne, the answer to my question—Who is Plath's writing?—should come as no surprise, since it retains the very terms engaged by those two critics. For Rose, the writing itself, in the final analysis, is both a Jewish survivor and a woman.

2

Books That Kill   What are the stakes of imagining, as I have argued Jacqueline Rose does, that the text is the bearer of onto-logical categories we usually think of as belonging to persons? I have suggested that in Plath's case the stakes are largely liter-ary; when the text is imagined as a Holocaust survivor and as a woman, the poetry gains a certain value within the context of both multiculturalist and poststructuralist critical contexts. But the implications of speaking of the text in these terms stretches beyond the literary-critical world. To see how, I want to turn back for a moment to the subject of Plath and to the criticism of David Holbrook. Holbrook suggested in the mid-1970s that Plath's poetry was dangerous because it glorified death and suicide and made violence glamorous. "If we give assent to the libidinal attachment to death in [Plath's last poem] *Edge*," he reasons, "what values can we invoke to con-demn those who blow up children with terrorist bombs?" But Holbrook does not limit his claim to the rather banal, and yet implausible, idea that if we represent death as glamorous peo-ple will no longer see reasons to oppose violence, for he imag-ines that Plath's own death was the "direct consequence" of *Edge*, a poem that speaks of a woman and her two children made perfect in death.[1] In asserting this direct causal relation-ship between the representation of death and its production, Holbrook is in fact following out what by now will look like a familiar assumption about Plath's poetry—that its referent is Plath herself—since it is her actual death that, for Holbrook, proves his point that the poetry is dangerous. Indeed, Holbrook heads his first chapter with that familiar question: "Who is Sylvia?" Holbrook's answer, in contrast to the kinds of answers I consider in chapter 1, is purely psychological: Sylvia Plath, he asserts, was "schizoid," and because her poems reflect that schizoid mind, whose tendencies ended in suicide, the poetry itself becomes as capable of inducing violence as the mind that produced it.[2]

Because Holbrook's conception of who Plath was is straightforwardly psychological, it does not intersect with the arguments about personification I engage in the previous chapter. But his ideas about a relationship of causality between poems and events in the world are worth noting, not so much within the context of Plath criticism as within the context of contemporary discussions about nuclear war. The connection is most explicit in the language he uses to characterize the danger of Plath's writing: he suggests that Esther Greenwood's breezy speculation about jumping out a seventh-story window in *The Bell Jar* reproduces "the terrible 'objective' language of 'body-count' and 'overkill.' "[3] The term *overkill*, of course, was the invention of policy analysts and engineers trying to describe the new capacity to kill that nuclear weapons presented. By equating Ester Greenwood's thoughts about suicide with these terms, Holbrook implies that representing death—in this particularly detached matter—in a novel is in some way the same as representing nuclear disaster. Or to put the point slightly differently, the representations in fiction and poetry are tied to results in the world in the same way that the work of nuclear analysts is tied to results in the world; the assumption about the latter linkage, implied though not specified here, is that describing nuclear outcomes will eventually bring them about. This is precisely the point that, for Holbrook, Plath proved: describing death and the desire for it in one's poems and novels will eventually bring about one's own death.[4] By extending this point to the culture in general through the comparison with the rhetoric of nuclear arms, Holbrook establishes his larger cultural critique.

It is this notion—that by representing something we bring it about—as much as Holbrook's explicit reference to the language of nuclear analysis, that places his argument within a discourse about nuclear destruction that grew, with varying intensity, from the time of the development of the hydrogen bomb in the early 1950s through the resurgence of the Cold War during the early 1980s. I begin with Holbrook because I want to demonstrate that the beliefs about representation I discuss in chapter 1, especially the belief that the figures in Plath's poetry are equivalent to Plath herself, reach beyond a certain literary discourse centering on one postwar poet. Such beliefs—and the logic they produce about both persons and texts—are characteristic of political and philosophical discussions on the Cold War as well as being evident in the literature and theory of that period.

We need only look to the most prominent pundits on nuclear policy to see the point. In the preface to Herman Kahn's *Thinking about the Unthinkable* (1962), Raymond Aron mobilizes a version of Holbrook's comparison between fiction and nuclear analysis, albeit for reasons diametrically opposed to Holbrook's. He uses the comparison to defend, not indict, the seemingly cold-blooded way Kahn discusses disaster (a manner for which Kahn had received much criticism). Aron suggests that the relationship between the analyst and his hypothetical scenarios is the same as the relationship between a reader and a detective story. The reader, Aron contends, "calmly accepts recitals of choice murders" just as the analyst calmly considers the possibility of millions of deaths. "Without the ability to neutralize his feelings," Aron explains, "the analyst's profession would become impossible."[5] Aron's point is that one cannot be expected to feel about representations of persons the same way one might feel about actual persons, and moreover, that the hypothetical persons whose deaths Kahn imagines are more like fictional characters than they are like actual persons. The very detachment of the tone used to describe death—precisely the kind of detachment that Holbrook criticizes in Plath's writing—reveals, for Aron, the fact that neither fiction nor nuclear analysis should be imagined to have a real referent.

For Aron the comparison between detective fiction and nuclear analysis indicates no causal relationship between representation and events in the world; indeed, the comparison is meant to negate such a relationship. If there is no literal correspondence between nuclear analysis and actual events and persons, then it will no more produce the outcomes it imagines than the detective story produces actual murders. But some readers of Kahn's work held a view something more akin to the one we find in Holbrook's analysis of Plath. Kahn, writing in 1962, notes that his effort (in *On Thermonuclear War*, [1960]) to describe the concrete details of nuclear outcomes was intended as an effort to "learn as much as we can about the risks" of nuclear war by detailing specific engagement scenarios and their probable outcomes, thereby making it easier to "act intelligently" in our defense policies.[6] Instead, he says, the book ended up raising questions among his critics not only about the content of the analysis—"questions of strategy, policy, or research techniques"—but also about its very existence, questions about "whether any book should have been written on this subject at all" (18). These critics were concerned not about the implications of fighting a nuclear war but about the implications of representing one. Some readers, Kahn goes on to explain, betrayed a "supernatural belief" in the "magical power of words" (28) that made describing nuclear destruction tantamount to producing nuclear destruction. Others, more sophisticated, argued that to write about nuclear war was to produce a self-fulfilling prophecy. The question for these (unnamed) critics is not so much what kind of representation the representation of nuclear war might be—that is, whether it is more like a novel or more like a history—or what the relation is between the representation of something and the thing itself, but what we are doing when we represent nuclear war, what act we are performing. For the critics Kahn rebuts in *Thinking about the Unthinkable*, the act of representing nuclear war is not so much the act of the "thinking" about a nuclear war as it is, proleptically, the act of fighting one. And not surprisingly, nuclear analysts like Kahn and his colleagues at the RAND Corporation, who devoted their professional lives to such efforts to represent nuclear outcomes, increasingly became associated with a hawkish nuclear stance, as if the willingness to represent outcomes were indeed in some sense related to the willingness to produce those outcomes, to actually use nuclear weapons.

The interest in the relation between nuclear destruction and fiction remained central to nuclear discourse from the time of Kahn's landmark *On Thermonuclear War*, up through the 1980s. For Jonathan Schell, representing nuclear outcomes in his best-selling antinuclear polemic, *The Fate of the Earth* (1982), it was crucial to assume that his representations of destruction were nonfiction; he imagined a transparent relation between his representations of human death and the actual persons who would face such deaths. The assumption of nonfictionality in fact defines the purpose, and the hoped-for effectiveness, of his polemic. While Schell, like Kahn, describes nuclear destruction in extended concrete detail, far from being "cold-blooded," Schell wants to produce sentiment in the reader, empathy for the suffering of the actual persons and for the whole destroyed world that he represents. In this regard, Schell uses in his nonfiction the very tools deployed by the sentimental novel (and like the sentimental novel, his writing seeks to reform his readers' morals). I will have more to say about Schell's analysis below, but for now I just want to note that Schell, Khan, Aron, and others who write about nuclear war all find themselves preoccupied with the question of how the representation of nuclear disaster relates to actual disaster in the world. Answering that question determines, for these writers, the morality of one's writing.

The contest I have briefly described in these texts over the relation between representation and the actual world, and in particular, between representations of deaths and actual deaths, presents us with a question: What do we imagine is destroyed when we imagine nuclear destruction? or more specifically, What do we represent when we represent nuclear destruction? Kahn gives us one kind of answer, an answer framed in terms of numbers of cities, numbers of lives, military capability, and so on. Writers like Jonathan Schell—a group I would take to include some fiction writers who imagined themselves to be producing literal, though prospective, representations of nuclear holocaust—took essentially the same approach to representing nuclear destruction as Kahn did, while giving it an affective spin entirely opposed to Kahn's. Kahn and Schell provide the same answer to my initial question, then: what we represent when we represent nuclear destruction is the possible destruction of actual things. What we are doing when we represent nuclear destruction is, for Kahn, "thinking"; for Schell it is thinking and feeling. Thus, Kahn's account of his critics, Aron's analogy between fiction and nuclear analysis, and Schell's desire to produce feeling in the reader all suggest that the effort to represent nuclear destruction, even in the most literal and technical way, immediately asks one to make particular kinds of assumptions about the relation between representation and the world. It is thus not the causal connection between writing and death described by Holbrook and by Kahn's critics that makes this discourse important to an account of personified texts, but the literal connection between texts and persons required by such causal claims. By the same token, it is not the denial of causal claims in Aron's and Kahn's writing that is important, but rather the fact that these writers turn to fiction as a defense against those claims precisely because fiction, by definition, does not posit a literal referent.

Book People   This is not to say, however, that fiction that engages the idea of nuclear war has answered the questions raised above about what representation is or does in the world and what its relationship to persons and their deaths might be. Indeed, it is precisely the relation between persons and representations that preoccupies Ray Bradbury's dystopic novel *Fahrenheit 451* (1953), the story of Guy Montag, a "fireman" whose job is not to put out fires, but to burn forbidden libraries. While falling short of representing the kind of nuclear destruction that was technologically possible by the time Kahn wrote *Thinking about the Unthinkable, Fahrenheit 451* nevertheless imagines a world in which the pursuit of nuclear capability—what was then called atomic weaponry—has determined the current state of the society and, in particular, has in some sense caused the government's repressive policy on books. This is a world in which the department of English Literature at Cambridge has been replaced by an Atomic Engineering School, which suggests that literature or imaginative representation, if not exactly destroyed by nuclear war, is at least replaced by the desire to wage such a war.

In this context, the narrative tracks Montag's transformation from book burner to book reader, a transformation that begins when he realizes that "a man was behind each one of the books" he had burned in his career, that "a man had to think them up."[7] While this formulation suggests that the relation between a book and its author confers a value upon books that makes the destruction of them suddenly seem wrong to Montag, it is in fact a more general identification between persons and books that is at issue, for Montag's realization comes when, upon arriving at a house whose library he is supposed to burn, he sees its owner refuse arrest, choosing instead to be burned with her books. That is, he realizes the value of books when he experiences their destruction as equivalent to the destruction of a person through the woman's extraordinary act of identification. Indeed, the very faculty of identification, in Montag's opinion, marks Clarisse McClellan, the sixteen-year-old neighbor who first begins to waken his imagination: "How like a mirror, too, her face," he thinks after their first meeting; "What incredible power of identification the girl had. . . . He felt that if his eye itched, she might blink." "How rarely did other people's faces take of you and throw back to you your own expression, your own innermost trembling thought?" (11) Though Montag locates the faculty of identification in Clarisse, it is clear he is describing his own faculty of identification—his own ability to see himself in her as if she were a mirror, to imagine what is truly himself as coming from outside himself. Insofar as Clarisse bears this structural relation to Montag, Clarisse is for Montag what books are for the woman who chooses to burn with her library. In realizing this relation between himself and Clarisse, Montag reveals himself to be a reader, though at this point in the story, he has not yet read any books.

If identification allows Montag to know himself as other, and thus makes it possible for him, as he says later on, to "become" himself, it is the failure to identify that prevents his wife, Mildred, from knowing, and hence becoming, herself. Mildred spends all her time in the television "parlor"—a room whose walls are television screens—listening to what she calls her "family," the group of actors that appear in the programs she watches. While it might seem that she thus identifies with something outside herself—with the people and events in the programs—in fact she is capable only of identifying with her own name. She subscribes to a service that inserts her name in the characters' conversation, and by doing so cuts herself off from the imaginative process of self-knowing that transforms Montag. Hence, what is remarkable to Montag about his wife is her complete ignorance of what we might call, to use

Montag's phrase, her innermost thoughts, thoughts that somehow impel her, in the first pages of the novel, to suicide. Bradbury does not describe her suicidal action, only the empty pill bottle on the floor and her inert body on the bed, thus reflecting formally what he soon reveals about Mildred's own story of the events; for after Mildred is revived by medical technicians, she herself cannot give an account of her act or its causes, responding with disbelief when Montag tries to tell her that she overdosed. Bradbury does not state, finally, whether Mildred was impelled to suicide by "inner thoughts." Montag speculates that it was her complete lack of thoughts that caused the overdose: "Maybe you took two pills and forgot and took two more, and forgot again and took two more, and were so dopey you kept right on until you had thirty or forty of them in you," he suggests to Mildred. She misses the point. "What would I want to go and do a silly thing like that for?" (19) she asks, but in doing so proves Montag right. She could not, in a sense, ever "want" to do anything. Her question is rhetorical not because she lacks the thoughts that might compel her to commit suicide, but because she has no thoughts at all. The details of Mildred's medical rescue suggest that she is only a named body. When her stomach has been pumped and her blood replaced, the medical technician tells Montag that now "all the mean stuff" is safe in a tank (15). Though "mean stuff" here might be taken in a literal sense, to be the chemicals from the overdose, the implication is that her blood—rather than her mind—also somehow contained whatever "mean stuff" impelled her to suicide in the first place.

The problem with Mildred—that she is only what she is, that she finds herself only in her own name—turns out also to be the problem with both ordinary conversation and with contemporary art in Bradbury's future world. Clarisse observes to Montag, for example, that "People don't talk about anything." She argues that ordinary conversation is simply the activity of naming a set of objects, like "cars or clothes or swimming pools. . . . They all say the same things and nobody says anything different from anyone else." She goes on to note that, at the museums, the paintings are "*All* abstract. . . . My uncle says it was different once. A long time back sometimes pictures said things or even showed *people*" (31; original emphasis). The problem, for Clarisse, is that the abstract painting is simply a painting. It does not point to, or include, something outside itself. By failing to present the viewer with the representation of a person, it also fails to elicit the response of identification that would make the viewer, in effect, into a reader. And while the name of a car points to a referent, that name is at the same time reducible to its referent. Clarisse is noticing something that Mildred, too, notices, when she

(Mildred) insists to Montag that, while "books aren't people" the family of characters in the TV parlor "is people" (73); that kind of representation *is* what it represents. The "program," like the abstract painting then, "says nothing" but simply is itself.

It turns out that intellectual content—saying something rather than saying nothing—is the official problem with books. As Beatty, the fire chief, explains to Montag, books first became a problem because they contradicted each other, causing dissension and unhappiness among the people. Thus, the movement to get rid of books was led by general market forces; people stopped buying them, and so writers stopped writing them. The government, realizing the advantages of a population interested above all in consensus, made what was largely a fact already—that few read books—into the law of the land. Beatty's historical account makes it clear that for Bradbury the society's problem is its desire for conformity. That desire translates into a desire for representation empty of content, or rather, for the end of representation as such.

Because of this emphasis on the dangers of conformity, *Fahrenheit 451* is widely considered to be a polemic against censorship, a reading supported by Bradbury's own "Coda," appended in 1979, which criticizes publishers for wanting to edit his stories to be more appealing to women and minority readers. In its concern with conformity and censorship, *Fahrenheit 451* is thus what some would think of as a characteristic novel of the 1950s, engaging some of the same social issues Norman Mailer was concerned with in *The White Negro* (1957), issues that made Sloan Wilson's *The Man in the Grey Flannel Suit* (1955) a best-seller and that drive Saul Bellow's *The Adventures of Augie March* (completed, like Bradbury's novel, in 1953).[8] But what is most significant about *Fahrenheit 451* in the context of a literary, as distinct from a social, history is the way it imagines the relation between persons and books in a nuclear world.[9]

The novel's final formulation of the relation between persons and books appears when American cities fall under atomic attack at the end of *Fahrenheit 451*. Having evaded the police, Montag joins a group of outcast intellectuals in the countryside, a group whose members introduce themselves first by their former occupations. Here we find a pastor, a professor of philosophy, and also "Fred Clement, former occupant of the Thomas Hardy Chair at Cambridge" before Cambridge became the Atomic Engineering School (150). Soon we discover that these are not merely outcasts, but men who are busy preserving books by memorizing and then destroying them. "*I* am Plato's *Republic* . . . Mr. Simmons is Marcus [Aurelius]," the group's leader, Granger, tells Montag. While at first Granger names the men as titles of books, he switches to authors in the next round of introductions: "I want you to meet Jonathan Swift, the author of . . . *Gulliver's Travels!* And this other fellow is Charles Darwin, and this one is Schopenhauer" (151; original emphasis). The structure of Montag's transformation earlier in the novel makes him what Granger calls a "perfect" new member. Montag not only realized that there was a man "behind each book," but also, as his first important subversive act, began to memorize the Book of Ecclesiastes. "While none of it will be me when it goes in," Montag reflects, "after a while it'll all gather together inside and it'll be me. . . . finally me, where it's in the blood, where it pumps around a thousand times ten thousand a day" (162). Montag becomes himself by making the content of the book not only the content of his mind but the very content of his body, the content of his blood in the same way that "mean stuff" was the content of Mildred's blood.

Bradbury thus personifies books in *Fahrenheit 451* both by giving them human bodies and by conferring upon them the kind of moral value Bradbury assigns to the self-conscious person. If my examples suggest that this kind of personification makes books and persons each into the other, Granger—recalling the language of Ecclesiastes—carves out a hierarchy of significance between the two terms: "We're nothing more than dust jackets for books, of no significance otherwise" (153), he explains to Montag. And as the city burns, and millions die in the atomic attacks, the significance of human life does seem slight. Though Montag registers some grief for Mildred, Bradbury is nevertheless leaving us with a comic ending. "When the war's over," Granger says, "perhaps we can be of some use in the world" (152). Indeed, in Montag's fantasy about Mildred's death he imagines a redemptive scene in which the nuclear attack knocks out her television program just seconds before she is killed, allowing her to see herself, for once, as other in the reflection of her face in the blank wall screen. With the end of the nuclear age, Bradbury seems to suggest, literature will return, and it will return by the same means by which human life will be regenerated—by being passed down not just by the process of learning but also "in the blood," from parents to children. Thus, while personification traditionally can confer upon the personified thing all manner of characteristics—form and agency, as in the famous example of Milton's Sin and Death, or sentiment, as in Wordsworth's landscapes—Bradbury's version of personification endows books with the ability to regenerate themselves and with an ultimate moral significance. Beyond this, *Fahrenheit 451* suggests that such a way of imagining representation is tied up with the idea of nuclear destruction, though in this novel the dynamics of that relation are left largely unexplored.

While the vision of nuclear destruction in *Fahrenheit 451* suggests that nuclear war makes this special relation between persons and books—a relation Bradbury clearly sees as preceding the nuclear age—both necessary and apparent, it does not, finally, make the personified books into the victims of nuclear war. They are instead imagined as the survivors of it. In the 1980s we find a vision of nuclear destruction that, in the effort to represent a war that could have no survivors, turns to the technology of personification as a way of imagining its victims, for when Jonathan Schell mounts his argument against all use of nuclear weapons, he begins by granting a certain privilege to imaginative representation. There are practical reasons for this. We must imagine nuclear war because we have never experienced it, and because the thing Schell sees as the most terrible outcome of nuclear holocaust, human extinction, can never exactly be experienced at all—there would be no one alive to feel the feeling of being extinct.[10] But imaginative representation is also crucial to Schell's argument insofar as the most important victims of a possible nuclear war by his account are not ourselves, or those we know, or others alive elsewhere in the world, but "the unborn." By the unborn, Schell does not mean children already conceived but not yet born at the time of nuclear conflict; he means the countless generations of children who, because of the conflict's consequences, might never be conceived. By making the unborn the center of his argument, Schell makes representations of possible persons—representations that, in being hypothetical, look much like Herman Kahn's representations—into war's primary victims. Schell himself acknowledges this as a problem, pointing out that extinction "doesn't seem to happen *to* anybody" (138). Despite Schell's acknowledgments that the unborn are not persons, that they cannot, for example, experience suffering or the loss of an existence they never had, by making the unborn the center of his argument Schell implies that future persons—who are always and only representations—are very much like actual persons in two important respects, in that we can be obligated to them in the same way we are obligated to actual persons and that we can, and should, feel the same way toward them as we do toward living persons. By failing to personify the unborn in this way, Schell implies, we short-circuit the emotional attachment to them that could encourage such moral obligation.

Schell is certainly not alone, in contemporary public discourse or in the history of philosophy, when he imagines that we have obligations to the unborn; indeed, assumptions about such obligations often structure environmentalists' arguments and have found a kind of limit in the contemporary utilitarian philosophy of Peter Singer. Singer argues, for instance, that the interests of unborn children—which for Singer, appears to mean their capacity for leading a happy and fulfilling life without undue suffering—can weigh decisively against the expected unhappiness of actual children who are born with severe handicaps, whose very existence, according to Singer, may prevent the hypothetical, and hypothetically healthy, unborn child from being born. Here, in contrast to Schell's scenario, one's moral obligation to the unborn justifies killing actual persons. Their death does not cancel the unborn, but rather is imagined to make it possible for the unborn to come into being. In whatever particular form it takes, the interest in treating the unborn as equivalent to actual persons gives enormous moral weight to what can only ever be the representation of a person. Thomas Nagel has pointed up the problems with such a position, suggesting that we cannot be obliged to bring the unborn into existence even though life itself, once we have it, can be considered the highest good.[11]

The personification of the unborn in Schell's analysis may seem more instrumental than necessary to his polemical efforts, more important, that is, to the production of affect in the reader than to any analysis of nuclear policy and the culture that produces it. But his cultural analysis theorizes and makes possible the status of representation suggested by the emphasis on the unborn. In an effort to get around the problem that nobody can be said to experience extinction, Schell argues that extinction is both a future event that would eliminate the category of human loss altogether and a kind of human loss we already experience. According to Schell, "we the living experience [extinction] now. . . . [it] saturates our existence and never stops happening" (147). One way we experience extinction, he suggests, is in Action painting or performance art, which, according to Schell, seek to shift the emphasis from the art object to the production of art. That shift produces what Schell calls "a blurring of the boundary lines" "between the artist and his work of art," a blurring which in turn "do[es] away with the enduring, independently existing art product" (164).[12] Schell's point is that in ceasing to think of art as the production of artifacts, artists are in fact ceasing to imagine a future human audience, and by ceasing to imagine that audience, are in fact rendering it extinct. While this claim personifies the representation of future persons along the same lines that the unborn are personified, it also makes the art object itself look, in important respects, like a person, in that it is imagined to have a life of its own, to be autonomous in the same way persons are autonomous. For the "independently existing art product" makes possible a "communion with the dead and with the unborn" (164)—or to put it another way, the traditional art object as Schell defines it makes a community of living beings out of living persons and living representations.

Deconstruction's Literary Victim There is nothing particularly new or special in Jonathan Schell's way of thinking about art as being the immortal embodiment of human value. What is new is how that assumption about art enters into this particular discourse about the destruction of persons. Insofar as Schell imagines nuclear arms as a threat not only to persons but also to the "independently existing art product" and, moreover, to the personified representations of the unborn, he is imagining a nuclear holocaust as a holocaust of representations. In this sense, it is structurally similar to the nuclear holocaust that Jacques Derrida imagines in his 1984 essay, "No Apocalypse, Not Now (full speed ahead, seven missiles, seven missives)," which appeared in the "Nuclear Criticism" issue of *Diacritics*. The essay was originally part of a symposium on criticism and nuclear threat, and so Derrida works in the course of the essay to argue for the relevance of criticism to the nuclear predicament. Derrida builds his case on the claim that nuclear war itself is "fabulously textual" and that it threatens "an irreversible destruction, leaving no traces, of the juridico-literary archive—that is, total destruction of the basis of literature and criticism."[13] He sharpens the latter claim in a way that helps us immediately to see the difference between his vision of nuclear destruction and Bradbury's, even though both visions center on the destruction of texts. Derrida writes that "a total and remainderless destruction of the archive . . .would take place for the first time and it would lack any common proportion with, for example, the burning of a library" (27).

While for Bradbury literature—the epitome of what he most often simply calls "books"—is a container for the thoughts of persons, and its referentiality is not at issue, for Derrida referentiality is at issue, and the critique of representation is at the core of his project. Thus, Derrida distinguishes between what he calls "literature," and other discourses like "poetry . . . the epic . . . and *belles-lettres* in general," suggesting that, in the face of nuclear destruction, the latter "might reconstitute their living process and their archive, at least to the extent that the structure of that archive . . . implies . . . reference to a real referent external to the archive itself" (26). What makes literature distinct, he explains, is that it "has not been possible without (1) a project of stockpiling, of building up an objective archive over and above any traditional oral base; (2) without the development of a positive law" that, for example, gives authors rights or produces a distinction "between the original and the copy." "Literature," Derrida claims, while it cannot be "reduced to this form of archivizing and this form of law" nevertheless "could not outlive them and still be called literature" (26).

That Derrida describes the archive in the terms of nuclear arms—as "stockpiling"—is more than mere cleverness. In fact, the equation between the project of literature thus defined and the project of nuclear war, between the way language works and the way nuclear weapons work, structures Derrida's entire argument. Here, the "missives" and "missiles" of his subtitle become, in a certain respect, the same thing: "Just as all language, all writing . . . sends itself . . . so today's missiles . . . allow themselves to be described more readily than ever as dispatches in writing." And the effect of making that analogy is not, he argues, to "reduce [missiles] to the dull inoffensiveness that some would naively attribute to books" (29) or to say that " 'all this horror is nothing but rhetoric' " (24). It is, rather, to "expose" "the power and the essence of rhetoric" (24) and "that which, in writing, always includes the power of a death machine" (29). For Derrida, rhetoric, or what he calls the "fable" of nuclear destruction, produces the actual stockpiling of weapons. He thus poses a causal relationship between language and nuclear violence that might remind us of the one in Holbrook's criticism of Sylvia Plath, except that Derrida's version relies not on the assumption of a literal correspondence between language and the world but the exact opposite, a complete failure of reference.

By this account, then, rhetoric and literature—whatever else they might be for Derrida—are also respectively the weapon and the victim of nuclear holocaust. He asserts more than once that nuclear holocaust is thus "not necessarily the destruction of humanity, of the human habitat" (26). If thinking of literature as the victim of nuclear holocaust begins to suggest the kind of personification I have described in Jonathan Schell's argument, that suggestion becomes even more compelling when we examine the terms in which Derrida describes the existence of literature in the nuclear age. In the nuclear epoch, Derrida writes, "literature comes to life and can only experience its own precariousness, its death menace and its essential finitude" (27). These are classic terms for describing the experience of conscious beings, terms at least as old as the Book of Ecclesiastes that Guy Montag memorizes. The notion that something might "come to life" and then become conscious of its own mortality only makes sense when we endow that something with a particularly human ability to "experience."[14] Insofar as only persons can be properly said to experience their own precariousness, Derrida has personified literature. Here, it is not moral value that personification transfers to the literary text—as we see in both Bradbury and Schell—but consciousness and mortality.

If Derrida is indeed personifying literature through the covert analogy between persons and literary texts, what then can one say about the ostensible subject of his essay—"nuclear criticism"? Or to put the question another way, what becomes of literary criticism if literature is thus personified? First, we need to say more about what literature is for Derrida, because, insofar as nuclear destruction destroys not a set of texts but rather "the basis" for literature, literature is more than a set of texts. It is some combination of the laws that make texts individual and the archive of these individuated texts. And in general, Derrida has seemed uninterested in ways of thinking about literature—as, for example, a canon or a library—that presume a set of texts. Insofar as this is the case, his effort to distinguish literary texts from other kinds of texts—"poetry, the epic, *belles lettres* in general"—looks misleading because it evokes, precisely, sets of texts that can be distinguished from one another. But that effort looks less at odds with his project when we consider what nuclear criticism is. For one thing, it is difficult to distinguish from deconstruction, for Derrida claims that the "the hypothesis of . . . total destruction watches over deconstruction" (27). And the purpose of both nuclear criticism and deconstruction, it seems, is to reveal the nonreferentiality of literature, not just literature of the nuclear age but literature of any age. This is why Derrida argues that "the nuclear epoch is dealt with more 'seriously' in texts by Mallarmé, or Kafka, or Joyce"—that is, in texts that he takes to be uninterested in referentiality—"than in present-day novels that would offer direct and realistic descriptions of a 'real' nuclear catastrophe" (27–28). But for the question I asked earlier—What do we imagine is destroyed when we imagine nuclear destruction?—Derrida's most interesting claim appears in a prophecy about the place of nuclear criticism in the university. "I foresee" writes Derrida, "that soon, after this colloquium, programs and departments in universities may be created under this title, as programs or departments of 'women's studies' or 'black studies' and more recently of 'peace studies' have been created" (30).

What does it mean to see a department of nuclear criticism—which is to say, a department of deconstruction—as the equivalent of departments of women's studies, black studies, or peace studies? Derrida suggests that such departments are "in principle and conceptually, irreducible to the model of the *universitas*," but defers a "demonstration" of the point (30). I can only speculate about the demonstration Derrida defers. Perhaps he is suggesting that these departments are not "reducible to the model of the *universitas*" because their concerns are not universal, though it is hard to see how peace studies would fit that description. But there is another demonstration that can be made here. Insofar as what Derrida calls "nuclear criticism" serves to personify literature by endowing it with consciousness, and insofar as Derrida does make literature recognizable as a set of individuated texts, it also transforms one's notion of nuclear holocaust from the destruction of humanity to the destruction of a group of personified texts. To put the point in positive form, the preservation of "literature," promoted by the project of nuclear criticism, consists of the effort to see it as valuable in and of itself, not because of its universality or because of its instrumentality in a real world to which it refers, but because of its self-contained particularity. And that project does seem assimilable to the project of at least two of the departments included in Derrida's list, and equally at odds with the universalist concerns implied by the model of the *universitas*. Departments of women's studies and black studies were founded in an effort to highlight the value and explore the dynamics of a particular kind of subjectivity, a particular kind of consciousness to be found in the living experience and history of particular kinds of persons. Derrida not only endows literature with personal consciousness, with the ability to experience, and with the capacity to become nuclear war's victim, but thus also assigns it a particularity of consciousness and experience, and a vulnerability, that make it assimilable to the aims of multiculturalism as epitomized by departments of women's studies and black studies.

It must be acknowledged, however, that if we put the question of "nuclear criticism" to one side for a moment, Derrida may seem the last critic one would want to implicate in the project of personifying texts, since in arguing against the traditional view of the spoken word as signifying presence—in arguing against what he calls "the metaphysics of presence" and the "logocentric" view of language—Derrida and deconstruction more generally have done much to distance persons from the texts they produce. Indeed, discussions of personification by critics such as J. Hillis Miller and Paul de Man have seen it as a trope of death and absence, as a "cover-up" or "compensation," as Miller puts it, for the death, absence, or fundamental otherness of real persons.[15] For Miller, the habit of reading—particularly, the habit of imagining characters like Pygmalion and Galatea as persons—invites us to repeat the very mistake that Pygmalion made, the mistake of taking literally the prosopopeia made visible by one's own art. This view of prosopopeia as a kind of foundational mistake lodged at the heart of reading practice is common to Derrida, de Man, and Miller, though the degree to which these critics think the mistake is avoidable varies. Miller casts this problem as an ethical one which he suggests we nevertheless cannot hope to avoid, while both Derrida and de Man are more insistent that, done right, reading can transcend the self-deception about presence that personification makes possible.

But it is in the very effort to articulate a reading practice and a definition of literature that would avoid this mistake that deconstructive critics have opened the door to an expansion, rather than the limitation, of personification's claims. Judith Butler suggests how this can be the case when she criticizes the grammar of structuralist defenses of the constructed subject, which substitute something else, such as power, culture, or discourse, in the place of the person as grammatical subject. Butler points out that "as a result, construction is still understood as a unilateral process initiated by a prior subject, fortifying that presumption of the metaphysics of the subject that where there is activity, there lurks behind it an initiating and willful subject." Therefore, "on such a view, discourse or language or the social becomes personified, and in the personification the metaphysics of the subject is reconsolidated."[16] She goes on to argue that deconstruction evades this problem, but I have already shown, in at least one instance of Derrida's writing, that this is not the case. And there are other instances, to be found in discussions that do not have to do specifically with genocide, that equally demonstrate the point.

I have shown how Derrida's effort to articulate literature as autonomous, as nonreferential and self-contained, leads his argument to imply an equation between persons and texts. Another example of this, which contains passages that are strikingly similar to some I have quoted above, can be found in "Demeure," Derrida's essay on a recovered fragment from Blanchot; here, too, he speaks of the loss of a text as death.[17] I am not the only reader to have noted a more general version of this tendency in Derrida's work. Wlad Godzich finds this to be the unspoken counterpart to de Man's critique of Derrida in "The Rhetoric of Blindness."[18] Godzich points out that Derrida's notion of text as "production" leads one back from the autonomous text to the phenomenal world from which it is supposed (by both Derrida and de Man) to be separate. I would cast this criticism differently: it is not so much Derrida's failure to establish the autonomy of the literary but the effort to do so in the first place that enables the return of the phenomenal world, its persons included.

De Man's attempts to do the same thing—more successful attempts, according to Godzich—demonstrate how deconstructive personification works in a context not specific to the discussion of nuclear holocaust. When de Man argues in "The Rhetoric of Blindness" that Derrida is blind to his own insights about Rousseau, for example, he also suggests that this kind of blindness is inherent in both literary language and in the critical discourse that draws close to the literary. The very fact of blindness, de Man goes on to say, suggests that "the cognitive function resides in the language and not in the subject."[19] The idea that language can "know" what the subject of language does not is elaborated in "The Resistance to Theory," where de Man argues that because reference is a "conventional" rather than a "phenomenal" link between signifier and signified, language thereby gains "considerable freedom from referential restraint."[20] This very autonomy in the realm of reference suggests that if language knows, what it knows is itself, and indeed, de Man says later that "literature is fiction not because it somehow refuses to acknowledge 'reality,' but because it is not *a priori* certain that language functions according to principles which are those, or which are *like* those, of the phenomenal world. It is therefore not *a priori* certain that literature is a reliable source of information about anything but its own language" (11). It is not clear exactly how convention fails to be phenomenal—are not agreements about meaning just as much a part of the phenomenal world as other kinds of things?—but even if we do not enter into that question any further than simply asking it, we can note nonetheless the generic consequences of de Man's belief in referential freedom: it is this "autonomous potential of language" that constitutes, for him, "literariness."

What is important here is not only the definition of literature that arises from de Man's work, but also the rhetoric of freedom that returns again and again throughout his writing. Literary freedom goes beyond the description of literature as "free" from referentiality to denote what looks more like a mode of being characterized by freedom from any kind of determination, referential, institutional, or otherwise. That kind of freedom is defended perhaps most energetically when de Man takes up the question of autobiography, a kind of writing that claims to be both literary and by definition referential, and which thus challenges all at once the literary freedom de Man posits. In "Autobiography as De-Facement" he argues both against the claim that autobiography is literary and against the assumption that autobiographical writing is referential in the way readers (and writers) ordinarily believe. While he argues, ultimately, that autobiography is not a literary genre, because it cannot define itself in even minimally general terms, he begins by making an evaluative argument as opposed to a theoretical one, suggesting that it cannot be a genre because it is does not possess the requisite "dignity." Those who seek to call it one, de Man argues, do so in an effort to "elevate" it "above the literary status of mere reportage, chronicle, or memoir" into "the canonical hierarchies of the major literary genres." These hierarchies, populated by lyric poetry, epic, and tragedy, are characterized for de Man by "the monumental dignity of aesthetic values" with which autobiography is, by virtue of its "self-indulgence," incompatible.[21]

This evaluative argument—which seems superfluous if we are to take the theoretical argument that follows, about failure of definition, as decisive—is revealing because it soon becomes clear that de Man seeks to separate autobiography from the literary genres not so much because it is unlike other genres as because it is too much like them. De Man argues that autobiography properly understood is a characteristic of every text: that autobiography only "makes explicit the wider claim to authorship that takes place whenever a text is stated to be *by* someone and assumed to be understandable to the extent that this is the case."[22] Not surprisingly, de Man goes on to contradict this finding, calling the "figure of reading" he has described as autobiography an unstable one, one that is the product, not the producer, of the text that demonstrates it. Indeed, the way de Man describes autobiography as part of every text is precisely the way of understanding the text that de Man argued against, most famously, in "The Purloined Ribbon."[23] As I pointed out earlier, according to de Man it is not the knowledge of the person who wrote the text, but the "cognitive function" of language itself that language communicates.[24] For de Man, a text is understandable not to the extent that he understands it to be by someone, but to the extent that it understands itself as language. It is not so much by someone, then, as about itself. This account of the literary makes it look like autobiography in a way that de Man does not acknowledge, for if meaning is generated by language itself, and the text is then about language, then the very structure of autobiography is reproduced, with language standing in as both the author and the subject of autobiography. The structural analogy reveals how uncomfortably close literature is on this account both to autobiography and to persons as such. Perhaps this is why de Man places what seems like a gratuitous evaluative argument against autobiography so prominently in this essay: evaluative terms may be the only ones left with which de Man can adequately distinguish autobiography from literature.

To read de Man's analysis this way is perhaps simply to assert, rather than to argue, a certain difference from de Man—he sees personhood as the product of rhetoric, I see it as the product of rhetoric plus embodiment. But what I want to point out here is not that I think de Man is wrong about what persons are; rather, I want to point out that he sets up various structures like autonomy, cognition, authorial agency—which we ordinarily assign to persons, whether or not de Man is right about what persons are—as belonging to the literary text. We can see, then, that autobiography understood as a characteristic of all texts actually does threaten the autonomy of the text, even if de Man argues at the same time that autobiography is as much absent from every text as characteristic of every text. It threatens the autonomy of the text not by virtue of being a genre (because, according to de Man, it is not one) or by trying to represent things outside of the text that are really (on de Man's reading) a function of the text. The text's autonomy is threatened by the very fact that someone has written it.

Given this threat, it is perhaps not surprising that the part of "Autobiography as De-Facement" that seeks to demonstrate the "abstractions" of the first part takes up an essay preoccupied with death: Wordsworth's *Essay on Epitaphs*. What is most important, for my purposes, about de Man's reading of Wordsworth is the point at which de Man finds error in Wordsworth's effort to contrast two kinds of language, language that is "clothing" for thought and language that is "incarnate" thought.[25] While Wordsworth posits a significant difference between the two, relying on a common understanding of clothing as different from the body and going so far as to characterize the former as a "poisoned coat" that kills its wearer, de Man denies a difference between the two. The clothing and the body are the same, he argues, in that both are the "visible outside" of some interior entity (80). This claim looks odd for two reasons. First, it conflates clothing and the body in a move that looks surprisingly similar to the descriptions of the body as clothing in Sylvia Plath's medical poems, taking the substance of the person to be not ontological (what she is) but representational (what she looks like). Second, and more importantly, it seems to suggest, for language, a dualistic structure—a body that veils the soul—that repeats the structure of reference that de Man eschews. It suggests an animating core of meaning and significance (which, by virtue of being a soul, bears metaphysical value) within the "veil" of language. The pathos of de Man's reading—of its conflation of language with the body, and its tacit suggestion of a rejected dualism—appears at the end of the essay, where, in returning to a more polemical discourse against autobiography, de Man writes that "death" is a "displaced name for a linguistic predicament" and that writing, even the prosopoetic writing of the epitaph or of autobiography, does not bring to life or give face but in fact is a "defacement of the mind" (81). Insofar as prosopopeia is, as de Man claims in "Hypogram and Inscription," "the master trope of poetic discourse,"[26] and insofar as autobiography is characteristic of every text we understand to be "by" someone, the ultimate destruction of significance (death) lies within the capacity of literary language. When language makes a person, or a face or countenance, the face of the person outside of language becomes inaccessible. The very autonomy of the text in de Man's account threatens to replace, or rather to erase, not only the writer, then, but also the text's own existence as writing.

Thus, we arrive at the same belief about the relation between language and persons whether we argue, with de Man, that language is utterly autonomous from the phenomenal world of persons, or imagine, with Bradbury, that language is utterly synonymous with it. In either case, language can come to look like a person. In the literalist's case, its ontology is defined by an actual person with whom it is conflated (this is apparent not only in Bradbury's book-memorizers, but also—to refer back and forward to chapter 1 and chapter 3—in the idea of the feminine text or the murdered diary); in de Man's case, it gains an ontology separate unto itself which bears the significant marks of persons—most importantly, consciousness and autonomy. We can see this last point most clearly in "Autobiography as De-Facement," where, like Derrida, de Man also finally imagines the literary as vulnerable and mortal.

It should be clear, then, that I am not giving a reading of deconstruction equivalent to the common critique that de Man is, at least in part, writing against in "Resistance to Theory," the critique that considers deconstruction to be "pure verbalism" and "a denial of the reality principle in the name of absolute fictions."[27] My reading of deconstruction suggests instead that de Man's (and Derrida's and Miller's) own ways of characterizing literary language have invited readers to understand language as itself personified to the degree that it is endowed with autonomy, consciousness, and mortality. If we personify as we read, it is not so much because, as Miller says in *Versions of Pygmalion* and elsewhere, we take characters to be persons, but rather insofar as we do not take language to be referential. Taking language to be representational, we have several kinds of explanations available to us for why we think of characters as persons—we might say, for example, that they represent the idea of a person originating in the author's mind, or that they are representations that remind us of real people we have known, or that the author intended the character to represent a particular person existing in the world. However we might evaluate these kinds of explanations, we can begin to see what is closed off by deconstruction, and further, how positing the literary as autonomous and nonreferential in both Derrida and de Man involves, in place of such explanations, not only a recourse to the figure of the person, but also the personification of the literary itself as mortal, threatened by an authorial presence and by referentiality, not to mention by nuclear war. Despite the explicit efforts of de Man, Derrida, and Miller to question the literalist deceptions of prosopopeia—efforts that are not far in spirit from the questions I myself wish to raise—deconstruction can been seen, if not as responsible for, then certainly as contributing to, an understanding of texts as personified literary victims. I have already laid out one example of how views of language made possible by deconstruction enable personification of writing in Jacqueline Rose's work, discussed in chapter 1, and I will give further examples of it, which involve de Man specifically, in the work of Shoshana Felman and Cathy Caruth, discussed in chapter 4.

Nuclear Holocaust and the Holocaust   When we think through Derrida's off-hand prophecy about a department of nuclear criticism in "No Apocalypse, Not Now," literature comes to look not only like a personification, but like a personification with the characteristics of what we would think of as an identity group, based on the particularity of its subjectivity. And at this point it becomes clear that, while Derrida and Schell can both be said to imagine that something like literature is the victim of nuclear holocaust, Derrida's version revises Schell's universalism. Derrida's personification makes nuclear holocaust look less like the universal destruction of life, destruction that registers no distinction between plants, animals, and humans, let alone between one kind of person and another, and more like another vision of holocaust: ethnic holocaust, or genocide.

Indeed, even Bradbury's version of holocaust suggests that such a shift is somehow inherent in the notion of nuclear holocaust. Montag, after all, imagines that when he memorizes a book he puts it "in the blood." If this looks like a racial paradigm, we might want to say, on one hand, that the race Bradbury is imagining is the human race, for it is the implicit universality of the texts, their value across time, that, in Bradbury's view, makes them worth preserving. But on the other hand, the race with the book in the blood looks in many respects less like a Western-civ stereotype of humanity than an equally stereotypical image of the Jewish people. As Granger explains to Montag when Montag first joins up with the "Book People" (as Bradbury calls them in the afterword, added in 1982), they are "the odd minority crying in the wilderness" (152). According to tradition, of course, the "odd minority crying in the wilderness," and, for that matter, "The People of the Book," is the Jewish people, a connection Bradbury reinforces with numerous details. It is the text of Ecclesiastes that Montag comes to embody—that is, the text of a great Hebrew prophet— and indeed, the "Book People" are a minority with a quasi-messianic purpose, to carry on the knowledge of a higher truth until the world is ready to receive it from them and embrace it, ready, that is, to write down the memorized texts and rebuild the destroyed libraries.

It appears that this "minority" is also an exceptional one in the eyes of its creator, for within the novel Bradbury has the fire chief, Beatty, explain that it was the "minorities" themselves—with their demands for inclusion and representation—who were the first to attack books. Bradbury's coda, added in 1979, is even more hostile to the claims "minorities" make upon art: "There is more than one way to burn a book. And the world is full of people running about with lit matches. Every minority," Bradbury complains, "be it Baptist / Unitarian, Irish / Italian / Octogenarian / Zen Buddhist, Zionist / Seventh-day Adventist, Women's Lib / Republican, Mattachine / Foursquare Gospel feels it has the will, the right, the duty to douse the kerosene, light the fuse" (176–77). While this list is made up largely of religious groups, the first examples of such groups Bradbury mentions in the coda are women, who wanted more women's roles in *The Martian Chronicles*, "blacks," who complained that the novel's black characters were "Uncle Toms," and Southern whites, who complained, to the contrary, that it was "prejudiced in favor of the blacks" (175). Bradbury obviously distinguishes between minorities who distort what he sees as the purpose of art (writing in particular) and the kind of minority he imagines the Book People to be, a group whose minority view is precisely that artistic freedom must be preserved. The Book People, then, are different from all other "minorities" Bradbury mentions in that they are custodians of humanity's interests, rather than custodians of the interests of a racially or otherwise defined group, and in this sense the Book People seem not a minority at all in the sense that Bradbury's coda insists upon. To put the point another way, the Book People make humanity look like a minority.

Bradbury is not alone, in the 1950s, in imaging the survivors of nuclear war as in some sense Jewish, and indeed, as the embodiments of texts. Walter Miller's *A Canticle for Leibowitz* (ca. 1959) imagines a postnuclear world in which knowledge has been preserved only at great pains by a Catholic monastic community, the Albertian Order of St. Leibowitz, founded by a Jewish nuclear weapons engineer turned priest, Isaac Edward Leibowitz. Like Bradbury's Book People, the monks of the order are "Memorizers" (they are also known as "Bookleggers" because of their smuggling activities), their mission having been, from the time of the founder, to preserve texts both by memorizing them and by burying them in casks in the southwestern desert.[28] Leibowitz himself, because of his identification with books, is eventually martyred; he is hanged and burned by a mob hostile to knowledge, and he dies like the old woman who is burned with her library in *Fahrenheit 451*.

Miller's Leibowitz thus institutes not only the preservation of knowledge but also the absolute identification of the person with the text. Miller has another Jew—the immortal Benjamin, the Wandering Jew, last living survivor of the first nuclear war—ensure the continuance of Leibowitz's legacy by sewing up the case for Leibowitz's sainthood hundreds of years later. Benjamin shows a novice monk where to find the crucial evidence for the canonization—the body of Emily Leibowitz, the saint's wife, on the *outside* of a buried fallout shelter, proving that Leibowitz was indeed free of the obligations of marriage when he became a priest. The success of the application for sainthood ensures not only the continued existence of the order and the continued preservation of the knowledge contained in the order's archives (called the "Memorabilia" in recognition of how the texts were preserved) but also provides a kind of immortality for Leibowitz. In canonization, Leibowitz is acknowledged to be an active presence in the world, working miracles and interceding with God for those who invoke him, as much alive, in a certain sense, as Benjamin (indeed, Benjamin is at one point in the novel mistaken for the saint himself). The function of the Judeo-Christian tradition, with its technology of canonization, is thus to act as the memory of civilization or, to put it more precisely, to embody the knowledge that civilization produced.

This is the case in spite of the fact that embodiment can appear insignificant in this novel. The order's abbot, for example, places the body firmly below the soul in the hierarchy of importance. As he explains to the aptly named Dr. Cors, a doctor serving in a euthanasia camp set up after massive nuclear attacks, "you don't *have* a soul, Doctor. You *are* a soul. You *have* a body, temporarily" (295; original emphasis). The very chronology of the novel, which stretches over some thirty-six centuries, ensures that most individual characters will not persist, and Miller makes a point of depicting the meaningless deaths of several whom the narrative has followed, most notably the pathetic Brother Francis, who is killed by bandits and eaten by buzzards. Miller frames descriptions of death with sardonic scripture-style reflections on the cycle of life: "The buzzards laid their eggs in season and lovingly fed their young. . . . The younger generation waxed strong, soared high and far on black wings, waiting for the fruitful earth to yield up her bountiful carrion" (118). But there are a number of bodies that do persist in *A Canticle for Leibowitz*. Benjamin, of course, but also the monastic order, his Christian counterpart, described by Abbot Zerchis as an "organism . . . whose cells were men, whose life had flowed through seventy generations. . . . The organism lived as a body, worshipped and worked as a body, and at times seemed dimly conscious as a mind that infused its members and whispered to itself and to Another in the lingua prima, baby tongue of the species" (275–76). Miller is not simply repeating a well-used Pauline trope here, of the believers as the body of Christ, where the analogy to the parts of the body denotes both a oneness and a difference between parts according to their given function. For one thing, Miller makes it plain that the community is not the body of Christ, or even of the Church, but the body of "the species." He is imaging a specifically biological version of the trope, a point that becomes clear when we consider the function of the novel's dominating theme: nuclear war.

It is the biological legacy of nuclear war—genetic mutation—that allows the human race to become a race in the way that Miller imagines the Jewish race, that is, for it to be understood, as the monks are, as continually self-renewing cells of what is a kind of body with distinctive traits. One of the several abbots that appear in the narrative demonstrates how this works during a conversation with Benjamin about collective identity. Abbot Paulo notes that when Benjamin says "I" he means "we," as in "my people." Collectivizing oneself in this way, according to the Abbot, is to assume for oneself the "burden" of past generations. Abbot Paulo rejects what he calls the "illogic" of adopting this assumption of racist persecution—that any member of the race can be called to account for the actions of any other member of the race. But when Benjamin, with a certain logical consistency, treats the Abbot himself as the embodiment of the "Them" who have persecuted him (or his people) in the past, the Abbot's own Catholicism requires that he assent to the collectivizing logic Benjamin represents. The Abbot realizes that he, too, is "a member of a oneness . . . a part of a congregation and a continuity." And so while he first claims that, in contrast to Benjamin, "the distinction between self and nation is clear," the Abbot eventually revises that claim, for the nation he decides he belongs to is "Man." "Man" is distinguished as a race (the human race)—and subject to Benjamin's collectivizing logic—because all men are doomed to carry the burden of Adam's sin (171–72).

That original sin is, for Miller, epitomized by nuclear war: the first strike in the second nuclear war (there are several over the course of the novel) is announced by the coded cry "Lucifer has fallen!" as if the use of the weapons indicated the first entrance of evil into the world. What makes nuclear war more than simply the epitome of original sin, however, is its ability, through radiation, to actually deform the body. Miller makes it clear that such deformity marks all persons: not only the "monsters," like the bicephalic Mrs. Grales, but also the seemingly normal men like Abbot Zerchis, whose hand bears a faint scar where a sixth finger was removed at birth. What Abbot Paulo calls the "burden," assumed by Benjamin according to the collectivizing logic of racialism—that the "I" is the "we"—becomes the genetically inherited sign of sin, the mutation in the race of Man. It makes the sins of the fathers, through the genetic mechanism of biological reproduction, into the sins of the children. While Miller's interest in genetic mutation is clearly religious, it is worth pointing out that it results in a kind of workable Lamarckianism, by which the cultural habits and actions of one generation transform the genetic material passed on to the next generation. In the world Miller imagines, the willingness to wage a nuclear war is passed down through the generations, sometimes lying latent in men, sometimes erupting into a new nuclear conflagration. To make the sins of the fathers into the sins of the children does not require, Miller seems to imagine, the "illogic" of racialism; it requires only the natural logic of biology. Genetic mutation takes the place of racial illogic.

Genetic mutation is the model for how representation survives nuclear war. In the largest sense, as Abbot Paulo reflects, God's "objective meaning in the world," requires "incarnation" in the "cultures" of humans. The Abbot claims, for example, that "Truth" is "crucified" when the cultures of humans are obliterated. Within the Catholic paradigm of the novel, crucifixion, of course, implies "a resurrection" (145–46). The monks and Benjamin are, above all, knowers and memorizers, the resurrection of embodied truth. In the body of Benjamin, knowledge and the body are entirely conflated, with eminently practical consequences. Because he is immortal, he knows things others do not and can ensure that, like his own body, cultural knowledge can persist in the body of the Leibowitzan order. Most importantly, the knowledge residing in his immortal consciousness stands ready to identify the Messiah (or more accurately, to identify who is not the Messiah). The implication is that without his immortal body and the knowledge he carries, "truth" would not have its "resurrection."[29] In the monks' case, truth lives not only in their minds, which memorize texts, but also through the material texts they preserve and reproduce. Like Bradbury's Book People, the biological life of Benjamin or of the monastic community allows the text to persist in the way the body can persist: through the miracle of immortality, through the renewal of genetic reproduction, or through the affiliative reproduction of the monastic community.

This text with a body is, in light of Miller's evident religious commitments, a version of the Gospel of John's "Word made flesh" and of Catholicism's miracle of transubstantiation. For Miller, the conflation of actual flesh

and what he variously refers to as knowledge, truth, meaning, or text is simply
the extension of that transubstantial logic, whereby the symbol—the bread—
becomes what it means—the actual body of Christ (thus ceasing to be a symbol). If this seems inconsistent with what I have argued about the centrality
of Jewishness to Miller's way of imagining this Christian community, it is
worth noting that the personified text is part of the Jewish tradition as well
as the Christian, as I mention in the introduction; the Torah is greeted and,
in procession, walks among the people gathered at *shul*. But there are historical
reasons more local to the 1950s, as well, for what we can see in Miller's novel
as a convergence of Christian and Jewish traditions. As Peter Novick has
explained, the very concept of the Judeo-Christian tradition was a product
of several political forces in the postwar period: the American reaction to
Hitler, strategic alliances between Christian and Jewish organizations in the
United States, and Cold War efforts to blame not Germany, but "totalitarianism" (which could then, of course, include the Soviet Union) for the Nazi
genocide.[30] Though the notion of a "Judeo-Christian tradition" might appear
to be universalizing, Novick's account makes clear that the idea on one hand
delineated important ideological and national distinctions (totalitarianism vs.
democracy, Israel vs. the Arab Middle East, U.S. and Europe vs. U.S.S.R.)
and on the other hand, created, in that concept, one larger particularity that
(supposedly) could transcend the nation without including our former ally or
excluding our former enemy.[31] Thus, Bradbury's and Miller's efforts to imagine the targets of nuclear holocaust as if they were targets of an ethnic holocaust exemplify a certain contemporary Cold War account of who, and what,
the Nazis tried to destroy.

What is perhaps more interesting than the simple fact that Bradbury and
Miller imagine nuclear holocaust as ethnic holocaust is that they do so using
a technology of personification that makes biology central, imagining the survivors of nuclear war as being in some sense the human embodiments of texts.
Biology became central to later writers interested not in nuclear survivors,
but in survivors of the Jewish holocaust. Terrence Des Pres, for instance,
argues that those who did survive in the concentration camps possessed what
he calls (taking the phrase from an actual survivor's testimony) a "talent for
life," a talent that, Des Pres explains, belongs not to "a particular class, race,
culture, or nation" but is instead a particularly human ability to keep life "as
the biologists see it" going even in the most extreme circumstances. He suggests that "the survivor's behavior is biologically determined."[32] Given this
definition, "survivors" are not only those who emerged alive from the Nazi
concentration camps or from the gulags in Siberia, but also those who hung

onto life until bad luck, disease, or violence ended their lives. While for many Holocaust scholars, the "survivors" include the children of those who escaped with their lives and others who never went into the camps (a kind of logic I take up in chapters 3 and 4), for Des Pres "survivors" include those who never got out.

Des Pres is more interested by far in living human beings, in persons, than he is in texts; his work does not in any sense personify texts in the ways I have shown Bradbury, Derrida, de Man, Schell, and Miller do. And he does not extend the implications of his argument to nuclear holocaust.[33] What is significant about Des Pres's work, from the standpoint of my analysis, is its commitment to understanding the Jewish Holocaust in biological terms, in terms of the species. The historical specificity of that understanding is perhaps reflected in the fact that this element of Des Pres's work on survivors dropped away in his later thinking on the subject. The commitment to the importance of biology, evident as the Cold War intensified in the mid-1970s, is also elaborated at the very end of the Cold War in Robert Jay Lifton and Eric Markusen's comparative study of nuclear and ethnic holocaust in *The Genocidal Mentality* (1990). There the authors argue—in language reminiscent of Miller—that the solution to the problem of genocide is a "species consciousness," to be cultivated in all people through moral education. Such education would aim, the authors suggest, at convincing people that their moral obligations, in particular, their moral obligation not to take life or to inflict harm, extend not just to the members of their own race or nation but to all members of the species. We even see the concern for biological persistence in Holbrook's study of Plath, whose fantasy of committing suicide with her children in "Edge" he finds especially dangerous because it represents a failure of "care and concern" for one's biological offspring, a kind of care and concern that turns out to be Holbrook's favored solution to the problems posed by Plath's poems.[34] What survives genocide, then, for Des Pres and for Lifton, is the species. For these writers, unlike Bradbury and Miller, the Jewish people are universalized as an example of the human species. To put it another way, the species does not look like a circumscribed racial or ethnic group—analogous to the Jewish people or, for that matter, to any people—despite the fact that Des Pres and Lifton are describing and analyzing the Jewish Holocaust.

3

The biological emphasis of writers like Des Pres and Lifton turned out to be short-lived among those interested in thinking about ethnic holocaust and, in particular, about the Jewish Holocaust. It was short-lived because, although the Nazis themselves were committed to a racialist biological view of their victims, murdering Jews regardless of their actual cultural practices, writers in the 1980s and 1990s chose to focus less on the destruction of living persons than on the destruction of culture and, more specifically, of representations. Thus, though the biological concerns of nuclear discourse began to recede from writing about ethnic holocaust in the late 1980s, the personification that accompanied that biological discourse became all the more important as a way of thinking about the moral terms in which one was to evaluate the destruction of culture. We see personification at work, for example, in the final panel of Art Spiegelman's graphic novel, *Maus I*, where the protagonist, Art, calls his father a "murderer" for burning the diaries of his dead wife, as if the destruction of Anja's record of her experiences at Auschwitz were somehow equivalent to the kinds of destruction that took place at Auschwitz (see figure 1).[1] Although the equation between the destruction of representations (the diaries) and the destruction of persons (the Jews) may seem at best hyperbolic, the equation in fact plays a role not only in imaginative representations of the Holocaust from the late 1980s and 1990s but also

159

Figure 1. The final page from Art Spiegelman, *Maus I: My Father Bleeds History*.

in contemporary critiques of the very idea of an imaginative representation of the Holocaust.

Thus, Berel Lang argues in his essay "The Representation of Limits" that all literary representations of the Holocaust violate the facts of history, and that violating the facts of history is immoral in the same way that violating persons is. Literary representations violate the facts of history because the mere idea of such "imaginative representation" makes the implicit claim "that the facts *do not* speak for themselves, that figurative condensation and displacement and the authorial presence these articulate will turn or supplement the historical subject (whatever it is) in a way that represents the subject more compellingly or effectively—in the end, more truly—than would be the case without them."[2] So the facts that would otherwise "speak for themselves"— facts that, Lang claims, "do not depend on the author's voice for their existence" (316)—are silenced by imaginative representation, or, more precisely, the historical representations through which the facts should be allowed to speak are silenced by imaginative representation.

Lang describes the treatment of facts in literary representations in terms of oppression, oppression that mirrors what Jews suffered during the Holocaust. "The denial of individuality and personhood in the act of genocide; the abstract bureaucracy that empowered the 'Final Solution,' moved by an almost indistinguishable combination of corporate and individual will and blindness to evil, constitute a subject that in its elements seems at odds with the insulation of figurative discourse and the individuation of character and motivation that literary 'making' tends to impose on its subjects" (316). The historical fact that is here "at odds" with literary representation is that Nazi brutality reduced people to nonpersons, denying them the marks of personhood; since "figurative discourse" endows the victims with personhood— with "motivation" and "individuation of character"—it thus "defies" the historical facts "which might otherwise have spoken for themselves." And so these marks of personhood become an *imposition* upon the subjects of literary representation, who are in this case the very persons upon whom the Final Solution was imposed. Literary representation denies the historical facts their specific content, their individuality; in essence, it denies them the marks of personhood. As I shall show, such treatment of historical representations— of the facts those representations contain—is understood by Lang as a kind of murder, not simply a denial but a repetition of the Holocaust.

Once I put the point in this way, it becomes easier to see how Spiegelman's personification of Anja's diaries and Lang's personification of historical representations can be located within a larger cultural project. Indeed, the very idea of culture may be understood in terms of this project, for the most common site upon which we relocate the pathos that ordinarily belongs to the human victim—the victim of murder—is neither the diary nor the history but the culture. What worries many who are invested in the future of certain cultural groups is that, as Eddy Zemach puts it in his essay "Custodians," "Cultures can die."[3]

Expressions of this anxiety cross the generic spectrum from popular fiction to scholarly essays and can refer to almost any culture. In the Native American community, for example, the threat to the continuance of the culture has historically taken the form of white families adopting Indian children. Thus, the plot of Barbara Kingsolver's best-selling *Pigs in Heaven* pits a loving and well-meaning white woman who adopts—illegally, it turns out—an abandoned Cherokee child against an equally well-meaning Cherokee lawyer who sees such illegal adoptions as a threat to the survival of Native American culture.[4] Kingsolver gives us a solution that only fiction could provide: the adoptive mother turns out to be part Cherokee after all, and by the end of the book *her* mother marries a man who turns out to be the child's grandfather. Yet the very structure of the solution, improbable as it may seem, is not far from the kind of solution scholars such as Eddy Zemach advocate to counteract what they and others see as the impending death of Jewish culture.

Of course, for the Jewish community the threat to continuance has been not adoption but assimilation and intermarriage. Sociologists of the American Jewish community divide up into "optimist" and "pessimist" schools, or "accommodationist" and "assimilationist" schools, according to how likely they think it is that there will be in the future as there has been in the past something identifiable as a Jewish ethnic group in America. The essays in *The Americanization of the Jews*, which detail both the history and the possible futures of Jewish culture in America, are mostly of the "pessimist" bent. Paul Ritterband, for instance, cites declining fertility, increasing intermarriage, and increasing geographical dispersion of Jews in America as "emblematic of the devolution of the Jews in our time." "Jewishness," Ritterband writes, "is attenuating."[5] Charles Liebman is equally skeptical about the viability of what he calls "a group that defines itself as Jewish and that is recognizably Jewish" in America. He fears that although in the future a group might continue to "define itself" as Jewish, the members of the group might nevertheless "become so assimilated that they are culturally unrecognizable as Jews."[6] The historian Arthur Hertzberg points to the decline of anti-Semitism and the increasing distance of present-day Jews from the immigrant generation as forces that could result in the disappearance of the ethnic community.[7]

In the face of this outlook, advocates of continuity feel compelled to step forward and offer rationales for consciously resisting such change. Zemach, one such advocate, argues that "the question is not whether one is to accept a culture; it is what culture, and what group that incorporates it, with which one chooses to associate oneself. That decision is most significant: Choosing not to align oneself with a group, say, not to join the local Jewish community, shapes the community's destiny, for one makes it an even smaller minority. . . . Cultures can die."[8] Against the possibility that a culture will "die" or be lost, people must be recruited to propagate the culture. If in Kingsolver's novel the death of culture is warded off by the enrollment of "new" Cherokees, we can see that for Zemach the solution is similar. Cultural death can be warded off by recruiting Jews to the practice of a Jewish cultural tradition; cultural death can be avoided by the enrollment of "new" Jews.

But the question remains, why should any culture survive? Why should Jewish culture in particular survive? If recruitment to an identity is possible because we think of cultural identity as something that can be claimed and lost, as something that is not simply equivalent to one's present beliefs and practices, it can be necessary only insofar as we believe that certain cultural practices are not only ephemeral but also inherently valuable, and in fact more valuable than those which threaten to replace them. This is always a difficult case to make, as advocates of recruitment rarely wish to denigrate other cultural practices in the process. Thus, while Zemach notes that certain desirable practices such as philanthropy or intellectual achievement have become associated with Jewishness, and that Jewish liturgy serves as the container for a valuable "anthology of hundreds of years of literature," his rationale for recruitment turns on the notion that cultural practices are inherently valuable in the same way that we think human life is inherently valuable. He implies that we should strive to avert the death of most any culture (not just Jewish culture) simply because it is a death.[9] Though this may provide a rationale for *adopting* any particular cultural practice, and especially any "dying" minority practice, it cannot provide a rationale for abandoning whatever practice the new one replaces, for that abandonment would always mean contributing to a cultural death, albeit a different and perhaps, in the case of a strong majority culture, a distant one.

In his controversial book *Why Should Jews Survive?* Michael Goldberg takes on this objection while continuing to argue for the survival of Jewish culture.[10] He answers his title question in a way that is at once historicist and religious. Goldberg points out that cultures arise and die out all the time without significant losses to humanity as a whole and argues that the only

coherent reason for Jews to resist this cycle—to consider themselves exceptional as a people—is the covenantal relationship that the Jewish people traditionally claim with God. Goldberg thus argues against both those like Zemach
who find inherent value in perpetuation and those who argue that Jewish
culture in particular must perpetuate itself in order to both mourn for and
defy the Holocaust.

It is this latter group with which he is most concerned, because he believes
that the Holocaust (and not the interest in perpetuation) has structurally replaced God in the Jewish community. Goldberg traces how traditional religious characteristics of the Jewish people—such as the belief in chosenness
or uniqueness—are secularized by transferring those characteristics to the
experience of the Holocaust; hence the intense scholarly interest in theorizing
its uniqueness. He claims that, when the Holocaust is simultaneously heralded
as the death of God, it comes to fill the place of God and thus constitutes an
instance of idolatry that parallels the ancient Jews' worship of Ba'al. Why
should Jews survive, then? According to Goldberg, the Jews as a people should
survive in order to fulfill the Messianic promise God has made through them
to all the world.

Although his account is a coherent one, to a generation of thoroughly
secularized Jews in America, Goldberg's rationale for survival sounds at best
old-fashioned, and at worst absurd. But most would admit that Goldberg is
right on one count: the Holocaust has indeed become a cornerstone of Jewish
identity in America.[11] In light of this, the passing of the generation who actually experienced the Holocaust presents a problem for the construction of
Jewish identity. If the answer to the question Why should Jews survive? is
going to remain tied to the Holocaust, and if connection to the Holocaust
rather than commitment to Judaism stands near the center of American Jewish
identity, the passing of that generation threatens to sever the community's
ties to an important source of its identity. That new ways of connecting to
the Holocaust are being constructed is obvious in the proliferation of movies,
books, classes, and museums that tell the Holocaust story, and in the separate
efforts of Yale's Fortunoff Archive and of director Steven Spielberg to collect
videotaped testimonies of survivors.[12] Since these new connections remain
independent of the life of individual survivors for their future existence, they
promise to remain available to all for all time.

What is less obvious, and more interesting, is *how* these representations
of the Holocaust forge connections between that event and present-day people
and by what discursive technologies this recruitment to identity occurs. I will
begin with a recruitment technology that relies on the equation between per-

sons and representations that I have been outlining throughout these pages: the technology of the list.

From History to the List   In "The Representation of Limits" Berel Lang works to build a theoretical structure upon which all representations of the Holocaust can be based and against which they can be judged, although he explicates and argues for a formula meant to help writers and readers think about the moral aspects of any particular project (though all of Lang's examples involve discussions of the Holocaust). Lang calls the formula and its product "the moral radical of historical representation" (308).[13] To illustrate the use of the moral radical, Lang proposes that there is a moral difference between the functionalist and intentionalist accounts of the Final Solution.[14] The former, he claims, assigns responsibility to a system, thus exculpating the individual and rendering the Holocaust "collectively unintended" (309), while the latter holds the individual responsible and maintains that the Holocaust was intended in all its extremity. Though everyone would agree that the difference Lang describes is a historical one—a difference between one version of how things happened and another—we might at this point want to ask what makes the difference between functionalist and intentionalist versions of the Holocaust distinct from other divergent versions of history. Why does the difference become a moral issue for the interpreter? While functionalist and intentionalist versions of history certainly point to different moral judgments of Hitler and his officials, it is not clear why the historian becomes less moral if the judgment against Hitler—based on an analysis of historical events—becomes less severe while judgments against others, though more diffuse, become more severe.

Lang contends that the morality of any historical account rests upon the "consequences" of the particular version of history; presumably divergent accounts of the Holocaust are distinct from divergent accounts of other events—consider, for the sake of argument, the 1980 presidential election— because any given interpretation of the Holocaust means more or is somehow more powerful in the culture than any given interpretation of the presidential election. But while Lang asserts that "it is clear that differences on this issue [of intention] have significant moral and social consequences" (308), he never specifies what these consequences might be. What does become clear is Lang's preference—a moralized one—for connecting events or statements as tightly as possible with nameable individuals and their intentions. What is at stake, then, between functionalist and intentionalist accounts is perhaps not so much the existence of consequences as the existence of intentions, intentions upon which judgments about moral responsibility can be built. In this case it is Hitler's intentions that are at issue, not those of the historian, for at this point in Lang's argument it is the historian's response to unspecified "social consequences" of his or her work rather than the historian's intentions that matter. But in the next stage of the argument the question of intention appears to shift from Hitler to historian, and the object of responsibility shifts from the community—from a group of people—to representations.

This shift takes place through Lang's second example of the formula's application, in which he uses it to judge histories of the Final Solution that insist there was no systematic killing of Jews by Nazis. The (again unspecified) risk calculated by Lang's moral radical increases dramatically with this kind of denial. He argues that the degree of risk incurred justifies an equally extreme response from what he calls a "moral community." The "moral community" Lang invokes in his example of a justified response is a conference of Holocaust historians meeting at Northwestern University. During the question and answer period following a presentation by Saul Friedlander, the notorious Holocaust denier Arthur Butz challenges Friedlander's version of history, implying or claiming (Lang does not print Butz's question) that the Holocaust as Friedlander represented it did not occur. Friedlander refuses to answer the question, and Lang reads that response as a moral decision. According to Lang's gloss on the incident, Friedlander acted as the voice of a moral community that wisely resists the kind of risky history for which Butz was arguing (312). Though Lang's example centers on a community of scholars, Butz's failing is importantly not a scholarly one. Arthur Butz is, according to Lang, a person who had "separated himself" from the moral community (312); he is not simply an incompetent historian. Since Lang seemingly cannot account for the "social and moral consequences" of Butz's version of history, what is the risk he runs and whom does he stand to harm by producing incompetent history? Or to put the question another way, why, precisely, is Butz not mistaken but immoral?

Lang suggests that if Friedlander were to have answered Arthur Butz's question he would have had to believe that "questions are detachable from those who raise them," and that "historical representations have no intrinsic or necessary moral standing" (312). His refusal rightly, according to Lang, resisted not simply the question but also these assumptions. Lang believes that these assumptions "are rightfully disputed, not uniquely in their bearing on accounts of the 'Final Solution.'" For the same reason that he favors the intentionalist over the functionalist account of the Holocaust, Lang believes that statements as well as actions must, of moral necessity, be attached to people and their intentions. For Lang this is a question of social responsibility. But by implying that the whole "moral community" recognizes that historical representations have "moral standing" in and of themselves, he transfers morality from the relation between persons—social responsibility—to the relation between persons and representations. If these two relations become nearly indistinguishable in Lang's essay, it is because persons and representations are themselves nearly indistinguishable. By the end of the essay, Lang has moved from the attachment of representations to persons (through intention and responsibility), to the "intrinsic . . . moral standing" of facts, to the "moral *presence*" (313; original emphasis) of facts. Thus, the moral indictment against Butz will not be the seemingly commonsense one—that Butz is immoral because his revisionist history is not merely mistaken but rather is designed to feed anti-Semitism. Lang does not in fact need to impute to Butz anti-Semitic intentions (intentions to harm people) if he can cast Butz's history as an anti-Semitic act (actually harming the equivalent of people).[15]

We can understand in a new way, then, why mainstream historians such as Lang, not to mention the general public, are outraged over Holocaust revisionism as if it were a form of murder, and why the profession (though not Lang himself) has made concerted efforts to suppress it in spite of scholars' allegiance to the idea of free speech.[16] We can also make sense of Lang's claim that artistic representations, in obscuring morally present facts, also obscure or erase the real (historical) victims and therefore reenact the genocide. Thus, the responsibility that Lang wants to assign to historians is not, since Lang never specifies precisely how it could be, a responsibility toward present society. After all, figures like Arthur Butz are so marginal in their beliefs that they pose little threat to social order even if they do spark public debate and justified outrage. Rather, on Lang's reading, the risk a historian or anyone runs in discussing the Holocaust is that of harming these morally present facts.

Because Lang is committed both to the moral presence of facts and to the immorality of imaginative representations of those facts, he advocates the chronicle as the most moral form of history for the Holocaust; it is a form that simply lists historical events in chronological order, leaving only the selection of events to the discretion of the historian. This form is supposed to allow the facts "to speak for themselves" and is meant to remove the agency and voice of the historian as much as possible from the scene of representation. Lang is not so naive as to think that the chronicle avoids questions of the historian's agency altogether, but he considers debate about which events to include to be taking place on the safest moral ground.

On the theoretical level the chronicle as Lang describes it lists facts in the same way that—in a popular form of Holocaust memorial—the ritual reading of names lists victims. Indeed, insofar as the facts are endowed by Lang with the "moral presence" of persons (and it is because they are so endowed that they must be chronicled rather than narrated), the chronicle already is a list of names. The history that Lang reduces to chronicle is a history that he has transformed into memorial.

Thus, if history becomes chronicle and chronicle becomes memorial, the historian assumes the position of the mourner as he or she "remembers" the events and the people lost. The technology of the list thus connects the historian to the event not only as a scholarly mind thinking about a subject but, more importantly, as a person grieving for a lost family member or friend. This same connection is constructed and encouraged by another repository of Holocaust history, the United States Holocaust Memorial Museum, an institution that has also managed to merge the practice of history and the practice of memorial.[17] The purpose of much of the museum's design is to bring the visitor into a personal and emotional relation with the events the exhibits describe.

Most obviously, this personal relation is constructed through the "identity card" each visitor is given before entering the permanent exhibit. From the main concourse of the museum, the ushers direct visitors into the cordoned-off space in front of elevators that take all visitors to the opening of the exhibit on the fourth floor. In that space is a table piled with identity cards sorted by gender, each containing the photograph and story of a person caught up in the Holocaust. The usher encourages visitors to take an identity card according to their gender (initially, these cards were to be matched with visitors according to age as well) and instructs them not to open the card, which is actually a four-page "book," until the end of the first level of the exhibit. The four pages of the identity card tell the story of the featured person in chronological order, each page of the story to be turned at the end of the corresponding level of the exhibit.

Because the visitor is invited to identify with the victim of Nazi terror not only by reading his or her story (by learning about the victim) but also by carrying identity papers (by behaving like the victim), the visitor becomes both a mourner and the double of the person whose story he or she carries. The visitor can then search for his or her "own" name among the memorial lists that cover the museum's interior windows. One member of the museum staff reports that the success of this identification process and the personification of the I.D. cards themselves became apparent early on when machines, originally meant to print out an update to the person's story at the end of each level, malfunctioned and occasionally destroyed the I. D. cards visitors had inserted. Some visitors became extremely upset, as if the person whose story the card held—and with whom the visitor had identified—had at that moment been destroyed. (Because of this and other problems, the machine-generated updates were eventually abandoned.)[18] And we should note that the I.D. cards are not the only aspect of the museum that works to produce such an experience. As Marianne Hirsch has pointed out, the museum's "Tower of Faces," where hundreds of family photographs from the Lithuanian shtetl of Ejszyzki are displayed, is a particularly powerful space for the kind of identification I am describing. Here, the conventions of family photographs, which produce what Hirsch calls "familial looking," invite all visitors to "become a community: descendants of those killed decades ago in a small shtetel thousands of miles away."[19]

This arrangement surprises us far too little. At Maya Lin's Vietnam Veterans memorial—just up the Mall from the Holocaust Museum—if visitors look for a specific name among those listed on the black marble, the name is one they know from their town or it is their own surname. It is a name they knew before they arrived. Experience, not a pamphlet or an exhibit, provided them with it. Those of us who did not know the dead, who have no personal connection to them, may scan the names for a while or simply take in the grim impersonality of the list. This memorial—and in fact most public memorials—are designed to be both personal and impersonal. In contrast, the U.S. Holocaust Memorial Museum provides for every visitor a familial or personal connection to the victims which most of us lack. This works, of course, for Jews and for non-Jews.

While lists at the U.S. Holocaust Memorial Museum can, with the help of identity cards, provide the visitor with "ancestors" who experienced the Holocaust, Steven Spielberg's film version of the novel *Schindler's List* takes the technology of the list and runs it backward in time, providing not Jewish ancestors but Jewish descendants for a non-Jewish moral hero.[20] In fact, much of the film is taken up with maneuvering the list into the position where it can perform such work, since list-making begins as a thoroughly repressive tool. In the opening scene we see the registration—the listing—of rural Jews in a Krakow train station as the first stage of their journey toward Auschwitz. Later, Itzaac Stern is almost carried away on a train to the death camps because his name is accidentally put on a deportation list. But whereas these scenes of list-making explore how the list gives or denies power to individuals (those who are on the list are powerless, those making the list powerful) the final, and definitive, scenes of list-making cast the list not as a repressive tool but rather as a genealogy. When Schindler makes his final list of the Jews he is to buy name by name from the horrible Amon Goeth, Schindler says to Goeth, "I want my people," to which Goeth replies, "Who are you, Moses?"

Lest the viewer miss the implication, the final scenes of the film expand upon the Biblical paradigm: Spielberg moves from a black-and-white scene of the survivors from Schindler's factory marching over a Polish field into a color picture of the real, present-day descendants of those now announced on the screen as "The Schindler Jews." One by one these descendants place stones on the grave of Oskar Schindler in the traditional Jewish manner. Text appears over the scene of the graveyard telling us that there are fewer than a thousand Jews left in Poland today. The next frame tells viewers that there are over four thousand "Schindler Jews" and their descendants living today. Spielberg thus invokes both the genealogies of Genesis and Exodus and the real persons to which the film refers, blurring the boundary between representation and reality to produce his final interpretation of the Schindler story: by making a list, Schindler claims "his people"; by saying their names and laying their stones, the Schindler Jews claim him—a Gentile—as their ancestor, the man who gave them life.[21]

The last image of *Schindler's List* takes that point yet one step further. The last hand to place a tribute—not a stone, but a flower—on Schindler's grave at the end of the film is not, like the other hands, named as belonging to one of the "Schindler Jews." The unnamed hand is reputed to be Spielberg's, but in its anonymity it stands in for any hand, for the reverent viewer's hand. Though Spielberg may rest his connection to Schindler on the fact of his own racial Jewishness, the hand we see is in no way marked as Jewish, and the object it places on the grave is not the stone of Jewish tradition, but the flower, associated with Christian and other religions', as well as secular American, memorial practices.[22] In the end, anyone can form a connection to Schindler in this way, regardless of their relation to Schindler's acts during the war and regardless of their race or religion; anyone can lay a stone or a flower on Schindler's grave and thus claim him as their forefather.

It is clear that *Schindler's List* and the Holocaust Museum, insofar as they recruit both Jews and non-Jews to identify with the Holocaust victims, cannot be said to recruit to a specifically Jewish identity. The purpose of devices that produce identity with the victims in the film and the museum is a moral one; the film invites any viewer to honor the morality of Schindler's efforts to save lives, and the museum invites the visitor to a historical awareness that will result in his or her commitment to prevention, to the slogan "never again."

In other words, we are invited to honor Schindler and abhor Hitler, not because one saved Jews and one killed Jews, but because one saved lives and one took them. The film and the museum share the assumption that—as the generality of "never again" implies—the Holocaust could happen to anyone, to any group. The non-Jew could be a victim, too. If the line thus blurs between Jewishness and non-Jewishness in these particular presentations of the Holocaust, then recruitment looks only incidentally like recruitment to Jewish identity. In *Maus,* on the other hand, because the line between Jewishness and non-Jewishness is dramatized by the animal heads, we see a version of the recruitment phenomenon that can tell us more about what it might mean to recruit to a more specifically Jewish identity through a representation of the Holocaust.

Maus: Other Technologies of Connection   The technologies of connection we see in *Maus* in fact do, like the Holocaust museum, recruit both Jews and non-Jews to identify with the Holocaust. The very device that governs the drawings—the device that makes the books so distinctive—demonstrates the ways in which anyone can come to identify with the event. For example, when, at the beginning of *Maus II,* Art considers which animal to use in drawing Françoise, his wife—whose French Gentile origins seem to raise a question for Art of what kind of head she should have—she reminds him that she converted to Judaism, and so must be a mouse, too (see figure 2).[23] Although Françoise's conversion is nominally religious, Jewish faith is not represented as part of Françoise's character. Her mouseness finally connects her not to a religion or even a cultural practice but simply to the family of her husband, to various Holocaust survivors, and most importantly to the mouse victims of the story Vladek tells and Art draws. Conversion brings not a new faith or a new culture but a new body contiguous with the Jewish bodies populating the story. In this case, Jewishness—signaled by the mouse head— is inseparable from connection to the Holocaust: it is not even clear (because she has a mouse head even as Art is deciding how to draw her) whether she is connected to the Holocaust because she is Jewish or whether she is Jewish because—through her husband—she is connected to the Holocaust.

It is important to note that, although Françoise's conversion and her resulting identity as a mouse gives her relation to the past a certain pathos (she is identified with the victims), any of the options we see Art doodling in his sketchbook (a frog, a moose, a rabbit, a French poodle) would have given her some relation to the event, as the animal heads do for all the characters, regardless of their personal relation to the Holocaust. An American neighbor

Figure 2. From Art Spiegelman, *Maus II: And Here My Troubles Began*.

of the Spiegelmans in the flashback scene that opens *Maus I* is depicted as a
dog, a choice of animal proleptically motivated by the Holocaust story Art
will eventually draw (in that story American dogs are the enemies of the German cats). Even American place names must be read in relation to the Holocaust; Vladek's vacation home, flanked by a house owned by another survivor
couple, is located in "the Catskills." We need not ignore Spiegelman's black
humor in order to register the logical point made by his pun: that all important
aspects of the present take their identity from the past event, though these
identities differ from those constructed by the U.S. Holocaust Memorial Museum's I.D. cards. Identification with the victims—something assigned to
everyone at the museum—is in *Maus* reserved for those who are Jewish (I
will discuss what that term means in *Maus* below, but for now it must remain
an open question). *Maus* finds the source of present-day identities not only
in the victims of the Holocaust, then, but also in other participants in World
War II.

Although Françoise argues successfully for her identification with the victims (her logic convinces Art to make her a mouse), *Maus* as a whole provides
no consistent system by which such eligibility can be established for all characters. Even when Art chooses Françoise's identity, it appears that the choices

between identities—choices about which animal heads designate which identities *and* choices about which characters get which heads—is motivated primarily by the cartoonist's imagination. The sketchpad full of other possibilities for Françoise's character foregrounds these as imaginative and perhaps arbitrary choices in spite of her protestations to the contrary. Art made her a mouse, but perhaps not because of her conversion. Indeed, it seems imaginable in *Maus* that some Jews may not be identified with the victims at all: in *Maus II* when asked how he would draw Israeli Jews, Art suggests porcupines (*Maus II*, 42), which in its very humor also draws attention to the choice as choice rather than necessity. Humor, not Holocaust history, makes the suggestion seem right.

While these passages seem to suggest that one's connection to the past is the product of imagination—here, the cartoonist's imagination—Spiegelman is in fact committed to a connection based on the facts of history. The central choice of mouse heads for the Jews is motivated by a very specific history: by the ways in which Nazis represented Jews prior to and during the war. The epigraph to *Maus II* makes that motivation explicit by quoting a German newspaper of the mid-1930s: "Mickey Mouse is the most miserable ideal ever revealed. . . . Healthy emotions tell every independent young man and every honorable youth that the dirty and filth-covered vermin, the greatest bacteria carrier in the animal kingdom, cannot be the ideal type of animal. . . . Away with Jewish brutalization of the people! Down with Mickey Mouse! Wear the Swastika Cross!" (*Maus II*, 4; ellipses in original). All persons in the present are in effect identified in relation to the Holocaust—to the paradigms of Nazi discourse—rather than in relation to some other source of identity in the present. Present-day Germans in *Maus* have identities linked with Nazism, for example, rather than with the political parties to which they might plausibly belong in the present. And Jews remain mice in present-day America, retaining with that identity all the connotations of victimhood that made the identity appropriate for Vladek's Holocaust story.[24] Thus, it is worth noting that, despite certain inconsistencies (evident in Françoise's mouse head and the idea of Israeli Jews as porcupines), this structure also serves to make Jewish identity within *Maus* look most often like a racial identity, like the product of biological origins. By making Nazi propaganda and the history of the Final Solution the source of identity distinctions, Spiegelman imports into his present-day identities the racial essentialism that defined Nazi policy. In short, Art is a mouse because his parents are mice.

While the epigraph thus suggests that *general* identities in *Maus*—German cats and Jewish mice—are motivated by history rather than imagination, other features of the text suggest that even *particular* identities—a mouse named Mala and a cartoonist-mouse named Art—are motivated by history, albeit a family history. The dedications and credits at the opening of each *Maus* volume emphasize this motivation. The acknowledgments in *Maus I* list people—Paul Pavel, Mala Spiegelman, Françoise Mouly—who later appear as characters in the strip. The opening of *Maus II* reads like a note about the author as it describes how "Art Spiegelman, a cartoonist born after WWII, is working on a book about what happened to his parents as Jews in wartime Poland" (*Maus II*, 6). Though the opening of *Maus II* serves as a summary of *Maus I*, it also serves to blur the distinction between the author and his character, Art, between other characters and their real counterparts, and between the inside and outside of the cartoon itself.

Occasional photographs also contribute to this blurring of boundaries between the cartoon characters and real people. *Maus I* contains just one, and that one photo is actually part of a cartoon within the cartoon: when (the character) Art's mother commits suicide, he draws a comic entitled "Prisoner on the Hell Planet" in which the characters are represented in distorted, but human, forms. In its upper left-hand corner, a hand grips a snapshot of Anja with her son next to her. The comic itself, actually produced by Art Spiegelman after his mother's suicide (it first appeared in *Short Order Comix* 1, 1973), and the photo within it remind the reader that this is a true story, that the characters represent real people, that the comic is, as Spiegelman has insisted outside as well as within the covers of *Maus,* nonfiction (see figure 3). In *Maus II* a dedicatory photo of Vladek and Anja's lost son, Richieu, produces the same effect. Far from disrupting narrative, as Marianne Hirsch has suggested, the photographs attempt to make history and comic one seamless reality within narrative.[25]

Though the analysis above makes the logic of Spiegelman's drawings appear to be fairly simple—they relate the present to the past, the real to the artificial—the theoretical work that enables these relations is as complicated as Berel Lang's historiography. Since people do not in fact have mouse heads, how does *Maus* argue for the truth—the biographical and autobiographical genre, and the nonfiction status—of its story? Why does Spiegelman go to the trouble of consistently calling attention both to the figurative aspect of his work and to its transparent connection to real persons and real events? We can begin to formulate answers to these questions if we look at chapter 2 of *Maus II*, where Spiegelman interrogates the relation of the animal head to the identity of his characters by introducing a new element in the drawings: the mouse mask. The head and the mask, it turns out, are not the same thing,

Figure 3. Family photo of Art and his mother, inserted into the short comic (included in *Maus I*) about Anja's suicide.

and it is precisely in the distinction between them that *Maus*'s claim to non-fictionality and its central claims about identity lie.[26]

Chapter 2 opens with a human-headed Art wearing a mouse mask, sitting at his drafting table feeling depressed and incapable of continuing with his book. In by-now-familiar Holocaust-history fashion, he recounts the dates of certain events as if they were part of a chronicle: "Vladek died of congestive heart failure on August 18, 1982," "Françoise and I stayed with him in the Catskills back in August 1979," "Vladek started working as a tinman in Auschwitz in the spring of 1944." The events of the present and past, of Holocaust history and family history, are mixed up together, creating a confusion of time frames that finally produces the ambiguous phrase "we're ready to shoot!" (*Maus II,* 41): Is it the camera operator ready to start filming an interview or a Nazi guard ready to shoot a prisoner? Outside the window of Art's studio, we see the guard tower of a concentration camp; on his floor lie piles of naked and emaciated mouse-headed bodies. From panel to panel Art shrinks in stature, becoming childlike in the face of past events and present commercial success (see figure 4).

What binds the events and images of present and past together is, of course, Art's mental state, his depression. In the cartoon (as in most popular

Figure 4. Art wearing the mouse mask, from *Maus II*.

psychology) depression is the disease of being controlled by a traumatic personal past, a disease of being unable to forget painful experiences or recognize
present experiences as happy and distinct from the past. But Art's depression
links him not only to events he himself experienced, such as his mother's
suicide, but also to tragedies he did not experience, such as the murder of
Jews at Auschwitz. Depression, here indistinguishable from the structure of
remembering, becomes another technology through which a person's identity
transcends the limits of that person's current experience and personal past to
encompass experiences—like the Holocaust—that are historically remote
from the individual. Though depression looks here like the disease of too
much connection with the past, the fact that Art's malady is signaled by the
mask would suggest otherwise.

   If depression makes Art feel distant from the person—or mouse—he is
in the rest of the story, if it makes his and even other people's historically
grounded identities feel like masks, the cure for depression as Spiegelman
imagines it will be not less connection to the past but more. In other words,
Art's problem turns out not to be the past but his inadequate connection
to the particular past that his organic mouse head (the head that is not a
mask) embodies. Art's session with his survivor-psychiatrist—conducted in

masks—will solve this problem by forging a new kind of connection between Art and the experience of the Holocaust. Instead of being connected to the past by depression, Art will be able to connect through narration, through continuing to tell a true Holocaust story. In *Maus* the narrative connection is in turn imagined as a bodily one; when narrative is restored, the mouse mask turns back into the mouse head. To put my initial formulation another way: what appears at first to be the symptom of depression—Art's inability to write—turns out to look like the cause of depression, for the session with Pavel suggests that the restoration of narrative in fact cures depression.

One part of the session with Pavel, then, is dedicated to solving the kinds of philosophical problems with narrative that also trouble Berel Lang. How, both Art and Pavel wonder, can Art accurately represent such extreme suffering? Should Art really speak for the victims? Pavel suggests that "the victims who died can never tell THEIR side of the story, so maybe it's better not to have any more stories" (*Maus II*, 45). Initially Art agrees; "Samuel Beckett," he points out, "once said: 'Every word is like an unnecessary stain on silence and nothingness,'" but a panel of unproductive silence causes both of them to reconsider Beckett's point. "[Beckett] was right," Pavel says; "Maybe you can include it in your book." Once they agree that one can—ethically—tell Holocaust stories, the practical problem of access—that Art cannot imagine what it was like in Auschwitz and cannot visualize the tin shop in which his father was forced to work—can be solved by using the narration they have just endorsed. Through narrative, experience and memory are transferable between persons: Pavel shouts "Boo!" startling Art; "It [Auschwitz]," he says, "felt a little like *that*." (*Maus II*, 46; original emphasis). Then Pavel provides from his own memory, not of the camps but of his childhood, the details Art needs to draw the tin shop. In the practical work of forging narrative connections with the past, then, one's *own* memory becomes irrelevant; someone else's narrative provides the material for one's own.[27]

The relation of Art's story to Pavel's story can thus be characterized as use: Art uses Pavel's story to tell his own. But the relation between Art's story and the story of the most important survivor—Vladek—looks quite different, although it is built on the same assumptions about transferability that enable Pavel to graft his experience onto Art's. Initially what troubles Art is the apparent difference between his story and Vladek's (the stories of their experience), and it is that which first keeps Art from telling his story (his cartoon story, which is, of course, a story of his and Vladek's and now Pavel's experience). He feels that his life-story is less important than his father's; "No matter what I accomplish," Art complains to Pavel, "it doesn't seem like much compared to surviving Auschwitz" (*Maus II*, 44).

Pavel's response to Art's complaint is crucial to *Maus*, for Pavel—and, as I will show, psychotherapy itself—provides the link that will connect Art firmly and finally to the Holocaust. Though Pavel reminds him, "you weren't in Auschwitz . . . you were in Rego Park," the psychiatrist goes on to suggest that Vladek, perhaps feeling guilty about surviving, had to insist that he was always right in order to make sense of his survival, "and he took his guilt out on YOU" he tells Art, "where it was safe . . . on the REAL survivor" (*Maus II*, 44; ellipses in original).[28]

But how can Art be a survivor? How can the children of survivors be survivors themselves? Trauma theory—as articulated by both literary critics and clinical psychologists—has provided the answer, the technology by which the trauma of the Holocaust can be transmitted between persons. The belief in specifically intergenerational transmission of trauma turns out to be a powerful technology for recruitment to Jewish identity; we can see its power not only in imaginative representations like *Maus* but also in the clinical literature that attempts to address what many therapists believe are problems unique to the children of Holocaust survivors. Dina Wardi's account in *Memorial Candles*, for example, demonstrates both the assumptions that underlie the belief in intergenerational transmission of trauma and the practical ways—the technologies—by which therapists and their clients construct "healthy" ways of connecting to the traumas that the parents suffered. Her work centers around group therapy sessions in which young adults—many of whom are the children of Holocaust survivors—produce personal narratives that, more often than not, construct the Holocaust as the source of their pain.

First, it is instructive to note that debate on the issue of "second-generation" survivors has centered on the question of whether all children of survivors or only those who become ill—"the clinical population"—are afflicted with the traumas their parents experienced, which amounts to a question not so much about whether "intergenerational transmission of the trauma" is possible but about how that transmission works.[29] But Wardi takes the idea of transmission beyond just the children of survivors: admitting in the introduction that her own parents are "not actually Holocaust survivors, nor did any member of their extended families meet his death in the Holocaust, except for a distant relative of my father's," she will nevertheless claim that "like every member of European Jewry of that period, I too am a daughter of survivors in potential." "Indeed," she goes on to ask, "which member of the Jewish nation is not a child of survivors in potential? It therefore seems to me that the problems raised in this book touch the essence of the Jewish nation in the post-Holocaust generation."[30]

The problems raised in *Memorial Candles*, the problems that Wardi sees as crucial to Jewish identity and Israeli nationhood, appear to be an elaboration of the problems condensed in Art's session with Pavel. For example, many in Wardi's therapy group, like Art, lack concrete information about their parents' Holocaust experience; also, like Art, they fill in the gaps with bits and pieces of other people's stories. In a chapter focusing on problems with sexuality, Wardi argues that the *possibility* that some of the survivor-mothers were sexually abused in the camps (none of the participants in her group are recorded as actually knowing that their mothers were sexually abused) becomes part of the trauma transmitted to the children. In their discussions, the therapists and participants use what they learn from films and books to fill in the details of what might have happened to their parents. These details seem to allow them to come to terms with the imagined trauma; that is, the details help them respond emotionally to possible or imagined events.[31] The therapy group thus provides a context in which the memories of other people can be grafted onto the memories of the "second generation" in order to help this generation "identify" properly with survivors. To put it another way, the group becomes a context in which the members can see themselves, as Art is encouraged to do, as "survivors."

The idea that trauma can be transmitted intergenerationally is not new, nor is it new in its application to Jewish identity. Freud's *Moses and Monotheism* posited a similar transmission of guilt—in this case guilt for the murder of Moses, the Jews' primal father—but Freud is specific both about the ways in which he needs the transmission to work in order to account for his conclusions and about the problems with the idea of transmission.[32] Wardi, on the other hand, embraces an unspecified notion of transmission without registering the slightest strain. Sometimes she says that children "absorb" the traumas of their parents, sometimes that they "internalize" them, sometimes that the children fail to learn that they are not their parents and therefore become their parents. It becomes the job of therapy to teach them what parts of themselves are not in fact themselves but are rather their parents, and which of their feelings are "theirs" and which are "their parents'."[33] It is clear that what interests Wardi and Spiegelman is not transmission itself but how transmission can be used or, to put it more neutrally, what transmission *does*. Spiegelman uses the phenomenon of transmission to resume narration and, in the work as a whole, to build a Jewish identity around the Holocaust. Wardi uses the idea of transmission both for therapeutic purposes—to encourage in a clinical population the behaviors that we think are "healthy"—and, as I quoted above, to account for the "essence of the Jewish nation."[34]

~~~~~~~~~

In *Maus*, then, belief in "intergenerational transmission of trauma" means not only that the survivors of the camps can produce the survivors of Rego Park, but also that the survivors of Rego Park can be understood as being survivors of the camps. The relation to the past that psychotherapy thus enables—that helps Art "feel better" (*Maus II*, 46; see figure 5)—replaces the depressive relation to the past with what *Maus* imagines as a healthy, true relation to the past. This new relation makes Art's cartoon story ("A Survivor's Tale") *his* in the sense that the story of his father's experience is his father's: when Art becomes a survivor, the story of his father's experience becomes the story of Art's experience, which is why the session with Pavel transforms the mouse mask to a mouse head. The mouse identity is no longer *his* but *him*. So, to reformulate once again the relation between narration and depression: if depression appears to be caused, and not simply signaled, by a failure of narration, and if the cure for depression is in fact the resumption of narration, it is because narration—the survivor's tale—produces the "REAL" person, the "REAL survivor." To put this in Wardi's terms, telling your story in therapy ideally results in making the parts of yourself that were not in fact you ("feeling your parents' pain," for example) into parts that are you ("feeling your own pain"). The idea that personal narrative—in therapy or in comics—produces a real person is simply the inversion of the logic by which Art can contend that the destruction of Anja's diaries was an act of murder.[35]

Once we see how narrative—how telling *true* stories, in Spiegelman's case—works in relation to identity we can see why Spiegelman argues that

Figure 5. Art growing taller as he walks home from his session with Pavel, from *Maus II*.

Maus must be classified as nonfiction, why it must be taken as literally true, why Jewish mice are the product not of imagination but of history. Spiegelman's letter to the editor of the *New York Times Book Review* protesting the placement of *Maus II* on the fiction best-sellers list makes the point even clearer. Spiegelman makes two distinct arguments about why *Maus* is not fiction. First, he appeals to the facts included in his book: research, he claims, has ensured that the facts included in the story are true to history, and thus the content of the story—as distinct from its "novelistic structure"—must be classified as nonfiction.[36] But this appeal to research and to the precedence of content over form cannot by itself produce the conclusion Spiegelman is looking for. Plenty of fiction writers conduct research to ensure the verisimilitude of their novels, and many base their narratives on true stories, but this does not make fiction into nonfiction; *Anna Karenina* is still fiction despite its verisimilitude and despite the fact that it was based in part on a true story. Rather, Spiegelman's conclusion rests on his claim that to put *Maus* on the fiction list is to participate in Holocaust denial. He writes, "it's just that I shudder to think how David Duke—if he could read—would respond to seeing a carefully researched work based closely on my father's memories of life in Hitler's Europe and in the death camps classified as fiction." His comic cannot be classified as fiction, then, because to do so is, like David Duke, to make the Holocaust itself a fiction and to make oneself racist. To put the point in the terms of my discussion of Lang, above, this is also to say that Spiegelman's letter makes the *Book Review*, like Arthur Butz, immoral rather than incompetent. The *Book Review* is in danger not of being wrong about genre but of being anti-Semitic.[37] When telling true stories has the power to make the artificial person (Art in the mouse mask) into the true person (Art with the mouse head), calling the true story artificial threatens to cancel the true person. In other words, there is more than one way to kill the diaries: you can burn them, or you can call them fiction.[38]

Why, then, does Spiegelman flirt with fictionality by populating his nonfiction with fantastical animal-persons? It is tempting to say that in doing so Spiegelman is casting the connections between Art and his father that I have been detailing here in an ironic light, as if to say, through the self-reflexivity of the comic, that all such relations are the product of artifice, that they cannot be taken literally, and that there is no such thing as authenticity. The photograph of Vladek in a camp uniform in *Maus II* epitomizes this potential reading: in it, we see Vladek, the really real survivor, dressed up after his liberation in a camp uniform he rents for the occasion of the photograph. A reading that hinged on this photograph and on the general self-reflexivity to be found in the comic would make Spiegelman's work of a piece with a way of using irony that is characteristically postmodern and is evident in everything from television advertising to Richard Rorty's discussions of community in *Contingency, Irony, and Solidarity*. Irony used in this way reminds the reader or viewer that any claim carries with it its negation, since we all know that not everyone would accept the claim as truth. Irony becomes the mark of philosophical relativism and performative identity. In Rorty's discussion of community, this kind of irony leads to a very desirable form of tolerance; in the worst of television advertising, as the media critic Mark Crispin Miller has argued, it enables sexist and otherwise objectionable images and claims to be transmitted with a wink that reassures the viewer that they need not object since no one actually believes what is being said even while it is being said.[39] What I have tried to show is how what looks, in *Maus*, like that form of self-reflexive irony in fact produces sincerity, and indeed, a kind of literalism, made apparent not only in the structure of the comic itself but also in Spiegelman's insistence on its nonfiction status.[40] In *Maus* Spiegelman claims as a literal truth something that photographs or realistic drawings would fail to convey: he claims that not only Jewish identity but all identities arise from the Holocaust and, more specifically, from telling Holocaust stories, for it is Holocaust-centered identity that the animal heads make visible, make literal, and it is telling Holocaust stories that makes the heads themselves "REAL."

4

The question of whether those who did not experience the
Holocaust become real survivors when they tell true stories
about the Holocaust, the question I have argued *Maus* raises
and then answers with its own version of the personified text,
captured broad public attention in the scandal surrounding
Binjamin Wilkomirski's memoir, *Fragments: Memories of a
Wartime Childhood.* When the memoir was published in 1995,
it was hailed as a powerfully moving account of the author's
experiences as a child during the Holocaust, an account whose
disjointed narrative and simple, almost abstract style was said
not just to represent, but actually to demonstrate, the effects
of trauma on its author. But at the time of its German publication there were already questions about the authenticity of
Wilkomirski's story. The author's legal name turned out to be
Bruno Dössekker, and his Swiss birth record indicated that he
was born not in Riga, Latvia, as he had claimed in the memoir
to have been, but in Biel, Switzerland, and that he could not
have been as old as he had claimed he was during the war.

Because of these questions about his identity, Wilkomirski
added an afterword to the book before publication, citing the
birth record and explaining that it was simply part of the new
identity "imposed" upon him by Swiss authorities after the
war.[1] This confession seemed not to bother early readers of the
memoir, who praised its seemingly artless and unsentimental
representation of brutality. As André Aciman put it in a review
for the *New Republic,* Wilkomirski's "aesthetic vision" was

characterized by "incomplete or mistaken readings of reality, accompanied by rude, painful awakenings."[2] While this style could be attributed, he suggested, "to the writer's desire to describe the events of the Holocaust purely from a child's perspective," that would only mean that Wilkomirski had employed what Aciman called an "old" stylistic "trick." Instead, the reviewer argued, "the fragmentary nature of Binjamin's account is not so much a product of the grown man's style as it is a product of the young boy's experience" (31). It was this kind of claim—that the very "fragments" of Wilkomirski's narrative were the evidence of its truth—that led readers to accept it despite the doubts raised at the outset by Bruno Dössekker's birth record.

~~~~~~~~

Most readers will know the end of this story: the book's publisher, having hired an independent historian to investigate the matter in 1998, decided that there was enough doubt about the truth of the memoir to justify taking it out of print. It was duly withdrawn from publication in the fall of 1999. Some continue to defend it, suggesting that to doubt its authenticity is not only to underestimate the thoroughness of the Swiss bureaucracy in covering up the traces of a child's original identity, but is also to perpetuate the brutalization the child Binjamin suffered at the hands of the Nazis.[3] But two extensively researched essays published in the summer of 1999—Elena Lappin's in *Granta* and Philip Gourevitch's in the *New Yorker*—and a later book-length study of the case by Blake Eskin, entitled *A Life in Pieces* (2002), seem to have convinced most readers that Wilkomirski, if not the calculating liar that Daniel Ganzfried (a Swiss writer and his earliest critic) describes, is at least a seriously and sadly deluded person who has invented for himself a terrible history.

Upon reflection, we might simply say that the story of Wilkomirski's memoir reveals how our desire for such memoirs of difficult lives has created an atmosphere conducive to fraud. In this chapter I demonstrate that there is, in fact, more to be said about the relation between the phenomenon of the false memoir and the common interest in trauma. For producing a fake is possible—and attractive to the would-be con artist—not only because the Holocaust memoir has become a form that has a certain cultural presence and worth, a worth evident in the various prizes and speaking tours that accompanied the general celebration of Wilkomirski's book.[4] Producing fakes is also possible simply because the Holocaust memoir *is* a form. As one reviewer of

Fragments noted (even before the questions about Wilkomirski arose), "a pe-culiar set of conventions has come to cluster around depictions of the Holo-caust. . . . the effect has been to turn the literature of genocide into a genre, with rules almost as constricting as those binding the Agatha Christie–style detective story."[5] This reviewer cites an "understandable and laudable" desire for representations of the Holocaust that are "consciously, even ostentatiously austere" as the origin of the genre as such (a fact underwritten, no doubt, by Adorno's famous assertion that to write poetry after Auschwitz is "barbaric"), but we might also note that the Holocaust memoir has become a genre—with all the conventionality that term implies—because trauma theorists in the academy have been working to elaborate, explain, and theorize about the things such memoirs have in common.

In saying this, I do not wish to argue, with regard to *Fragments,* that Wilkomirski read trauma theory and other memoirs in order to learn the con-ventions of the Holocaust memoir, his extensive personal archive of such books becoming, as Daniel Ganzfried has put it, a "laboratory" for creating his fraud.[6] While this may well be what happened (there are those, like his high school girlfriend, Annie Singer, who claim that Wilkomirski has always been a liar), there are other reasons why trauma theory would help explain the Wilkomirski story, help in a way that can account for the somewhat diffi-cult fact that many people—some of whom are closely acquainted with the author—believe that he did not set out to produce a lie, that he fully and sincerely believes himself to be the child-survivor his memoir describes. The misery apparent to practically all who have seen him since the memoir was published certainly suggests that if he is lying, he is not doing it for the emotional pleasure inherent in his new identity.[7] If his book is a fraud, it may well be an unintended one, and it is this aspect of the Wilkomirski story, I will argue, that a close reading of trauma theory can illuminate.

Perhaps I should more accurately say that it is this aspect of the Wilkomir-ski story that can illuminate what we find upon a close reading of trauma theory, for there is nothing very new or interesting in saying that fakes require generic conventions—require, that is, a formal expectation that can then be met fraudulently. Indeed, my point will turn out to be more, and more com-plicated, than this. I will argue that in the process of becoming a form, the Holocaust memoir and the representation of trauma in general has been described by two of our most prominent theorists of trauma and literature— Shoshana Felman and Cathy Caruth—as embodying a certain relation be-tween language and experience, a relation that ultimately asks us to understand *Fragments* not so much as a fraud, but as the epitome of the very assumptions that underlie trauma theory's analytic discourse. And further, I will show that these assumptions are not unique to trauma theory or to writing that specifically engages the Holocaust. These assumptions about language and experience are also integral to contemporaneous fictional understandings of the relation between memorization and memory, between what you know and who you are, between epistemology and ontology in an era dominated by the memory and the threat of genocide. This larger argument demonstrates why, after the Wilkomirski story has come to an end, the phenomenon of his memoir will continue to be worth thinking about.

A Survivor of Writing   To understand how trauma theory could be useful to Wilkomirski apart from the narrative models it describes—apart, that is, from its value as a kind of formal handbook—it is worth noting some of the features of the memoir itself, features that echo and, indeed, rely upon some basic assumptions about the relation between language and experience that I will address later in the work of Felman and Caruth. The book opens with a lament for the loss of what Wilkomirski calls his "mother" and "father" "tongues." He first introduces himself as an orphan, that is, not by explaining that his parents were killed but by describing his loss of language. He is an orphan, in these opening sentences, because he has forgotten the Yiddish that his family spoke. "I have no mother tongue, nor a father tongue either," he writes; "the languages I learned later on were never mine, at bottom. They were only imitations of other people's speech" (3, 4). While one might object to the notion that any speech is anything but the "imitations of other people's speech"—surely the speech Wilkomirski claims to have lost was learned by imitation—what is more important here is to understand the belief that underlies this statement. In order for it to make sense, personal identity must be somehow the equivalent of language, and moreover, language must be imagined as a quasi-biological entity: it is not what you learn, what you "imitate," but what is yours "at bottom," the very source, like a parent, of your identity.

Indeed, the priority of language as parent over the actual figure of the parent in *Fragments* is underscored by a strange episode in the postmemoir life of Wilkomirski himself. On one occasion he decided to embrace, as his father, an Israeli survivor who had seen in him a resemblance to his first and (at that time) only son, thought to have been lost in the Holocaust. While Wilkomirski agreed to a blood test that, in the end, could not prove the rela-

tion, and while he later said that he was simply looking for a sort of stand-
in father, his early enthusiasm for and evident desire to believe in the reunion
can make one forget that *Fragments* gives a graphic account of his father's
death (he was crushed by a truck) and, moreover, describes a large family in
which Wilkomirski was the youngest of several brothers, which is to say, not
his father's first and only son.[8] The episode makes it evident that for Wilkomirski the source of his identity was not, in a sense, an actual family. It was
more importantly the ongoing discourse about that family which began in the
memoir and continued to evolve even after the memoir was published. Standing at the airport in Tel Aviv during the reunion with his putative father,
Wilkomirski thus spontaneously revised the text of *Fragments:* "I still see in
my mind," he mused, "how my father was taken away in the direction of the
gas chambers."[9] While his willingness to revise the memoir in light of new
facts might suggest that he values some version of lived reality over the story
he has told about himself, that he wants to correct what might be erroneous
in his memoir, I would argue that the very fact of the story's constant evolution reveals its priority as the source of identity. Wilkomirski's narrative has
become his life (as Elena Lappin put it, he "is his book"), and, by the looks
of things, that narrative will continue to assimilate to itself all the new evidence
that might appear about Wilkomirski's past and all experiences that will constitute his future.

It is the personal identity thus conceived and elaborated in his memoir
that Wilkomirski appeals to in the afterword added at the request of his publisher when the first questions about his identity arose in 1994: "The document I hold in my hands . . . gives the date of my birth as February 12,
1941," Wilkomirski writes, "but this date has nothing to do with either the
history of this century or my personal history" (154). What makes the document false, according to this strangely vague statement, is not that it contra-
dicts the facts of his birth, but rather, that it does not fit within two preexisting
narratives, "the history of this century" and Wilkomirski's "personal history."
There is a psychological interpretation that can be made here: we can see how
Daniel Ganzfried, for example, might come to argue that Wilkomirski's desire
for personal significance drove him to invent himself as a Holocaust survivor.
The life he wants to call his own is one that matters to the history of the
century, not the comfortable and insignificant life of an upper-crust Swiss
son.[10] But there is also an assumption about language to be read in Wilkomirski's claim and, more specifically, an assumption about the relation between personal identity and "personal history." In this case, "personal his-

tory" can only be the memoir itself, for it is only in the memoir that evidence for Wilkomirski's claim about his identity exists. The belief required about language here has the same structure as the belief we see in the opening lines of the memoir, cited above: that personal identity inheres in language. In this version of the claim, it is not simply the kind of language one speaks that becomes the source of identity (the Yiddish mother tongue that makes you Jewish), but the narrative structure of one's language (its shape vis-à-vis the formal conventions of the survivor's memoir) that creates the personal identity that can then be appealed to over and against the competing "document" the author "holds in [his] hands."

One might object that ferreting out the fact that Wilkomirski thinks his story constitutes his personal identity does little more than demonstrate that Wilkomirski subscribes to a basically Freudian, and currently very common, version of the self, a self whose meaningfulness and identity across time is constructed through narratives that link together the discrete experiences of life into what we recognize as a story. Or, more interestingly, one might object that Wilkomirski is progressively rejecting an essentialist, biologically based notion of identity based on one's parentage. But to make either of these objections would be to mistake the order of priority at work here: the narrative comes first, the claim to experience—and to biology, which never ceases to matter even if it is subject to revisions—follows. Wilkomirski's friend Elitsur Bernstein (an Israeli therapist) makes this order apparent when he tells of receiving, by fax, the first part of what was to become the manuscript of *Fragments*. According to Bernstein, Wilkomirski had appended a question to the story he sent: "Could it have been so?"[11] Clearly, Wilkomirski's own beliefs about his "personal history" were produced, over time, by the production of the stories that then came to be called a memoir. And moreover, Wilkomirski is not alone in bearing this relation to his own narrative; his American readers were urged to replicate the relation themselves. "Beautifully written," proclaims the dust jacket of Carol Brown Janeway's English translation, "with an indelible impact that makes this a book that is not read but experienced." Philip Gourevitch, whose essay in the *New Yorker* called my attention to this blurb, suggests that what we are asked to experience here is not the memoir but the public "sensation" it had become. When we put the promotional claim next to Wilkomirski's implicit claims about language within the memoir and its afterword, and next to the account Elitsur Bernstein gives us of the memoir's origins, however, American readers are asked not so much to experience a media sensation as to replicate the relation to the narrative that its author instantiated. The public is invited to experience the Holocaust the same way Wilkomirski did: by reading his story.[12]

~~~~~~~~~~

Reading and the Transmission of Experience   Becoming a survivor by telling or reading a survivor story does not originate with Bruno Dössekker becoming Binjamin Wilkomirski, or with the readers of *Fragments* taking up the cover's invitation to "experience" the memoir. I have presented other examples of this structure in the previous chapter, specifically in *Maus* and in the psychotherapeutic practice of Dina Wardi. But perhaps the strongest precedent for such a transformation can be found in the very theory that tries to account for the way language and narrative works (or becomes fragmented) in texts like *Fragments,* that tries to account for why the story of trauma cannot in fact be read but must instead be experienced. This mode of transformation begins to appear in a peculiar parallel between Binjamin Wilkomirski's story of coming to discover his survivor identity and a story that Shoshana Felman tells about a graduate seminar she led at Yale. Wilkomirski, in interviews, has noted that he first began to understand what had happened to him when he studied the Holocaust in high school, seeing a film of the camps' liberation. It was only then, he claims, that he realized that the war was over, that he himself had been liberated; he only then began to understand what had happened to him. His high school girlfriend, Annie Singer, tells the story a different way, that when Wilkomirski was about eighteen he showed her "a picture book about the Holocaust" and at about the same time began to claim that he came from the Baltic states.[13]

Whichever version of this story one believes, it is clear that studying the Holocaust in school was a pivotal point in the transformation of Bruno Dössekker into Binjamin Wilkomirski, and this fact echoes, in important respects, the account of a classroom experience that constitutes the subject of the first chapter of Shoshana Felman's *Testimony* (1992), a work whose juxtaposition of psychoanalysis and de Manian deconstruction has made it the theoretical model for those who seek to analyze the relation between traumatic experience and literature. Felman tells, in the opening chapter, of the experience of a class of Yale graduate students taking her "Literature and Testimony" seminar, a seminar whose syllabus included Dostoyevsky, Camus, Mallarmé, Freud, and Celan and concluded with a screening of two videotaped Holocaust testimonies from Yale's Fortunoff Archive. Felman describes how the class, after viewing the first of the two Holocaust testimonies, experienced a "crisis" in which the students were "entirely at a loss, disoriented and uprooted."[14] What the students needed, Felman concluded, was to be brought "back into signifi-cance" (48), and to accomplish this she prepared an "address to the class" that would "return" to the students "the importance and significance of their reactions" (49).

The significance that Felman decides to give to the students' reactions turns out to have much in common with the significance the young Bruno Dössekker gave to his own responses to the Holocaust history he encountered as a student: namely, that those responses indicated survivorship. "We have in this second screening session," Felman told her students, "the task of sur-viving the first session. . . . I will suggest that the significance of the event of your viewing of the first Holocaust videotape was, not unlike [Paul] Celan's own Holocaust experience, something akin to *a loss of language*" (49, 50; origi-nal emphasis; I might add, of course, that the "loss of language" is also not unlike Wilkomirski's response to trauma as he tells it in *Fragments*). Encourag-ing her students to explore their emotional responses to the tapes, Felman gave a final writing assignment that asked them to reflect on those responses in relation to the literature they had studied that semester. "The written work the class had finally submitted," she reports, "turned out to be an amazingly articulate, reflective and profound statement of the trauma they had gone through and of the significance of their assuming the position of the witness" (52). While Felman is not exactly claiming that her students became survivors of the Holocaust in the literal sense, in the sense that Wilkomirski makes that claim for himself, her analysis of this classroom experience nevertheless suggests that the experience of listening to Holocaust testimony produces symptoms of trauma equivalent to the traumatic symptoms produced by actu-ally experiencing the Holocaust. Moreover, Felman suggests that the signifi-cance of the students' feelings was to be found in the significance we accord to survivors' feelings. The students could experience trauma by listening to testimony about trauma, Felman explains, because a " 'life testimony' is not simply a testimony to a private life, but a point of conflation between text and life, a textual testimony which can *penetrate us like an actual life*" (2; original emphasis). The text is not only like a life, then, but it can become the actual experience of another life, an experience that then becomes ours.

I want to pause in the argument here to make clear that my contention is not that reading or viewing Holocaust testimony is not a moving experience. My own response to reading and viewing testimony attests to the fact that encountering the survivor's testimony must be understood as a lived experience that can have intense emotional effects on the person who has that experience. My point is not that watching—or reading, or hearing—survivor testimonies is not in its own way traumatic, but that it is so *in its own way*. It seems important, if only in the interest of accuracy, to distinguish this experience of trauma, if one wishes to call it that, from the trauma that the survivor herself has experienced and then represents in her testimony.[15] Geoffrey Hartman has written wisely about what he calls "secondary trauma," giving us a way of thinking about these emotional effects that avoids conflating the reader with the survivor. Hartman argues, and I think he is correct, that secondary trauma consists, finally, not so much in extreme feelings of sympathy and identification, but rather in numbing. Hartman suggests that in presenting testimony we must be careful to avoid both psychological numbing to the violence the survivor describes and false identification with the survivor through secondary trauma.[16]

Felman's account of the classroom experience, and the more general account that she and Dori Laub give of the relation between those who listen to Holocaust testimony and those who give that testimony, might seem to suggest that to transmit the traumatic experience one must have experienced the Holocaust, as is the case with Paul Celan or with the survivors to whose testimony the Yale students listened. Other chapters of *Testimony*—in particular, the essay on Claude Lanzmann and his film *Shoah*—revise that notion in what appears to be a significant way, implying that trauma can be transmitted not only by survivors but also by those who, like Lanzmann, show an intense concern with the subject despite the fact that they are not themselves survivors. This suggests that the one who transmits that trauma need not have had the experience of trauma. Such a revision highlights the centrality of sympathetic identifications to the process of transmission, a point evident also in Felman's descriptions of those who receive the transmission; all these cases suggest that to receive traumatic experience one must feel an identification with the victims of the Holocaust and willingly immerse oneself in the literature of testimony, as both Lanzmann and the Yale graduate students had done, and, indeed, as Bruno Dössekker had done in his own student days. Initially, then, the mechanism of identification Felman describes in these cases seems to require, on the theoretical level, a commitment to the importance of sentiment and desire in the production of that identification, over and above lived experience of the trauma represented.[17]

But Felman's analysis of Paul de Man's wartime journalism, also in *Testimony*, suggests otherwise, suggests, rather, that it is neither shared experience nor sympathy that enables the identification or makes transmission of trauma possible. Paul de Man never connected himself to the events of the war after it was over, and neither he nor his family were the victims of Nazi brutality. Unlike Celan and Lanzmann, de Man made no claim to a connection with the Nazis' victims, and as we know, de Man willingly wrote for a collaborationist newspaper in Belgium from 1941 to 1942, an activity that, when discovered after de Man's death, stirred anger among his friends and colleagues and a wave of critical articles in the press.[18] This controversy prompted Felman— a student of de Man's—to produce what reads as a defense of her former teacher, in an essay first published in *Critical Inquiry* in 1989, immediately after the wartime writings came to light, and later reprinted as a chapter in *Testimony*. But the essay's inclusion (unchanged) in the later book, and its relation to the other chapters, indicates that it is more than a defense of de Man; like the other chapters, it argues for a relation between writing and trauma like the one imagined in the analysis of the Yale seminar, a relation that allows trauma both to exist in and to be transmitted by writing or speech.

Felman builds her analysis of de Man's wartime writing around the "series of disasters [that] preceded, in de Man's life, the outbreak of the war" (124). When de Man was seventeen, "his brother Hendrik died in a bicycle accident at a railroad crossing; a year later his mother committed suicide on the anniversary of his brother's death. Consequently, Paul de Man's uncle, also named Hendrik, became a sort of adoptive father to his nephew" (124). "Young Paul," as Felman calls him in these sections of her essay, under the (presumed) sway of his charismatic, politically active, collaborating "adoptive father," starts writing for the collaborationist newspaper *Le Soir* once the Nazis gain control of Belgium. Felman constructs a speculative psychological portrait of a young man who, in response to personal traumas, makes unwise decisions out of emotional need. She writes that de Man might have collaborated because "Hendrik's claims [about the Flemish language] and his political focus as a leader seemed to offer his young nephew . . . a renewed relation to the *mother tongue,* beyond the loss marked by the mother's suicide" (126; original emphasis).[19] Felman encourages her reader to feel sympathetic toward both Young Paul and Hendrik, suggesting that "what the young Paul must have found compelling" in the Nazi propaganda was the "ideology of *reconstruction* and *national salvation* . . . [which] might have seemed to hold the promise of making up for personal and political disasters" (127; original emphasis). The story of de Man's collaboration, as we are given it here, is not a history of de Man's beliefs about fascist nationalism—as one might reasonably expect— but rather an account of the psychological and emotional context in which his collaboration took place.

Having thus set up de Man's biography and his decision to collaborate as a story of trauma and its aftermath, Felman reads his early writing career as another traumatic story. In what appears to be an effort to align de Man with the many Holocaust survivors who have taken their own lives, Felman reads a hiatus in his published writing, after he was fired from the publishing house where he had been working in addition to his freelance journalism, as a self-punishing suicide.[20] "Might both de Man's eleven-year-old silence and his radical departure [from Belgium] be viewed as substitutes for suicide?" Felman wonders (134–35), imagining de Man as analogous to Ishmael from *Moby-Dick*, who goes to sea as a substitute for suicide (de Man had published a Flemish translation of Melville's novel in 1945). And further, Felman wonders, might that "silence" be "suicide as the recognition that what has been done is absolutely irrevocable, which requires one in turn to do something irreversible about it?" (135). Felman goes on, then, to read de Man's lifelong silence about his wartime activities not as "an erasure of the past" but as a "quasi-suicidal, mute acknowledgment of a radical loss—or death—of truth, and therefore the acknowledgment of a radical loss—or death—or self" (135). The suicide Felman finds in de Man's publishing hiatus and the acknowledgement of "loss" and an "irrevocable" act (which seem very much like guilt here) she finds in his later silence together give de Man's life not only the suicide that structures one version of the survivor's life, but a kind of survivor's guilt as well.

The method of reading that Felman uses to argue for this suicide and for the meaningfulness of de Man's silence reveals more about Felman's assumptions regarding the relation between writing and persons than it reveals about de Man's view of his own activities. Recounting how de Man helped to arrange the publication of the French Resistance journal *Exercise du silence*, for example, she proceeds to read the journal's content as de Man's own reflections on his collaborative activities; it is worth quoting at some length in order to see not only what her reading does, but how that reading is done. Felman argues that "*Exercise du silence* had announced both literally and metaphorically the annihilation of the self, not only because the volume chose symbolically to open with a letter by Baudelaire announcing his own suicide . . . but because the editorial introduction, entitled 'Exercise of Silence,' had included . . . thoughts on the death of the self and its reduction to silence (thoughts that can uncannily be read as prophesying the silent violence of de Man's imminent departure)" (135). Despite the uncanny prophecy about de Man that Felman finds in this journal, the absence of de Man's name as the grammatical subject in certain key moments reveals the gap between the suicidal intention Felman assigns specifically to de Man and the actual content of the journal: "*Exercise du silence*," we are told, "announced . . . the annihilation of the self"; "the volume" "chose . . . to open with a letter by Baudelaire announcing his own suicide." The text stands in for de Man in such a way that any characteristic of the journal can also be read as a characteristic of de Man, despite the fact that his relation to the content of the journal was quite distant. Perhaps I should clarify that he was not the journal's editor, despite the weight Felman assigns to the content of the journal's editorial introduction. He simply helped arrange to have the journal published.[21]

Felman does acknowledge that she is speculating, that this interpretation is "conjecture," but even in the process of acknowledging this she insists on connections she has posited not only between de Man and the content of *Exercise du silence*, but also between de Man and other texts he might be said to be connected with, in particular, *Moby-Dick*, which he translated, and the writing of Walter Benjamin, which was important to the criticism he went on to produce during his long career in the United States. "My conjecture is," Felman writes, "that . . . Benjamin's suicide might have resonated with the suicides that framed de Man's own life. Benjamin's aborted departure [from Europe during the war] might have evoked de Man's own radical departure and his violent annihilation—or erasure—of his Belgian self" (155). Felman concedes that this is "conjecture," but goes on to defend it with more of the same: "If the question remains open of whether de Man, like Ishmael, departed as a substitute for committing suicide, Benjamin commits suicide when he is in the process of departure and when he believes (mistakenly) this process to be disrupted" (155). In this instance, the conflation of de Man with Benjamin is offered as the grounding alternative to the "open" question of whether de Man was, in his emigration from Belgium, in fact performing Melville's Ishmael.

I am not the first to notice, or to question, the way Felman's essay thus represents de Man as a suicide, and moreover, as the equivalent of a Holocaust survivor. Kalí Tal, in *Worlds of Hurt* (1996), and Dominick LaCapra, in a 1992 essay published in *History and Memory*, mount parallel critiques of Felman's exoneration of de Man and her appropriations of survivor identity. LaCapra focuses on the equation Felman makes between de Man and Primo Levi and criticizes Felman for "filling in de Man's silences with views explicitly elaborated by others," a move he characterizes as "an extremely speculative form of contextualizing ascription."[22] Felman's whole effort to "elide" the difference between de Man and Levi constitutes, LaCapra argues, "an unfortunate lapse of judgment" (14) comparable to Ronald Reagan's infamous remarks at Bitburg.[23] He goes on to question both Felman and, in the second half of the essay, Derrida for using deconstructive readings to exculpate de Man. LaCapra argues that it is this use of deconstruction, not de Man's wartime activities, that poses a threat to the prestige of deconstruction as a theory.

Tal's critique, by contrast, centers on the way Felman's and her coauthor Dori Laub's ideas about testimony appropriate the experiences of survivors in order to elevate the psychoanalytic interpreter to a position of power. While Tal and LaCapra take issue with many of the same elements of Felman's essay that I have pointed to above (indeed, there seems to be a consensus about which passages cry out for interpretation), their purposes in mounting these critiques and their accounts of the essay's significance are quite different from what I wish to set out. In keeping with LaCapra's larger project—as we see it in *Representing the Holocaust* (1994)—he psychoanalyzes the relation between the scholar and her subject, suggesting that the dynamics of the transference best explain not only the kind of analysis Felman produces, but the kind of history that gets written about the Holocaust in general.[24] For Tal, Felman and Laub's work in *Testimony* is one instance of a more general phenomenon in which the survivor of trauma is "depoliticiz[ed]" and "medicaliz[ed]," thereby domesticating whatever social or political intervention she might wish to make.[25]

My point differs from both of these interpretations: I see Felman's reading of de Man not as an irresponsible use of deconstruction brought on by intense transferential forces, or as a manipulation with political consequences, but as the logical limit case of the trauma theory *Testimony* as a whole puts forward.[26] The "point of conflation between text and life," where writing or speech can come to embody and transmit the trauma of the "actual life" (2), not only allows those who sympathize with Holocaust survivors to draw their personal significance and their identity from the Holocaust, but also allows those—like de Man—who did not evince such sympathy, to have their significance, and indeed, a kind of moral status, drawn for them from the Holocaust.

The implications of this kind of transmission reach beyond Felman herself and her relation to de Man, for Felman's argument is only one version of a theoretical innovation we find in the 1990s, particularly in discourse about the Holocaust, that attempts to reimagine the relation between texts and persons in such a way that texts take on particular characteristics we ordinarily assign exclusively to persons. Other chapters in *Testimony* reveal, for instance, that while de Man can commit suicide by ceasing to write, those who bear witness to suffering reverse death. Felman claims that "the main role of the historian is, thus, less to narrate history than to *reverse the suicide*" (216; original emphasis),[27] suggesting, for example, that Simon Srebnik, a witness of the most extreme violence of the camps, comes back from the dead when he agrees to take part in Claude Lanzmann's film. Felman claims that "it is . . . only now, in returning with Lanzmann to Chelmno [where Srebnik was held prisoner], that Srebnik in effect is returning from the dead (from his own deadness)" (258). Later, she repeats the assertion without its accompanying parenthetical. Simon Srebnik's return from the dead is no longer metaphoric and abstract but real, now capable of personifying yet another abstraction: "Srebnik's return from the dead personifies . . . a historically performative and retroactive *return of witnessing* to the witnessless historical primal scene" (258; original emphasis).[28]

It becomes clear that Felman cannot—and does not wish to—contain the collapse of persons and representations by which de Man can commit suicide and Claude Lanzmann can raise the dead. Felman imagines, further, that language itself, in the abstract sense of all languages, is a Freudian subject who "splits" into German, French, English, Russian, and Hebrew in response to the trauma it—Language—experiences in the Holocaust (213). Whatever truth might lie behind her formulation—that the twentieth century included terrible and unprecedented events—and whatever stylistic tendency toward hyperbole might shape that formulation, I think it is worth taking her own language seriously. While Felman does not always imagine writing as itself a person in the way these final examples suggest, she does consistently imagine writing as the embodiment (rather than the representation) of the kind of experience—of "life"—that only persons can be said to have.

Trauma without Experience   In the two cases of holocaust discourse I have examined thus far, Binjamin Wilkomirski's false memoir and Shoshana Felman's *Testimony*, actual trauma—lived suffering—seems to be pertinent, even crucial, to the claims that traumatic memoir and trauma theory make about texts. No matter how far removed Yale graduate students may be from the actual violence of the Holocaust, that violence underwrites the substance of what they are said to experience, and I have shown how Felman points to the undeniable suffering in de Man's life—the death of his brother and the suicide of his mother—as the foundation of the story she will tell about the trace of trauma in his writings. And no matter how doubtful the facts behind Binjamin Wilkomirski's memoir have turned out to be, the violence described there is, for both Wilkomirski himself and his readers, the source of the story's power and its significance.

This concern with actual violence and the psychic pain it engenders seems consistent with ideas about Holocaust survivors that were prevalent from about the mid-1970s up through the early 1990s, a period defined by the Reagan-era resurgence of the Cold War. In this period, as I discussed in chapter 2, discourse about survivors tends to be more narrowly focused on what we might call literal survival—escaping from the camps with one's life—as epitomized by Terrance Des Pres's *The Survivor* (1976) and by Robert Jay Lifton and Eric Markusen's *The Genocidal Mentality* (1990).[29] But at the same time, Felman's work moves away from the emphasis on physical violence and literal survival that defines the Holocaust survivor for Des Pres or Lifton, focusing instead on the survivor's ability to "bear witness" to her own and others' suffering. In some respects, the turn away from biological life as the basis of survivorship turns back to the ground covered by Primo Levi in *Se Questo è un Uomo* (1958), who suggests that the survivor ceases to be a person in any significant sense while in the camps, precisely because of the minute and desperate measures to which the inmate is driven just to sustain the life of the body, measures that overtake any notion of civility or culture.[30] Levi's response is to tell the story of his oppression, to insist on producing meaning through representing those events. While Levi's work might thus appear to fall under Felman's category of "witness," Felman's commitment to deconstruction, which is to say the rejection of language as representational, already moves her away not just from Des Pres and Lifton, but also from Levi.

Indeed, the implications of that deconstructive shift from language as representation to language as performance—apparent in the idea that survivors can be produced on the basis of trauma that is experienced by being read—suggests that Felman's evident concern with the actual violence experienced in the Holocaust may be unnecessary to trauma theory at its most abstract level. This is indicated in part by the fact that trauma theory does not, as Levi does, treat the camps as the destruction of what makes persons significant as such, but instead imagines the existential crisis that structures the Holocaust experience as the very core of both culture and personhood—that is, as the very core of our common life. I am not referring here to the belief that the camps revealed something like the truth of human nature or the notion that they epitomize the cultural and moral bankruptcy of our century. Rather, trauma theory has suggested that the experience of trauma is what defines not only the survivor, but all persons.[31] The psychoanalyst Dori Laub argues in his own chapters of *Testimony*, for example, that "the survival experience, or the Holocaust experience, is a very condensed version of most of what life is all about," because "it contains a great many existential questions" (72). The implication, for Laub, is that "the Holocaust experience is an inexorable and, henceforth, an unavoidable confrontation with those questions" (72). In other words, the Holocaust is not unique but exemplary, and exemplary not so much of other genocides as of everyday life. The suggestion implicit in this notion of exemplarity, that the "Holocaust experience" is not confined to the events we have come to call the Holocaust, implies, further, that the experience of the Holocaust continues in the present. It is not the facts of the Holocaust—its history—that are "an inexorable and, henceforth, an un-avoidable confrontation" with existential questions, but the experience itself.

While Laub thus suggests that the specific historical events of the Holo-caust, which some experienced and the rest of us learn about, are in fact at the heart of everyone's continuing experience, Cathy Caruth pushes the point even further. For Caruth the traumatic nature of history docs not begin with the Holocaust, to continue "henceforth," but rather, the structure of trauma characterizes all history and experience despite the fact that the notion of lived trauma is almost entirely absent from her analysis in *Unclaimed Experi-ence* (1996).

It should be said, first of all, that Caruth, unlike Felman, is not writing about the Holocaust in *Unclaimed Experience;* she is interested instead in ex-ploring trauma and its relation to history and literature in a more general sense. It should also be said that, while she does not specify a historical site of trauma as her subject, neither does Caruth move to the other extreme, claiming that all experience, and all history, is traumatic; indeed, she specifi-cally disavows the notion that her work is "an attempt to identify experience with trauma." Caruth wants, rather, "to allow, within experience, for the very unexpected interruption of experience constituted by the traumatic acci-dent."[32] By defining trauma and experience in this way, in relation to one another, Caruth thus suggests that she has avoided the mistake of "defining, and thus anticipating, the difference between experience and trauma" (115). While Caruth's effort to avoid both identifying experience with trauma and roping off the traumatic experience from experience itself, as something dis-tinct, makes sense—"experience," after all, is simply what happens to us, and what happens to us includes both the traumatic and the nontraumatic—we need to look more closely at the other claim being made here, that to be able to categorize an experience is to be able to anticipate it, to be able to "anticipate the accident" (115). This, on the surface, looks implausible: just because we know what to call a train wreck does not mean we know when we might be in one or that when we are in fact in a train wreck we are any less surprised for being able to name it.[33]

But obviously Caruth does not mean precisely this. Rather, she seems to be suggesting that the accident is something that happens not just to people, but to language. To put it in the more general terms that Caruth develops in her reading of de Man, which makes up chapter 4 of *Unclaimed Experience,* experience and language are the same thing insofar as accidents of the sort she is describing as traumatic—epitomized, for Caruth, by Freud's account of the train wreck in *Beyond the Pleasure Principle*—include accidents within language. What Caruth calls the "impact" of the linguistic referent that de Man appears to deny in his theory becomes, on Caruth's reading, a moment of trauma that inheres in the very structure of language. Reference is thus a kind of accident for Caruth: not the sort of accident that de Man describes in "The Purloined Ribbon," where Rousseau's "Marion" accidentally refers (refers simply by chance) to an actual person, but an accident that is like "falling down" (74), like the "impact" of the falling body (7).[34] This abstract notion of falling, for Caruth, epitomizes the trauma inherent in language itself, the trauma that is explored and, indeed, concentrated, in the ambiguities and the indirectness of reference to be found in literary language, "a language that defies, even as it claims, our understanding" (5).

Caruth may well be right in her basic intuition that de Man's theories about language contain an unacknowledged pathos, in which one might read a kind of regret or loss associated with the mechanistic functioning of language and the concomitant evacuation of presence and meaning that de Man theorizes. But in finding this pathos and characterizing it as a fall (a characterization I do not find convincing, because it is never clear how falling can ever be more than an analogy for the functioning of language), Caruth simply replicates and amplifies the pathos without making its object—the failure of reference—any more plausible as an instance of trauma. By making trauma—that experience which cannot be fully understood or known because of its violence—inhere in the very structure of language as such and by asserting trauma's centrality to literary language in this way, Caruth in the end insulates her analysis from the more concrete notions of trauma that inform Felman's analysis. And she does so even as she, like Felman, argues that trauma is embodied, without mediation, in language.

We can see this most dramatically in Caruth's conception of history. History is not what we might think—it is not the violent events of the world; rather, history is the way psychoanalysis and literature imagine one's relation to the past. Caruth's examples of "history" thus include Freud's *Moses and*

Monotheism (which he originally subtitled "an historical novel"), the film *Hiroshima Mon Amour,* and Jacques Lacan's reading of Freud's account of the dream of the burning child. These are histories by Caruth's account because of the way they imagine the stories of people who have survived a loss and whose lives are still structured around that loss. History is "the inextricability of the story of one's life from the story of a death" (8). While what we would ordinarily call history does come into Caruth's reading of Freud's *Moses and Monotheism* insofar as she reads the work in relation to Freud's precipitous departure from Austria to England in 1938, that traumatic departure is immediately subsumed into the text of *Moses and Monotheism* itself. The text becomes "the site of a trauma" that is "historically marked" (20). Rather than the text marking a trauma Freud experienced, here history "marks" the textual trauma. What is striking in Caruth's account, then, is the way actual history—the things that happen in the world—is either excluded from the discussion or reduced to a kind of trace, just as actual trauma—the railway accident itself as distinct from Freud's account of it—is also excluded.

I take this strange insulation in Caruth's analysis to result from the understanding of trauma to which she is committed, an understanding that makes trauma not only "like literature" in that it is a kind of "not knowing," but also "like psychoanalysis" because of the latter's interest in "the complex relation between knowing and not knowing" (3). What history, literature, and psychoanalysis all share for Caruth, because of this very insulation, is the ability to "transmit" trauma whenever they "transmit" (115, 106, and throughout) or "pass on" (71, 107, and throughout) what is not known. The literary language of these discourses, because it does not describe an accident but in some sense must be understood *as* an accident, allows trauma to be transferred from one person to another. This counts as an explanation, for example, of the transmission of trauma imagined in *Moses and Monotheism* (an explanation, it must be said, Freud himself does not produce, though he does suggest that transmission takes place).[35] If, Caruth reasons, the experience of trauma is "possession by the past that is not entirely one's own" then trauma is an "individual experience" that "exceeds itself," and as such, "the witnessing of trauma" may not occur in the individual who experienced it but rather in "future generations" (136).

The impact of this claim—that the experience of trauma can be cut free of the person to whom the trauma happens—saturates Caruth's study; it can be seen even on the level of style, in her peculiar use of gerunds such as "the witnessing," "a seeing," "a falling," "a forgetting," "a not-forgetting." While such nominalization of academic writing has occurred in part as a grammatical effect of the critical desire to stop referring back to authors as a way of under-standing what we see in a text, in Caruth's case the implication would be more specific. Once what a subject does is detached from the subject—in these cases, detached from a person—the act of experiencing can become a thing in the world, like an object (and here we can begin to understand the book's title). Experience, like a lost glove, can be "claimed" or left "un-claimed." In other words, once "she forgets" becomes "a forgetting," the forgetting can belong to anyone, and indeed, can begin to have actions predi-cated upon it.[36] By cutting experience free from the subject of experience, Caruth allows trauma not only to be abstract in the extreme but also, by virtue of that abstraction, to be transmissible.

Ruth Leys has produced a thorough analysis and critique of this notion of transmissible trauma and the way it has played a role in the intellectual and institutional evolution of the psychoanalytic profession, linking it with the scientific work of Bessel van der Kolk and showing how Caruth's theories distort Freud's more complex (though admittedly ambiguous) understanding of trauma. And Leys has raised serious questions about the ethical implica-tions of Caruth's notion of trauma, pointing out that even Nazi perpetrators can, under its rubric, be seen as victims.[37] While my argument is in some ways parallel—and certainly indebted—to Leys's work in this regard, my own extended reading of Caruth is meant to show how her work, and trauma theory more generally, produces not so much a certain understanding of trauma as a certain understanding of language. This is an understanding in-debted to de Manian deconstruction but also departing from it at the very point where the autonomous literary language that de Man imagined is taken, by virtue of that very autonomy, to actually be the experience of persons.[38] Though I agree with Leys's ethical critique, which is akin to LaCapra's and Tal's critiques of Felman and my own implicit critique of Wilkomirski, I want to focus less on the ethical implications of trauma theory than on its position within a wider literary discourse about the destruction of persons in the sec-ond half of the twentieth century. For Caruth's understanding of trauma and language is neither new nor particular to the practices of deconstruction and psychoanalysis she explicitly engages. In the final section of this chapter I show how a certain fantasy about memorization that we find in Caruth—made possible by the deconstructive emphasis on the materiality of the signifier—is rehearsed in the two nuclear dystopias that I discussed (in other terms) in chapter 2, in Don DeLillo's novel of postnuclear culture, *Underworld* (1997), and finally, to return to where I began this chapter, in Binjamin Wilkomirski's false memoir of the Holocaust.

Memorizing Memory   Caruth's notion of transmissible trauma—trauma that can be passed unknowingly from one person to another —is perhaps best exemplified by a certain fantasy about memorization, and it is this fantasy that will connect her study to the novels I mention above. Caruth points out, as she concludes her reading of the film *Hiroshima Mon Amour*, that the Japanese actor in that film—Eiji Okada, who speaks perfect French throughout—in fact did not know a word of French. He memorized what could only be, to him, the sounds of French and delivered these sounds to the French woman in the film as if he were intending a meaning. It should not take much reflection to see why this happenstance is important to Caruth, for the story of Okada's memorization reproduces what she has been presenting as the characteristic—rather than exceptional—linguistic structure. Here the actor literally "performs" the words he speaks, appearing (though this could hardly be the case even if he did not know French) to produce them without knowing their meaning, telling his character's story of trauma—of his family being killed in the bombing of Hiroshima while he was away in the Army—without understanding that story even as he tells it.

For Caruth, this happenstance reveals not only the truth about language, but also a truth about the relation between cultural identity and language understood in these terms. She argues, for example, that a Japanese businessman, who in the film uses English phrases (which Caruth characterizes as being memorized from a guidebook[39]) in an effort to pick up the French woman in a bar, has willingly submitted himself to a culture not his own. In this particular case, he has submitted himself to the culture of English, the culture that was responsible for the destruction of Hiroshima; he thereby represents, according to Caruth, "a certain loss of self implicit in the speaking of another's language" (49). By contrast, Caruth suggests that the Japanese actor who memorizes without trying to learn, and who memorizes not English but French, maintains his cultural integrity while still connecting with the cultural other, his French lover. Unlike the speech of the businessman and of the fictional character Okada plays, whose "well-learnt French represents," according to Caruth, "the loss of the Japanese referent" (51), Okada's speech "cannot be considered in the same terms of loss and forgetting. Okada, in other words, does not represent, but rather voices his difference quite literally, and untranslatably" (51). Here, cultural integrity appears to entail the decision to speak—or, more accurately, to intend meaning—only in one's own language, the language, to use Wilkomirski's terms, that is not the "imitation of other people's speech" but one's "own, at bottom." The language of the other is preserved as incomprehensible by the operation of memorization as opposed to learning. But in a sense, we can see that memorized, incomprehensible language has become not the language of the other, but the language in which one is most oneself: on this model, language is not representation but ontology; not the vehicle for knowledge but the medium in which one "voices his difference quite literally," in which one simply is oneself.

Being oneself in this way in turn means being the subject of a trauma, since the meaninglessness of the actor's speech is aligned, for Caruth, with his character's story of having missed the destruction of Hiroshima and of his family and thus being unable to "*know*" (40; original emphasis) his own experience of trauma. If identity imagined in these terms preserves one's cultural integrity in the way Caruth argues, then cultural identity has the same structure as traumatic experience—cultural identity and trauma are incomprehensible experiences that get passed around. The valorized production of personal or cultural identity is thus not, as it is for a writer like Primo Levi, the commitment to telling the story of one's trauma, but is rather the commitment to actually passing on the experience of trauma without having the experience oneself. The way Caruth presents it, this looks like a vision of ultimate particularity—for both persons and experience—since particular experiences that constitute personal and cultural identity thus bear an unmediated or literal relation to language. And indeed, this is part of what Caruth is interested in showing us, since representation as such for her implies the replaceability of persons and experiences, and the potential universality of these things.[40] Caruth thus claims that Eiji Okada's "phonetic feat" made him particularly essential to bring back when *Hiroshima Mon Amour* had to be reshot because of technical problems and, further, that the film's own history in this way underscored the importance of particularity in the representation of trauma. But the traumatic structures Caruth has laid out actually mean that Okada's participation cannot be in any sense significant. For, apart from the certainly remarkable talent for memorizing sounds that he demonstrated, anyone could memorize the script, say the lines, and "transmit" the trauma. Far from preserving what Caruth presents—and values—as the unknowable particularity of the traumatic experience, this fantasy about memorization makes particularity meaningless and makes trauma available to anyone, not just without recourse to painful experience but without recourse to experience as such.

It is here, in the coincidence between memorization and the construction of identities centered on trauma, that trauma theory can be seen most clearly to take up questions characteristic of postwar novels that, in imagining American culture in the wake of a large-scale nuclear war, attempt in their own way to come to terms with the relation between literature and what we can—in the ordinary sense—call traumatic events. As I showed in chapter 2, Ray Bradbury's *Fahrenheit 451* and Walter M. Miller, Jr.'s *A Canticle for Leibowitz* both feature groups of people whose identities in the wake of nuclear war are a function of the books they memorize. In both of these novels, the memorized text is both mechanical and material—a set of words in a particular order, preserved and transmitted through what is described as a mostly mechanical action of the memorizer's mind or pen. Guy Montag finds that he has memorized Ecclesiastes despite his apparent inability to screen out the distraction of advertising jingles. His mind, as imagined by Bradbury, memorized of its own accord and without his knowledge, filtering out the jingles and preserving, photographically, the entire prophetic text. *A Canticle for Leibowitz* features memorizers and copyists who reproduce texts and diagrams whose basis in extinct scientific knowledge renders them even more remote from meaning than the words of Ecclesiastes seem to Montag. For *Canticle*'s memorizers, the text becomes an arrangement, as one copyist puts it, of "doohickii" and "thingumbob" (76). Miller pushes this conception of the text one step further in significance by imagining it not only as essentially material but also as sacred, and as such the embodiment of truth even when—or especially when—its content cannot be understood rationally.

We also see the structure of unintentional or nonrational memorization thematized in novels closer, historically speaking, to trauma theory than *Fahrenheit 451* and *Canticle*, particularly in Don DeLillo's work. In *Ratner's Star* (1976), for example, Ratner's rabbi confesses that he has resorted to memorizing the sacred writings instead of interpreting them, because he is not really capable of understanding what they mean. The image returns in *Libra* (1988), in a secularized version, when Lee Harvey Oswald memorizes the Marine Corps manual and the utterly arbitrary rules of the military prison where he serves time. But its appearance in *Underworld* (1997) makes explicit the relation between memorization and a postnuclear culture permeated with violence both intended and unintended. Here, we find one of the main protagonists, Nick Shay, memorizing the ideas in Catholic texts under the tutelage of his Jesuit mentor: when the priest asks whether Nick understands what is in the books he is reading, he replies that he understands "some of it. . . . What I don't understand, I memorize."[41] For Nick, memorizing ideas and even simply new vocabulary is, he thinks, "the only way in the world you can escape the things that made you" (543). In Nick's case, what "made" him was a difficult, impoverished urban childhood that, through a complicated set of circumstances, led him to kill a man—unintentionally—for which he was convicted of manslaughter. While it looks like "the things that made" Nick also made, in his brother Matt's case, a very different man, DeLillo is in fact imaging the two as alike in a crucial way; for Matt becomes a nuclear weapons engineer, epitomizing what it means for American culture as a whole—like Nick, who describes himself as a "country of one" (275)—to be made the unintentional agent of murder. The religious texts Nick memorizes appear to offer, for him and perhaps for DeLillo, the only alternative to the unintentionally criminal identities both Nick and his brother possess. The memorized texts preserve what appears, in *Underworld,* to be an unavoidable failure of agency and rationality in a postmodern world, while they substitute some other, and better, end result for the individual person whose agency is thus compromised. Memorizing for Nick—as for Bradbury's Guy Montag in *Fahrenheit 451*—takes what is not you, what you do not yourself intend or understand, and makes it you.

And this is precisely what I take Bruno Dössekker also to have done. He absorbed the accounts of camp life, the stories of extreme violence, the testimonies and histories and photographs, and they finally became him, finally made him Binjamin Wilkomirski. Despite the difference we understand between what we memorize (like the multiplication tables) and what we call our memories (to use Nick Shay's terms, our recollections of the "things that made" us), in the case of Bruno Dössekker memorizing and memory have become the same thing. Without setting out to memorize the map of Auschwitz, he nevertheless did, and in doing so, perhaps without intending to, he became a child survivor.

Having earlier set aside ethical questions of the kind that Ruth Leys, Dominick LaCapra and Kalí Tal raise about transmissible trauma, ethical questions that we cannot help but think about when we consider the case of Wilkomirski, I want to conclude by taking up those questions in a limited way. One of the most accomplished contemporary ethicists and theorists of personhood, Derek Parfit, provides a final example of the fantasy of transmitted experience and in doing so offers a response to such transmission that is diametrically opposed to the one implied in trauma theory.

Parfit is interested in what persons are and why what persons are might (or might not) matter. As he thinks through various propositions about what persons are in his *Reasons and Persons* (1984), he produces a version of the view of experience I have been describing in this chapter. We see this in one of the hypothetical examples he uses to tease out the logic of identity: the example of Jack and Jane's memory surgery. In the scenario Parfit imagines, Jack and Jane undergo surgery in which the memories of each are implanted into the other's brain. Parfit argues that after a while, Jane will not be able to tell which of her memories were the result of her experiences prior to the surgery and which were the result of Jack's experiences. Indeed, Parfit argues that, for all significant purposes, Jane will become the subject of Jack's experiences. The point is that since we can imagine Jane feeling that Jack's experiences bear the same relation to her sense of identity as her own, it would be incoherent to assert that identity lies in some singular entity that has experienced a certain set of things, that identity can be located within the subject of those experiences.

The example of Jack and Jane is just one scenario among several that Parfit uses to think through, and disprove, various ways of defining what persons are. The result of his analysis of existing theories leads him, finally, to what he calls the "Reductionist View." The Reductionist View states that "the existence of a person, during any period, just consists in the existence of his brain and body, and the thinking of his thoughts, and the doing of his deeds, and the occurrence of many other physical and mental events."[42] The ethical importance of the memory surgery example becomes clear when Parfit later describes the effects of believing the view of persons he arrived at, in part, through the idea of memory surgery. When one thinks of life as the Reductionist does, Parfit finds that "there is still a difference between my life and the lives of other people. But the difference is less." This, in turn, changes how Parfit thinks and feels about death: "After my death, there will be no one living who will be me. I can now redescribe this fact. Though there will later be many experiences, none of these experiences will be connected to my present experiences by chains of such direct connections as those involved in experience-memory, or in the carrying out of an earlier intention. . . . My death will break the more direct relations between my present experiences and future experiences, but it will not break various other relations" (281). What Parfit here calls "direct relations" are discussed in earlier parts of his argument as the narrative relations that we routinely generate to explain the events of our lives, narrative relations of the kind so evident in the example of Binjamin Wilkomirski. For Parfit this is not simply a linguistic activity, but also has to do with physical facts, such as the fact that the same brain perceives one event and then another, the same body does its deeds from one moment to the next. The Reductionist View suggests that these connections—both physical and narratological—are not morally significant even if they are emotionally compelling.

Without discounting the fact that our narratological sense of ourselves has a certain power (Parfit feels "better" about his own death, though we can still hear melancholy in this passage), he suggests that it is a kind of sentimentalism to believe that these narratological links between experiences are what matters in the world. What matters, rather, is that the sum total of experiences is predominantly good (Parfit clearly displays his utilitarian commitments here). For Parfit, unlike the trauma theorists and literary practitioners I have presented, seeing experiences as in some sense alienable from what we think of as the person (through the fantasy of memory surgery) leads to the devaluation of personal identity as such, let alone particular kinds of trauma-centered personal identity like the ones Wilkomirski and Felman construct or theorize. The "Reductionist," Parfit explains, "also claims that personal identity is not what matters," which is why a certain set of relations between experiences, produced by the narratives of an individual person, matters less to Parfit as he reflects upon his own death (275). In questioning the value of personal identity understood in terms of narratological links, he voids the cultural work trauma theory can be said to accomplish even while he shares its ambivalence about the tie between experiences and persons. The loose tie Parfit imagines, instead of conferring value on something like Wilkomirski's traumatic identity or the survivorship of Yale students, makes such identities morally irrelevant. It seems fair to ask, if Parfit reasons correctly (as I think he does) about what persons are, whether we should have any interest in imagining other people's experiences as our own.

5 Bellow, Roth, and the Secret of Identity

I want to begin by summarizing the final point I make in the previous chapter: one way around the ethical problems raised by the story of Binjamin Wilkomirski would be to begin with the philosophy of personal identity outlined by Derek Parfit in *Reasons and Persons*. There, Parfit argues (like the practitioners of trauma theory) that we can imagine a world in which experiences thought to define personal identity might be transferred from one person to another. But unlike the practitioners of trauma theory, in imagining such a world he argues that we must then conclude that personal identity—based on the narrative unity of such experiences—is not what matters about persons. (Instead, what matters about persons, according to Parfit, is that the experiences people have are as nearly free of suffering as possible.) Parfit's philosophical position, even though it makes the idea of transmissible experience central to the underlying logic of personal identity, would also make transmission of experience much less compelling as a literary-critical enterprise. If, as Parfit argues, personal identity based on claims to and narratives of experience is of no real value, then there would be fewer reasons to continue in the effort to make literature—rather than, say, the fantasy of memory surgery Parfit uses in his example—the conduit through which that transmission takes place. It would follow that, under such philosophical conditions, memoirs could not carry the cultural significance made apparent in the successive adulation for and outcry against *Fragments*. Fake memoirs and doubtful claims to experience could not raise the same ethical questions that they do with respect to Wilkomirski and for trauma theory, even if they continued to raise the same theoretical questions about representation and its relationship to persons. The effect of agreeing with Parfit, then, is to separate out the question of whether we should conflate texts and experience from the question of personal identity and all that personal identity currently carries with it in the way of political significance.

As compelling as I find Parfit's argument in the abstract, it seems hard to imagine that we will soon agree that personal identity does not matter, despite the efforts of writers like Paul Gilroy, Anthony Appiah, and Walter Benn Michaels to argue for the abandonment of particular versions of it such as racial identity. To put the point another way, it is hard to imagine, as Parfit does at the end of *Reasons and Persons,* that people will abandon the habit of narrating their experiences to themselves or of thinking that such narratives constitute something intrinsically and overwhelmingly meaningful about themselves. It is hard to imagine, again as Parfit does, that people might face death with the sense that the end of this narrative is not something to feel strongly about.

Adopting Parfit's view is one way to avoid assenting to the beliefs about identity, history, experience, and representation that I have argued, in the last two chapters, are entailed if one accepts the logic of some of the personal identities that have come to be so highly valued in our culture. But it is not the only way. There are certainly writers who have imagined a version of identity that takes history into account but does not imagine the person as determined by that history, who have imagined an art that is closely allied to life but that remains distinct from life, who have acknowledged the need of individuals to join themselves to others without making the individual subordinate to the kinds of coercive group identities Paul Gilroy has described, in *Against Race,* as "camps."[1] In this chapter I take up two such writers who set about imagining what I will present as alternatives to the personified text and its outcomes for beliefs about identity: Saul Bellow and Philip Roth.

I choose these two in part because their work engages the idea of the Holocaust. This will allow me to show how their understanding of persons plays out in the discourse about the destruction of persons that has been the subject of the previous chapters. I choose Bellow and Roth also because they are intensely interested in how the particular person relates to history and to identities that are shared by groups and generated by kinship, love, or politics. Far from discounting these sometimes coercive, sometimes empowering forces, both Roth and Bellow make them central to much of their fiction.

Finally, I focus on these two writers because they have clearly chosen to define themselves, above all, as writers. I will argue that this fact is reflected in the distinctions they draw within their fiction between representations and persons. If identities are representations or narratives—what Appiah calls "life-scripts"—and adopting an identity implies the conflation of the person with such a text, then the artistic commitments of these writers suggest that the writer may carve out a modicum of freedom—by dint of both perseverance and writerly talent—by crafting, rather than simply accepting fully made, a representation to inhabit.[2] To put the point in Althusserian terms, the writer is presented in these works as one who, instead of simply answering the hail of ideology, instead of simply acquiescing to interpellation, comes back with a revision of the name by which he is called. The most striking example of this is Roth's Coleman Silk, the protagonist of *The Human Stain* (2000). The space opened up by art is thus the space of flexibility in which the conflation of person and representation is acknowledged as an illusion that, while it perhaps cannot be defeated as a social reality, can certainly be played with or resisted. Ultimately, such resistance is most effectively imagined in Roth's notion of identity as secret. The chapter concludes with a discussion of how Roth's and Bellow's notions of persons intersect with the ideas about identity that drive criticism of their work and that animate theoretical discussions of gender, race, multiculturalism, and performativity.

These are the larger lineaments and implications of the arguments I make below about Roth and Bellow, but these points will emerge if we consider first how history relates to identity in the work of these two writers. I have demonstrated in the preceding chapters that how one imagines past experience in relation to the present person sets up a logic by which one understands identity as such. This holds true for Bellow and Roth as well. In the first section of this chapter I will ask how, and why, the history of the Holocaust matters in Bellow's work, particularly in his 1970 novel *Mr. Sammler's Planet*. In the second section, I will examine what Holocaust history and family history together have to do with identity and representation in Roth's *The Ghost Writer* (1979) and *The Human Stain* (2000).

"Everybody Has a History"   Central elements in Saul Bellow's first major novel, *The Adventures of Augie March* (1953), recall the issues I have engaged in the previous chapters. In this novel the young Augie March demonstrates a persistent commitment to what Bellow calls his individual "fate" in the face of others who try to enlist him as a necessary accomplice in pursuing their own fates. First, an employer, later, his Circean lover, Thea Fenschell, and then his brother Simon ask Augie to identify not so much with them as with their representation of him as a player in their personal dramas, creating a complex of what Bellow calls "cosmic" forces, an array of godlike persons (a revision of the *Odyssey*'s personlike gods) who try to detain him in his search for his own fate. Representations of Augie by these others turn out to be powerful instruments in what Bellow describes as their efforts to "recruit" Augie, for such representations are evident in a repeated scene: at each important turn of the plot, Augie is either urged or forced to don new clothing, urged or forced, that is, to inhabit a representation of himself that someone else has chosen.

When he finally abandons Thea in Mexico and then definitively rejects his brother's urgings to live in a borrowed suit and become part of the family business, we finally see what Augie's own fate might look like: he dreams of a house in the country where he would bring his aged mother, his simpleton brother, and his new wife, to live together happily ever after. While the Odyssean structure of the novel underscores the point that this fate is in fact a kind of return to origin, Bellow finally displaces the return Augie desires. At the end of the novel, Augie suddenly abandons this pastoral dream and goes to great lengths to enlist in the merchant marine, essentially recruiting himself to the cause of war, choosing for himself the new set of clothes—and the new identity—that he will now inhabit.

The story of Augie March thus thematizes several of the problems that I have been exploring throughout this book. Like Sylvia Plath's speaker in the "The Bee Meeting," Augie desires the recognition by others that comes with each new set of clothes he is given, while remaining conscious of the loss of self entailed in such recognition. Like Benjamin Wilkomirski, he inhabits representations as a way of manufacturing his identity. Other parallels between Bellow's work and the texts I have considered up to this point will become apparent later on, but I want to begin by suggesting that in taking up the questions in play in previous chapters, Bellow marks himself not only as typical of writers in this period, but more importantly, as atypical. His fiction imagines quite different answers to the questions I have been pursuing thus far, about what the relationship is between representations and persons, about history's hold over identity, and finally, about what the purpose of literature might be in a world overshadowed by death.

Bellow's atypical vision begins to become apparent in the way *Augie March* revises the Odyssean story. By displacing the pastoral return to family and origin with recruitment to the merchant marine, Bellow suggests that a return to origin is not so much closure or completion (as Augie clearly hopes it will be) as yet another kind of recruitment, a recruitment that is not privileged as more authentic or in any other way different from the others that have marked Augie's life. Unlike Art Spiegelman, to take one example, Augie's search for his real self does not bring him, as it brings Art, back to his parents and their experiences as the fount of authenticity (as in the moment where the mouse mask becomes the mouse head and Art becomes the "REAL survivor"). The displacement of the family suggests that Bellow sees the ongoing march of history as preferable to the sentimentalized past even if it requires, in the process of displacing that past, a type of group identification that is clearly distasteful to Bellow.

The need to enter history is highlighted by the fact that, in some ways, Augie's final act of identification seems unnecessary given the terms of the novel up to that point. Augie does not need the merchant marine to make him American, for that is what he claims he is from the opening sentence of the novel: "I am an American, Chicago born." And Bellow does not invite us to see the newly enlisted Augie as heroic, for at no time in the novel does Bellow try to make Augie seem like a hero in that traditional sense. In fact, Augie's patriotism is portrayed as impulsive, extreme, even silly—he undergoes a risky surgery in order to meet the physical requirements of enlistment—and Bellow chooses a low-status branch of the military as the object of Augie's patriotic efforts. All of this suggests that Bellow remains ambivalent about the seeming necessity (manufactured by Bellow himself, of course) for Augie to identify with a group as such. What is important about Augie's enlistment, then, is not that in choosing it himself he has finally become an individual and a man within a society dependent upon groups—a reading that would be consistent with the critical understanding of *Augie March* as *Bildungsroman*. What is important about Augie's enlistment is rather that it inserts him into the ongoing production, rather than the recovery, of history. As Bellow would put it later, in reflecting upon Walt Whitman, "on the open road, separateness was ideal because it ended in joining."[3] What Augie joins, in the end, is the life of the world.

Insofar as its central dramas revolve around a man's recruitment and his resistance to it, *Augie March* takes up concerns—about conformity and masculinity, among other things—evident, albeit in less interesting ways, in other postwar novels. Sloan Wilson's *The Man in the Grey Flannel Suit* (1955), for example, thematizes a corporate version of recruitment and imagines marriage, home, and the birth of the suburbs (in the subdivision of the family's ancestral estate) not, as Bellow imagines domesticity in *Augie March*, as another recruitment, but as the answer to it, as the assertion of masculine individuality in the face of corporate power and endless middle management.[4] I have already indicated, in chapter 2, how Bradbury's *Fahrenheit 451* can be read next to Wilson's novel as being about questions of conformity, and we could include in this group, as well, J. D. Salinger's *Catcher in the Rye* (1951) or Carson McCullers's *The Member of the Wedding* (1946). But Bellow's interest is finally less sociological—less about how to be a man in 1950s America—than it is metaphysical, about what it means for one to find and honor one's own "fate." This is not to say that Bellow's novels are themselves transcendental or ahistorical.[5] Rather, it is to say that what we have to historicize is not the social thematics of Bellow's work but its metaphysical concerns. The questions produced by the concern with fate—questions of identity and its relation to one's view of history—continue to preoccupy Bellow's writing, even in a novel like *Mr. Sammler's Planet* (1970), which, set in New York City of the late 1960s, imagines for its protagonist a social world in which conformity is not the problem, in which nonconformity is fashionable and the young, far from being conservative and nostalgic, are thirsty for social progress.

Because it thematizes the Holocaust—that is, because it engages a specific history that has come, as I showed in chapters 3 and 4, to define a particular kind of identity—*Mr. Sammler's Planet* invites us to think further about the conjunction of history and identity in Bellow's work, about what that conjunction accomplishes within Bellow's own literary project, and how it might compare with the connections between history and identity that I discussed in chapter 3. *Mr. Sammler's Planet*, extending the logic we find in *Augie March*, mounts a critique both of history as a determining force and identity categorization as such, and goes on to suggest an alternative to the racialized grounds of identification that structure both the murderous Nazism we see in Artur Sammler's past and the identity politics that surround him in late-1960s New York City.

Sammler, an elderly Polish refugee and a Holocaust survivor, is the central character and narrative consciousness of the novel. His history in Europe includes both a successful stint in London as a Bloomsbury intellectual before the war and, later, extreme victimization at the hands of the Nazis. Mr. Sammler and his wife are both shot into a mass grave in the Zamosht Forest, but Mr. Sammler later crawls out alive from under the bodies. He lives out the war first as a resistance fighter and then, when Polish anti-Semitism becomes as dangerous as Nazi anti-Semitism, he waits out the war in hiding, in a Polish mausoleum. In New York, where the novel takes place, Sammler lives a modest life supported by his nephew Elya. He spends his days reading, talking to relatives, or riding the Riverside bus watching a princely black pickpocket at work. The novel has come to be known for the scene in which this pickpocket, having caught the old man watching him, follows Sammler, corners him in the lobby of an apartment building, and exposes himself to Sammler in a gesture of threat. This scene, occurring near the beginning of the novel, is one of several subplots that distract from and impede Sammler's main activity throughout the narrative: getting to his nephew Elya's bedside in the hospital where Elya is about to undergo brain surgery he is unlikely to survive. These distractions give the journey to Elya's deathbed what little dramatic tension it possesses.

In considering how the history of the Holocaust functions within this plot structure, it is first crucial to note, given what I have discussed in previous chapters, how the Holocaust does not function: it does not produce a valorized Jewish identity such as the one we see in *Maus*. Neither is it committed to the Holocaust as a unique event or a uniquely Jewish experience. Rather, Bellow consistently undermines such ideas of uniqueness and ethnic particularity within the novel.[6] "Certainly," the narrative voice—the voice of Sammler's thoughts—tells us, "Sammler had not experienced things denied to everyone else. Others had gone through the like. . . . Why speak of it?"[7] In asking rhetorically why one should speak of this experience, Sammler not only questions the importance of the Holocaust for Jews in particular, but also hints at a certain skepticism about how, and whether, one's past experience is relevant at all to one's present life. Sammler will not even say, for instance, that he "survived" the scene at the mass grave; instead, he says that he "lasted," "since so much of the earlier person had disappeared" (91). It is possible that Bellow is suggesting that the trauma of the Holocaust in particular creates this kind of discontinuity between what one experiences as one's self in the present and what one thinks of as a past self, but elsewhere in the novel he suggests that discontinuity, or irrelevance, marks all elements of the past. When his niece Angela tries to explain a quarrel with her younger brother Wallace on the grounds of her childhood resentment at his being born, Sammler remains unimpressed. "Well," he replies, "everybody has a history" (153).

Sammler rejects the decisiveness of history as part of his more general resistance to what he calls "explanation," the endless effort to identify the causes or the origins of things. History may well explain the causes of something—for example, why Angela behaves as she does—but according to Bellow that explanation tells us nothing about how we should evaluate the present thing—whether Angela's behavior toward her brother deserves tolerance or condemnation. History, it turns out, is inadequate even to distinguish one human being from another, because "everybody," as Sammler insists, "has a history." History is thus invoked to produce a critique of history as a determining force. We need to ask, then, whether or why history—or to be more specific, the history of the Jews in Europe—is central to *Mr. Sammler's Planet*. For if it cannot ground its characters' identity, or give meaning to or reasons for the shape of their present lives, we might ask with Sammler, "why speak of it?"

We can begin to answer this question by returning to Sammler's own account of his history and his reflection that "others had gone through the like." While one might read "others" as referring specifically to other Jewish victims of Nazi violence, Bellow demurs from that specificity and substitutes another in its place: "Surely some Navaho, Apache must have fallen into the Grand Canyon, survived, picked himself up, possibly said nothing to his tribe," Sammler reflects; "Why speak of it?" (137). By substituting the Navaho or Apache, Bellow imagines the moment of being shot and falling (not yet dead) into the grave as equivalent to accidentally falling into the Grand Canyon. In one sense, the two might indeed bear a structural similarity, since both entail a fall that looks like death and a reemergence into life and the world above the pit. Figured in this way, the existence of Nazism looks as contingent, historically speaking, as a slip of the moccasin.[8] Bellow thus steers the reader toward a particular understanding of what is important about the Holocaust: not its contextualization within the history of the "tribe" and its tendency to reinforce categorization of persons into tribes, but its status as a generator of knowledge about death. This point is reinforced by the fact that Bellow makes no gesture toward a parallel we as readers might be tempted to make between the Jews in Europe and Native Americans—that they were both, as groups, the targets of genocide.

If history matters, as I am suggesting, because it produces exemplary instances of death, why does death matter for Bellow? For if everybody has a history, certainly everybody will have a death, too. But it is this very universality of death that, by contrast to the universality of history, makes it not irrelevant but significant, and makes it one of Bellow's persistent concerns across the half-century of his career. In *Mr. Sammler's Planet,* death is imagined, perhaps predictably, as the impetus for literary work. We are told, for example, that while hiding in the Polish mausoleum Sammler begins to read signs, finding "curious ciphers and portents" in the world around him, "for many larger forms of meaning had been stamped out, and a straw, or a spider thread or a stain, a beetle or a sparrow had to be interpreted. Symbols everywhere, and metaphysical messages" (89–90). Death, revealed through history as that which stamps out meaning, demands that one fall back upon what we might call literary resources, what Bellow here calls the symbol, and elsewhere in the novel calls the "sign," to make sense of existence.

Even when Sammler has left behind the grave pit, the forest where he shoots a German soldier, the Polish mausoleum, and the ruins of postwar Europe, death remains palpable and insistent. Thus, in the present of the novel—in New York City—symbolic resources to mediate death are still required. This becomes clear as Sammler's cousin Elya draws closer to death: Sammler sees "A vacant building opposite marked for demolition. Large white X's on the windowpanes." While he reflects that "most scrawls could be ignored," "these for some reason caught on with Mr. Sammler as pertinent. Eloquent. Of what? Of future nonbeing. (Elya!)" (89). Here, the sign of the large white X reminds Sammler, in the midst of the distractions of his present life—his encounters with the pickpocket, his tiresome conversations with his neurotic relatives and friends, his failed lecture at the university—that death is imminent. It is Sammler's exceptional ability to read signs, to sift through the "scrawls" to find what is "eloquent," to identify "ciphers" and "metaphysical messages," that his Holocaust experience has given him.

That experience is imagined as a determining force, then, insofar as his exceptional knowledge of death forms him as an exceptional reader, for Bellow figures death itself as successful linguistic connection, as the perfect exchange of meaningful signs, an exchange that requires the perfect reader-listener. The image of that listener appears in the way Sammler describes his own history. When "Sammler, with his wife and others, on a perfectly clear day, had had to strip naked" and wait to be shot into the mass grave, Sammler "failed, unlike the others, to be connected" (137). Sammler compares this failure of connection with "a telephone circuit: death had not picked up the receiver to answer his ring"; now, when walking on Broadway, and hearing "a phone ringing in a shop when doors were open, he tried to find, to intuit, the syllable one would hear from death. 'Hello? Ah, you at last'" (137–38). History for Bellow is useful in that death unfolds inevitably within it: "Things that happen, happen" (137), as Sammler says in preface to his reflection on the scene at the mass grave, and those things include murder. Elya, like all people, is "marked for demolition," consigned by his very humanity to "future nonbeing." In other words, the Holocaust provides a set of conditions—the conditions of mortality—under which Bellow can imaginatively explore how reading and listening produce metaphysical meaning.

While death in *Mr. Sammler's Planet* is imagined as a successful exchange of signs—the phone's ring, an answer, a mutual satisfied recognition, "Ah, you at last"—life is imagined as a kind of redemptive rehearsal of that exchange. Or at least, life when it is properly mediated by the symbolic can be that redemptive rehearsal. Bellow outlines this symbolic function as the plot of *Mr. Sammler's Planet* builds toward Elya's death. Sammler, who loves his cousin, worries incessantly about contacting Elya and is prevented time and again by the absurd antics of a whole galaxy of characters, including the exhibitionist pickpocket. As Sammler tries to evade these obstacles, we have the sense that Elya is running out of time and that what he most needs is Sammler's particular symbolic talents. As Sammler tries to reach Elya, he dwells on this duty: "About essentials, almost nothing could be said. Still, signs could be made, should be made, must be made. . . . Elya at this moment had a most particular need for a sign and he, Sammler, should be there to meet that need. He again telephoned the hospital. To his surprise, he found himself speaking with [Elya] Gruner. He had asked for the private nurse. One could get through?" (261). Here, then, is the "connection" that Sammler himself failed to make when Death, in the Zamosht Forest, failed to pick up the receiver: this phone call, the immediate connection to Elya, and eventually the prayer that Sammler offers at Elya's bedside affirm the human obligation that makes life meaningful.

This vision of human affirmation may sound naive when taken in the context of the novel's historical moment—a time of urban riots, the youth movement, and a faltering war, events present in the novel through a demonstration at the university where Sammler delivers a lecture—and so it is worth pointing out that Bellow has Sammler acknowledge that one can feel the limitations of the sign. "One must be satisfied with the symbols," Sammler reflects, as if there might be something more satisfying than symbols, something like the thing itself. He suggests that one must "make peace . . . with intermediacy and representation" (149). If violence and death can stamp out "larger forms of meaning" generally found in large social institutions such as law, religion, or government, one must be content in times of violence with smaller forms, with the sign and the symbol exchanged between individuals. Failing that, the person sinks into a state that truly threatens human meaning.

The term Bellow chooses to describe this degraded state makes it clear that the problem indeed occurs at the level of the sign, as I am arguing: Sammler calls it "bad *literalness*" (my emphasis). When Elya is gone, Sammler reflects, "there would remain . . . that bad literalness," a state he associates both with his time hiding in the Polish mausoleum and with the "china-cabinet room" in the New York apartment he had had to share with his crazy daughter, Shula. In both scenes of confinement, Sammler remembers "endless literal hours in which one is internally eaten up. Eaten because coherence is lacking. . . . Or eaten by a longing for sacredness" (92). On both occasions Sammler refers to, he is rescued from "literalness" by the return of human obligation and its attendant signs. In the first case, the defeat of Nazism restores those obligations, and in the second, they are revived by his cousin Elya's search for European relatives after the war and by his generosity toward Sammler when he was stuck living with Shula. Literalness is linked with dying in both situations: in the first, Sammler is subsisting inside a mausoleum; in the second, he is an old refugee, coming to America to live out a mere remnant of life preoccupied by thoughts of death. When Sammler is called back into the world of signs, death can be put off, or at least, its eventual arrival can be met with the signs of "coherence" or "sacredness."

This is how Sammler will meet Elya's death. He offers a prayer at the close of the novel that acknowledges the specific character of the man and sets that character in the context of larger virtues. " 'Remember, God, the soul of Elya Gruner,' " he prays,

> "who, as willingly as possible and as well as he was able, and even to an intolerable point, and even in suffocation and even as death was coming was eager, even childishly perhaps (may I be forgiven for this), even with a certain servility, to do what was required of him. At his best this man was much kinder than at my very best I have ever been or could ever be. He was aware that he must meet, and he did meet—through all the confusion and degraded clowning of this life through which we are speeding—he did meet the terms of his contract. The terms which, in his inmost heart, each man knows. As I know mine. As all know. For that is the truth of it—that we all know, God, that we know, that we know, we know, we know." (313)

This prayer is just comical and peevish enough to demonstrate the imperfection of such signs and the persons who use them, and just lyrical enough to allow those signs and their users a glimmer of redemptive power against the threat of literalness.

~~~~~~~~~~

The threat of literalness is described in this instance as the blockage of signs or of symbol-making, but elsewhere in the novel it is described as an excess of symbol-making, an excess that makes persons into the symbols used to represent them. In this version of literalness we can begin to see how Bellow mounts a critique of the personified text by associating it with the violence of Nazism. Initially, the vision of Sammler as symbol looks harmless, even respectful. We are told that to his relatives and friends Sammler "was a symbol" (91) of Old World manners, of suffering endured, a symbol because, as his grand-nephew's friend Feffer explains, he has "experiences" (109). But in being regarded this way, Sammler is, like Augie March, invited to inhabit a representation of himself whose purposes have little to do with his sense of his own life and the meaning he takes it to have and everything to do with the lives and meanings of others. While Augie acquiesced to changes of clothes frequently and threw them off again at will (though usually at someone else's request), Sammler's identity changes little in this respect over the course of the novel. He seems mired in the role he has been given to inhabit. And by contrast with Augie March, whose humanity is not seriously in question even if his social identity is, Bellow suggests that something of Sammler's humanity is foreclosed by the enduring symbolic categorization, a categorization reproduced obsessively by the array of characters who appear at Sammler's bedside to confess to him their most intimate—and usually sexual—experiences.

It is this process of confessing to Sammler, of telling their private and sordid stories, that casts Sammler not only as listener and as priest, but categorizes him in other ways as well. Angela, for example, tells Sammler in detail about her sexual adventures, because "she thought he was the most understanding, the most European-worldly-wise-nonprovincial-mentally-diversified-intelligent-young-in-heart of old refugees" (69). The label, which Bellow makes ridiculous by excessive hyphenation, transforms a string of clichés about the "old refugee" into a single noun that comes to stand in for Sammler. The label bears little relation to the Sammler that Bellow's narrative has us know, who in his private interior consciousness squirms with embarrassment at Angela's revelations and is full of judgments against the behavior of the young. This disjunction between Angela's label and Sammler's consciousness of himself replicates, at a more benign level, the disjunction between Sammler's life as an Anglicized Bloomsbury intellectual before the war and the reductive racial categorization to which he is subjected when he returns to Poland during the war. The categorization of persons in this latter case leads not just to the foreclosure of some element of Sammler's full humanity, as it does in his relationship with Angela, but to the foreclosure of his humanity as such. The symbol of the Jew, created by the Nazis (and by a whole history of European anti-Semitism), displaces all humanity in the persons so symbolized and renders them vulnerable to the mass murder Sammler witnesses.

Once again, Bellow makes it clear that it is not only Sammler who is vulnerable to others who wield symbols and not only the Jew who is victimized by this version of literalness. The black pickpocket is described by Sammler himself as if he were a symbol—as the black, sexualized embodiment of aesthetic performance and preoccupation with money. He is decked out in Christian Dior sunglasses, "cherry silk necktie" (10), and French perfume and slips his elegant black fingers into the purses of unsuspecting ladies to withdraw their dollars. He becomes the symbol of a vital but degraded life force that both fascinates and disgusts Sammler. If this were not enough to make the pickpocket a symbol, Bellow also has him wielding the phallus—the very basis of Freud's symbolic order. Precisely because he is a symbol of these things, the pickpocket, at the end of the novel, becomes the victim of Sammler's erstwhile son-in-law, the abusive Eisen. The potential of the symbol to be both the instrument of violence and the victim of it is driven home in this scene by the fact that Eisen, a nationalistic Israeli and thus a kind of symbol himself (of the "muscle Jew," the iron man), beats the pickpocket by hitting him over the head with a bag of metal-work Jewish symbols. Earlier, Sammler had seen the potential danger of Eisen's "crude-looking" medallions, suggesting that they were too heavy for the sick Elya Gruner to handle (170). The later scene seems to answer the rhetorical question Eisen had used to answer Sammler's objection: "How can art hurt?" (171). His question is answered as "the terrible metal" of Eisen's Stars of David "cut [the pickpocket] through the baize" of the bag (291). The art of symbol-making can be redemptive, this scene suggests, only when the symbol is not conflated with the person. Symbol-making becomes deadly when the vulnerable, embodied humanity of the person is reduced to symbol and thus is figuratively—or in this case, literally—bludgeoned by the symbol.[9]

As I have shown, Sammler, and through him Bellow, reveals certain problems with the categorization of persons, problems that foreclose the humanity of those categorized. Nevertheless, one cannot help but note that Bellow has Sammler himself name human categories and assign people to those categories throughout *Mr. Sammler's Planet*, and indeed, Bellow's narrators do this throughout most of his novels. It seems as if we could turn Mr. Sammler's reflections on this urge back on Bellow himself: "As Mr. Sammler saw the thing, human beings, when they have room, when they have liberty and are supplied also with ideas, mythologize themselves. They legendize." This activity, according to Sammler, "reproduces" "human types": "the barbarian, redskin, or Fiji, the dandy, the buffalo hunter, the desperado, the queer, the sexual fantasist, the squaw; bluestocking, princess, poet, painter, prospector, troubadour, guerrilla, Che Guevara, the new Thomas à Becket. Not imitated are the businessman, the soldier, the priest, and the square. The standard is aesthetic" (147). This list of human types might well recall some character types that are frequently deployed within Bellow's own novels.

In continuing to categorize people freely, as Bellow does both within his novels and in other writing, does he simply contradict and undermine (as opposed to testing or strengthening) a humanist, universalist resistance to categorization that I am arguing his novels advocate? In a 1992 essay, "There Is Simply Too Much to Think About," Bellow argues explicitly against the desire to erase categories, on the grounds that the differences such categories announce bear an intellectual and moral value. "Can it be that we are tired of whatever it is that we in fact are—black, white, brown, yellow, male, female, large, small, Greek, German, English, Jew, Yankee, Southerner, Westerner, etc.—that what we now want is to rise above all tiresome differences?" Bellow asks.[10] He suggests that "what we are by nature, . . . the given, the original, the creature of flesh and blood" (175), needs no alteration or improvement and that it is from the very imperfection and difference of the person that we can learn to "think." For Bellow the raceless, androgynous, "synthetic man," the "revised, improved American" is a form of "tyranny" (176). But insofar as my readings here are correct, we can see that it is not just the universalist type but all types that are tyranny for Bellow. If the "flesh and blood" givens that Bellow invokes here represent a kind of essentialism (not exclusively racial, but including race as an essential category), it is essentialism of a kind that is ultimately imagined to be so particular that it is closer to humanist universalism than it is to a multiculturalist view of particularism, where the particular is defined, most importantly, as group particularity. I take this to be the reason that Bellow's novels always focus on the thinking, self-contradicting, peculiar mind of a particular individual.[11]

I want to conclude by noting that, while most characters in *Mr. Sammler's Planet* seem like symbols in one way or another, Bellow does imagine that the person can exist independent of the literalism represented most dramatically by the symbol Sammler is taken to personify in Poland and by the pickpocket who is abused at the hands of Eisen. That possibility is what Bellow's novella *The Actual* (1997) tries to imagine. In this sense Bellow offers an alternative both to personified representation (being a symbol, like both Sammler and the pickpocket, which exposes both the person and the symbolic order to certain kinds of threat) or to a notion of identity that reduces what matters about the person to the things that can be categorized (being a person only insofar as you can be said to be a particular "type"). "The actual" of the title refers to Amy Wustrin, the first and lifelong love of Bellow's protagonist, Harry Trellman. Harry is a Jew "with an East Asian expression," which he first classifies as Chinese, and later, at his friend Mr. Adeletsky's suggestion, accepts as Japanese ("The old man was right, you know," thinks Harry, "I have Japanese legs, straight from one of Hokusai's bath scenes").[12] While Trellman's face immediately suggests classification, and even prompts Harry, earlier in his life, to try to "effect a transfer" (3) to Chinese culture, Amy's face, to the contrary, is utterly unique: "I stood back from myself and looked into Amy's face. No one else on all this earth had such features. This *was* the most amazing thing in the life of the world" (104).

The character of Amy Wustrin advances a fantasy about what a person who transcends representation, and thus categorization, would look like. But there is a problem with Bellow's ultimate alternative to symbol, category, and personification, for Harry Trellman cannot in the end remember what Amy, the actual, looks like. Upon encountering her again after a space of many years, Harry is unable to recognize her even though her face is unique and he has thought of her every day since their last meeting. It is as if, like Sylvia Plath, Bellow imagines that representation is so close to the person that it becomes—like Harry's Jewish face with its Asian look—one's very countenance. As a result, the face of the actual, of that which is not subject to representation as "type," may be invisible or unrecognizable. Bellow seems to overcome the uncertainty he introduces with Harry's failure to recognize Amy in the comic ending of this novella, when Harry and Amy are finally united in a marriage proposal over the grave of Amy's ex-husband. But the problem is perhaps evaded rather than solved. The existence of the person outside of a coercive kind of representation is better or at least more persistently taken up in the work of Philip Roth.

Roth's Family History   I have argued that Bellow's way of imagining history—as the context in which death unfolds—holds direct consequences for the way he imagines representation and its relationship to persons. While the mediation of death through signs (like Sammler's prayer for Elya) is redemptive, the conflation of signs and persons (denoting identities or categories) is damaging or even deadly. Philip Roth's work configures these elements differently, but, I will argue, leaves us with an even more pointed sense of their necessary interrelatedness and of their significance for human freedom. If Artur Sammler and Augie March are threatened or confined by representations of themselves that others have manufactured, then we can certainly say the same, and more, for many of Roth's protagonists. Roth's concern with this kind of constraint has been evident in his work from the time Neil Klugman chafed at the middle-class Jewish identity the Patimkins pressed upon him in "Goodbye, Columbus" (1959), through Nathan Zuckerman's defense of himself against his family's demands in *The Ghost Writer* (1979), up until Coleman Silk abandons his black family in favor of Jewish-inflected whiteness in *The Human Stain* (2000).

In *The Ghost Writer* Nathan Zuckerman, like Bellow's Artur Sammler, is asked to identify with the Jewish community in part on the basis of the Holocaust. But unlike Artur Sammler, whose "experiences" of the Holocaust are his own, Nathan's experiences of the Holocaust are given to him (or rather, foisted upon him) over the footlights of Broadway, in the musical production of Anne Frank's diary. Or at least, that is how Nathan is supposed to identify with the Jewish community, according to Judge Wapter, the comically powerful Jewish figure who, at the Zuckermans' request, pleads with Nathan to come back into the fold after Nathan publishes what the family thinks is an anti-Semitic story. In Wapter's letter to Nathan, he asks Nathan whether "there is anything in your short story that would not warm the heart of a Julius Streicher or a Joseph Goebbels" and "strongly advises" Nathan to see the production of Anne Frank's diary as a corrective, emphasizing throughout the letter that Nathan's allegiance must be not to art or to his individual success as a writer, but to the community of people—the Jewish people—defined by the history of anti-Semitism.[13]

By the end of the novel it looks as if Nathan has done just this, though on his own terms. While staying overnight as the guest of his mentor, E. I. Lonoff, he imagines that a mysterious and beautiful young woman he meets there is in fact Anne Frank herself. In a fit of imagination he constructs the story of her postwar life, her erotic relationship with the father-figure Lonoff, and her eventual betrothal to Nathan himself. Suffering from guilt at his parents' displeasure with his supposedly anti-Semitic story, angered at their having turned Judge Wapter loose upon him, and unable to write a letter to his father about these things, Nathan imagines himself married to the living Anne Frank he has constructed in his mind. And he proceeds to imagine his consequent redemption as a proper and loving Jewish son and his father's admission that he has "misunderstood" Nathan (159). But Roth's solution to Nathan's problem is not a solution, of course: Nathan realizes that the fiction he has evolved as the "unchallengeable answer" to the Judge's letter, "far from acquitting" him and "restoring" to him his "cherished blamelessness, . . . would seem to them a desecration even more vile than the one they had read" (171). Moreover, the structure of the novel undermines the idea that the story of the living Anne Frank and Nathan's fantasy of marrying her is really an attempt to acquiesce to identification with Jewishness. What Nathan is identifying with here is not so much a Holocaust survivor as a writer, and indeed, she is not so much another writer as a reflection of himself as a writer.

We can see this first in the way Nathan's story about Anne Frank is set off in the novel itself. It is encapsulated in a separate chapter entitled "Femme Fatale," in which no reference is made to the situation (Nathan's visit to the Lonoffs) that gives rise to the story. The ending of the previous chapter has Nathan standing on a volume of Henry James's collected stories, ear to the ceiling, trying to overhear a conversation between Lonoff and Amy Bellette, the young woman who sparked his fantasy. The chapter that follows "Femme Fatale" begins with Nathan already at breakfast the next morning in the Lonoffs' dining room, implying that the intervening chapter is in fact Nathan's next short story, composed in an all-night fever there in Lonoff's study (we are told that Nathan had "gone the whole night without sleep" [157]). The fantasy of marrying Anne Frank comes not within "Femme Fatale" but after it, in italicized passages that interrupt the account of Nathan's breakfast and mirror the italicized passages from the *Diary* that pepper "Femme Fatale." Placed this way, the story of Anne suggests that Nathan's fantasy is not the fantasy of marrying Anne Frank, the Holocaust survivor and guarantor of Jewish legitimacy, but of marrying his own fiction, since the living Anne exists only *as* his own fiction.

The representation of Anne within the story itself reinforces the sense that in marrying Anne Nathan is marrying his writerly vocation. She is pictured there as a writer above all else, and we are told that her book "was her survival itself. *Van Anne Frank.* Her book. Hers" (134). When she finally reads that book in print for the first time, she marks it up in the margins with comments that, she imagines, imitate what Lonoff, her writing teacher, would say about the prose. In presenting this image of Anne, Nathan models her on the character of the novelist Dencombe in the Henry James story "The Middle Years" that Nathan has been reading just before he begins to eavesdrop on Lonoff and Amy. In that story Dencombe receives a copy of his own latest novel in the mail and immediately begins to revise it in the margins. (Of course, the figure of Dencombe is also the figure of Henry James himself, the "passionate corrector" [114] of his own published works.) When praising Anne's work to Amy Bellette, Nathan likens her to "some impassioned little sister of Kafka's, his lost little daughter" (170). Amy Bellette, the figure who inspires the character of Anne, is named, too, in such a way that she embodies the idea of writing—Amy meaning "beloved" and "Bellette" translating phonically into "belles lettres." What Nathan identifies with in *The Ghost Writer* is not the Jewish community, his family, and the history they both hold out as the reason why he should identify with them, but with his nascent art and the individual "madness of art" revered by James, Lonoff, and Nathan himself.

The Ghost Writer* thus rejects both family and tribal history as determining forces, but it also rejects personification of texts, though that claim may seem counterintuitive or even willful given the novel's tropes of marrying one's own fiction and resurrecting the dead in the form of short-story characters. But this proximity to personification of texts is precisely what is fascinating about Roth's understanding of the relationship between persons and texts. Instead of turning texts into persons, Roth does the reverse, turns persons into texts. This is precisely how Nathan Zuckerman, in his letter to Roth at the end of Roth's autobiography, *The Facts*, describes his author's particular talent. Castigating him for making real people shallow and one-dimensional when writing in the autobiographical mode, Zuckerman reminds Roth that his "gift is not to personalize your experience but to personify it, to embody it in the representation of a person who is *not* yourself. You are not an autobiographer, you are a personificator."[14] The difference between the personification that Roth produces and the personified texts imagined by the writers I have discussed up to this point is that Roth's text remains text and the metaphor implied by personification remains metaphor rather than conflation. Roth's personifications retain all the limits and prerogatives that their status as texts confers, rather than reaching toward the moral status and prerogatives we associate with persons. If the metaphor collapses in Roth's work, it does so in the opposite direction: Zuckerman suggests to Roth that he has "written metamorphoses of yourself so many times, you no longer have any idea what *you* are or ever were. By now what you are is a walking text" (162). In *The Ghost Writer*, Nathan likewise turns his family and finally, Amy Bellette, into a story.

The proximity between life and fiction has in many ways defined Roth's career, as he has persistently turned elements of his life into fiction while simultaneously arguing for the difference between his life and his fiction. The proximity between fiction and life in Roth's work is described by Roth himself as an effort to get at truth, and it is worth noting the metaphor he uses for truth. He writes that "imagination . . . clubs the fact over the head, . . . slits its throat, and then with its bare hands, . . . pulls forth the guts. Soon the guts of facts are everywhere, the imagination is simply *wading* through them."[15] What Roth has called the "unwritten" world—the "facts"—is figured as the body, while the written world is figured as that body destroyed and rearranged into something else: truth. We might be tempted to align this understanding of truth with what Spiegelman says about the nonfiction novel in his letter to the *New York Times Book Review*, where he defends *Maus*'s status as nonfiction, but this would be to mistake the formal implications of both *Maus* and Roth's work. As I have argued in chapter 3, the fictional devices of *Maus* (especially the animal heads) create a logic of conflation between text and person such that the text becomes the person; in Roth's work, the person is eclipsed by the text, even destroyed by it. Nathan marries his story, not the resurrected survivor Anne Frank, while Art in *Maus* becomes himself the "real survivor," not a fiction about the real survivor.

The difference is encapsulated in an image that closes the title novella in Roth's first story collection, *Goodbye, Columbus and Five Short Stories* (1959). As Neil Klugman leaves Cambridge to return to Newark after his affair with Brenda Patimkin is finished, he stops in front of the plate-glass windows of the Lamont Library in Harvard Yard, searching for some sense of himself: "I simply looked at myself in the mirror the light made of the window. I was only that substance, I thought, those limbs, that face that I saw in front of me. I looked, but the outside of me gave up little information about the inside of me. I wished I could scoot around to the other side of the window, faster than light or sound or Herb Clark on Homecoming Day, to get behind that image and catch whatever it was that looked through those eyes."[16] Within moments, Neil gets his wish: "I looked hard at the image of me, at that darkening of the glass, and then my gaze pushed through it, over the cool floor, to a broken wall of books, imperfectly shelved" (136). At the moment when Neil rejects (or is rejected by) the Jewish family identity that Brenda and the Patimkins embody, he sees in the library window an alternative identity, one in which he is made up entirely of books. Though Neil is not yet a writer in "Goodbye, Columbus" this image makes clear his affinity with all the other Roth protagonists who are writers. Like Nathan Zuckerman in *The Ghost*

Writer, Neil might be said to marry not Brenda—the female embodiment of Jewish identity—but books.

~~~~~~~~

The history of the Holocaust is one kind of history that Roth rejects as a determinant of individual identity, but even in *The Ghost Writer* that history is mapped onto family history, for it is Nathan's parents who deploy Holocaust history (through Judge Wapter) and who try to persuade Nathan to see their point of view by inviting to the house various family guests who are meant to counteract the negative depiction of family history they see in Nathan's story. Indeed, far more than the Holocaust, family history as a determining force has been at the center of Roth's work.[17] In *The Facts,* for example, Roth describes the criticism he encountered from some sectors of the American Jewish community under the chapter heading "All in the Family," suggesting that Jewishness itself, even as a public discourse outside of his immediate family, must be understood as a force of family history.[18] Psychoanalysis provides the most powerful narrative model for twentieth-century understandings of how family history creates the self. Thus, the invocation of psychoanalysis in *Portnoy's Complaint,* coming at the end of Alex's dissection of his family's most intimate history, suggests how that family history comes—or will come, once Nathan begins to do the work of psychoanalysis—to constitute the core of Alex's identity.[19] Roth's parody of the psychoanalytic narrative in *Portnoy* suggests what will remain true for his fiction, namely, that psychoanalysis and the family history it configures cannot be accepted as the final word on individual identity. For Roth, family history has psychological force, but also carries with it biological and sociological forces with which it is equally important to contend. Nowhere is this more evident than in *The Human Stain.*

In *The Human Stain* Coleman Silk's identity is defined, it seems, by his particular family history: by his black parents and the biological blackness that, in the novel, is imagined as persisting in his "children, who carried their father's identity in their genes and who would pass that identity on to their children, at least genetically, and perhaps even physically, tangibly."[20] This is his sister Ernestine's formulation of Coleman's identity, but it is confirmed earlier in the novel in Coleman's voice as well.[21] Identity is thus imagined as racial in the discredited biological sense, which may account for the strange slippage in Ernestine's formulation, where the "genetic" is somehow not the same as the "physical." We might be tempted to normalize this by assuming that "physical" really means "visible" here, but the ambiguity suggests that the genetic racial essence attributed to Coleman and his children is in fact not biological (and thus physical) but the product of the representation—Ernestine's representation, Coleman's representation, American society's representation—of race. Indeed, family history as the Silks see it clearly revolves as much around genealogy as around genes. Coleman's family's history—the story of the Silk clan, told through the story of the family's reunions and their collective sense of genealogical history—is figured as what is lost to Coleman and his children even while their core identity ("who [the children] are" [321] and who their father "really was" [177]) is conserved genetically.

It looks, then, as if one's essential identity in *The Human Stain* is located in the genes, in the simple physical fact of being the child of two particular parents who are in turn the children of certain parents, and so on. It is in the realm of representation that one can resist that essentialism, and this is exactly what Coleman does, or rather, what he allows others to do for him. As he tells his girlfriend, Ellie, early in his life of passing, he allows people to "play it any way" they like in construing his race (133). He eventually creates around him a set of conditions—a Jewish wife, a career teaching Classics at a very white college, no visible family—that allows others to assume that he is something that, according to the genetic version of identity, he is not. In doing so, he becomes another version of Roth's writer-protagonists, for while he ultimately asks an aging Nathan Zuckerman to write the story of his life for him, Nathan sees him as an author in his own right. Addressing Coleman after Coleman's death, Nathan asserts that "of course" Coleman could not write the book of his life (344). "You'd written the book—the book was your life. Writing personally is exposing and concealing at the same time, but with you it could only be concealment and so it would never work. Your book was your life—and your art? Once you set the thing in motion, your art was being a white man. Being, in your brother's words, 'more white than the whites.' That was your singular act of invention: every day you woke up to be what you had made yourself" (345). Coleman's act of writing is, according to Nathan, not so much the fabrication of stories about being white as the very arrangement of a white reality.

This vision of identity is different from the vision of Jewishness that Roth lays out in *The Facts*. There he writes that "being a Jew had to do with a real historical predicament into which you were born and not with some identity you chose to don after reading a dozen books. I could as easily have turned into a subject of the Crown by presenting my master's degree in English literature to Winston Churchill as my new [Gentile] wife could become a Jew by studying with [Rabbi] Jack Cohen, sensible and dedicated as he was, for the rest of her life" (126). But in *The Human Stain,* Coleman does something that looks similar to Roth's tongue-in-cheek fantasy of presenting his degree in English literature to Winston Churchill and thus becoming a subject of the Crown. Coleman presents his degree in Classics to the white academic establishment, embodied in Athena College, and once admitted by that establishment becomes fully white, even to the degree that he is accused of being a white racist. The "historical predicament" that Roth refers to in *The Facts* comes in the later novel to include the historical predicament of passing: the possibility that others will take you for being a member of a race into which you were not born and the possibility that you will be aware of that new identity as somehow at odds with, as Coleman puts it, what you "really" are.

While it thus appears that racial essentialism—founded upon family history—is entailed in either vision of the historical predicament of identity (the one that accounts for passing and the one that does not), the idea of passing in *The Human Stain* in fact is imagined as working against racial essentialism. This is not because passing opens up the possibility for performative identities, for as Walter Benn Michaels has argued, the very idea of passing relies on the assumption that there is a difference between what you do and what you are, the latter continuing to be defined in essentialist terms. According to Michaels's argument, if this kind of performative identity is imagined without such undergirding essentialism, someone like Coleman could never "pass" for, but would simply be, white.[22] The rhetoric of biological essentialism certainly persists in the ways Coleman and others speak of themselves, and so Roth does not expose and discredit, as Michaels does, the essentialist logic of passing so much as he reimagines what the essential identity is that passing defines.

We can get at that revision by questioning what Zuckerman means when he says of Coleman that writing personally "could only be concealment." What would Coleman be concealing? The obvious answer, given the terms of the novel I have explored so far, is that he would be concealing who he "really was," a black man. But what is being referred to in the moments in which "real" identity is invoked? Roth, despite the essentialist discourse that runs throughout the novel, is in fact creating a character whose true identity has nothing to do with race—understood either biologically or as a social construction. In the passages I have mentioned in which Coleman or Ernestine refers to who the children "really" are, or who Coleman "is," Roth is careful to articulate a particular element of what that means. When Coleman speculates to Ernestine that, in not telling his children the truth about his family history, he has denied his most rebellious son, Mark, the "real thing" for which he could hate his father, Ernestine assumes he means that Mark might hate him for being black. But Coleman quickly corrects her: "Not that he would have hated me for being black. That's not what I mean by the real thing. I mean that he would have hated me for never telling him and because he had a right to know" (321). Similarly, when Coleman is tempted to tell his wife, Iris, about his family, after the birth of their last child, he finally does not because he realizes she could never forgive him, not for being black but for hiding it. Coleman intuited her probable reaction because Iris had recently singled out concealment within the intimacy of marriage as the problem with a friend's husband's adulterous affair. It was not the affair itself that Iris felt her friend should not forgive, but the secrecy that made it possible.

Even as a child, before Coleman decides to pass as white, concealment defines his sense of himself. He conceals from his strict father the fact that he has taken up boxing, which precipitates the first moment in which he denies his parenthood: his father insists that he stop, Coleman refuses, and his father asks him, in a bid for power, "Who then is your father?" Coleman initially replies, "You are, Dad," but when his father asks again, "I am?" Coleman resists, yelling "No, you're not!" and running from the house (92). He repeats that denial implicitly when a coach from the University of Pittsburgh comes to watch him fight at West Point under the direction of the neighborhood's Jewish coach, Doc Chizner. That night he feels that "something he could not even name made him want to be more damaging than he'd ever dared before, to do something more that day than merely win. Was it because the Pitt coach didn't know he was colored? Could it be because who he really was was entirely his secret?" (99–100). It seems here that passing for white is what empowers Coleman, but Coleman's reflections in this scene suggest otherwise, suggest that it is secrecy itself that empowers him:

> He did love secrets. The secret of nobody's knowing what was going on in your head, thinking whatever you wanted to think with no way of anybody's knowing. All the other kids were always blabbing about themselves. But that wasn't where the power was or the pleasure either. The power and pleasure were to be found in the opposite, in being counterconfessional in the same way you were a counter-

> puncher, and he knew that with nobody having to tell him and with-
> out his having to think about it. . . . All the answers that you came
> up with in the ring, you kept to yourself, and when you let the secret
> out, you let it out through everything *but* your mouth. (100; original
> emphasis)

It is not the secret of boxing, kept from his father, or the secret of his "colored" father, kept from the Pitt coach, but the inherent secrecy of individual
consciousness that defines who Coleman "really was." This is what he "knew
. . . with nobody having to tell him and without his having to think about
it." The mastery of boxing, likened elsewhere in this scene to the mastery of
"biology" (100)—which we can read as the subject in school but also as Coleman's own biology—revolves around keeping a secret. The phrasing of his
question, "Could it be because who he really was was entirely his secret?"
encapsulates the point. Coleman "really was" his secret. He "really was" the
fact of the secret itself not the content of it, the possibility of secrecy not the
substance of the secret. And this is why, as Nathan says, Coleman could not
write his own story of being persecuted at Athena College for an alleged racist
remark. If "writing personally is exposing and concealing at the same time,"
Coleman could only conceal because secrecy is his identity; he could only
reveal more secrecy.

Coleman Silk, then, resists identity categorization in a very particular way.
He "believe[s] that disregarding prescriptive society's most restrictive demar-
cations and asserting independently a free personal choice" is "a basic human
right" (155), one he exercises by passing for white. He rejects the force of
family history in "refus[ing] to accept automatically the contract drawn up
for [his] signature at birth" (155). The logic of that resistance is finally, as
we see in the boxing scenes, based on the assertion that identity lies in the
essential separateness of one's consciousness from all others, in the separateness epitomized by the idea of the secret. While that separateness suggests
that identity is absolutely particular, we could also say that for Roth it is
universal, defining a human identity in the same way I have argued mortality
defines human identity for Bellow.

This generality is most clearly indicated in Faunia Farley, Coleman's
lover. Her illiteracy at first makes her the antithesis of the writer and thus
unable to assert a social identity of her own making (indeed, she is subject
to many men over the course of her life and finally to the patronizing protection of Coleman's enemy, Delphine Roux), but we find at the end of the novel
that she was not illiterate, that she kept a diary. In Faunia's case, writing does

both expose and conceal: the contents of the diary presumably expose her inner thoughts, its existence exposes her illiteracy as a masquerade. At the same time, the secret of the diary conceals some kernel of self denoted by the idea of the diary—the story one writes in private of one's own private life. We never see the diary or know its contents (it is destroyed by her father's overbearing companion after Faunia dies). This absence—or privacy—marks not only the interiority and ultimate identity of Faunia, but also the loss entailed in her death and, because her secret interiority mirrors his, the loss entailed in Coleman's death. Faunia, who has no racial secret, and Coleman, who does, possess the same valued human identity centered on the fact of secrecy.

Perhaps this way of defining identity seems, in the end, banal, for what is more obvious than the fact that persons are possessed of a private consciousness? But in light of how representation is imagined to utterly defeat the separateness of consciousness in various discourses I have discussed in previous chapters—in trauma theory, in Jacqueline Rose's psychoanalytic criticism, and in representations like *Maus* that imagine the transmission of Holocaust-centered identity—Roth's insistence on that separateness seems both necessary and corrective. It is necessary to the idea of writing and language as craft rather than purely psychic product, and corrective to the idea of history—be it family history, Holocaust history, or any other kind of history—as the force that determines us at birth.

Identity and Freedom   Both Roth and Bellow have, like many of their contemporaries, been called upon to account for their work to the ethnic group from which they come. Roth, for example, has famously contended with elements of the Jewish community who saw his early work as "self-hating," and Bellow has publicly resisted attempts to categorize him as a Jewish-American writer.[23] This is one way in which the concerns taken up by these writers have been reflected back upon them in the reception of their work. Another way this has happened is in the literary-critical interpretation of their fiction. For example, reading the Holocaust as I have done in Bellow's fiction flies against recent criticism that begins from the very assumptions about identity that I have argued Bellow criticizes. S. Lillian Kremer has done the most to argue that Bellow's novels center on Jewish identity through the image of the Holocaust, by suggesting that Bellow's second novel, *The Victim*, is "holocaust literature" and by reading *Mr. Sammler's Planet* as a meditation on Holocaust survivors; Leila Goldman and Alan Berger have also produced versions of this argument.[24] Oddly, the novella *Seize the Day*, which makes only the slightest reference to the Holocaust, has become another locus for such efforts; Emily Miller Budick, for example, argues that we can read it as "*Yizkor* for Six Million."[25] Ethan Goffman's analysis of *Mr. Sammler's Planet* invokes the histories of Jewish oppression in Europe and the oppression of blacks in America to argue that that novel should be read as a caution against forgetting what it means to be "Jewish American."[26] For Goffman, forgetting what it means to be Jewish-American means forgetting that the Jews should identify with African-Americans; doing so is important because it establishes the contemporary cultural value of Jewishness in Goffman's argument—the value of distinction from what he calls the "dominant" cultural gaze.[27] Roth's work, too, has been read as being about the Holocaust. A recent study that sets out to reconsider Roth's work suggests that, taken as a whole, it centers on the "concentrationary universe" of the camps (the term comes from Primo Levi). The author argues that "Roth's varied works, when studied closely, point to a central obsessional issue, the issue of the Holocaust and its impact on twentieth-century American life."[28] This body of criticism, relying as it does on assumptions about the centrality of the Holocaust to Jewish identity, and the centrality of Jewish identity thus defined to Bellow's and Roth's work, makes it difficult to see the complexities of these writers' engagement not only with the particular history of the Holocaust, but with history as such and its relevance to identity.[29]

The criticism that has thus clustered around Roth's and Bellow's work reenacts the very forces of identity recruitment that both writers have resisted and that provide the counter-tension against which, as I have tried to show, each constructs a vision of personal and artistic freedom. But that freedom should not be understood as being based on a simple liberal universalism of the kind that, for example, was epitomized in the popular 1950s photographic exhibition "The Family of Man," the kind of liberal universalism that assumes we are all the same under the skin.[30] That version of universalism has been taken to task, in most respects rightly, by feminist and multiculturalist theory and by critics of classic procedural liberalism for failing to take into account the significance of historical situatedness, the ways that particular worldviews already determine what counts as "universal," and the fact that liberalism itself has a cultural content, one based on the primacy of the individual and the concept of rights. Bellow's and Roth's visions of identity are closer to that articulated (and debated) in the essays gathered together by Charles Taylor and Amy Gutmann in *Multiculturalism: Examining the Politics of Recognition,* where a number of philosophers—including Jürgen Habermas, Michael Walzer, K. Anthony Appiah, Susan Wolf, and Steven C. Rockefeller—attempt to theorize a liberalism that is neither Eurocentric nor by definition hostile to particular collective interests.[31]

Aligning Bellow and Roth with these writers is perhaps a strange move to make, given that in several of the essays Bellow is specifically invoked as the example of the liberalism—based on a Eurocentric notion of universal values—these thinkers want to reject. Taylor is the first to single him out for having once remarked that we will read what the Zulus write when they have produced "a Tolstoy."[32] For Taylor, this reveals "the depths of ethnocentricity."[33] It seems to me, however, that Bellow's certainly Eurocentric idea about what is of value in literature and culture—represented bluntly in this statement—is not far in its logic from that of the groups Taylor wants to make room for within a revised liberalism, groups that feel their particular cultural traditions carry something of ultimate human value that is not found in the culture or cultures that threaten to assimilate them. It may be implausible, considering the power relations of the world, to suggest that Zulu culture threatens to assimilate—and thus destroy—the cultural traditions that revere Tolstoy, but it is not logically different to say that Tolstoy has a value worth preserving over and even against the products of another culture than it is to say—using Taylor's example—that the French culture of Quebec has something worth preserving over and even against the English-speaking culture of the Canadian majority, such that it is reasonable to forbid French-speaking families to send their children to English-language schools. Bellow's comment about the Zulus may be racist, but not because he is suggesting that Tolstoy is more valuable than the cultural products of that tribe. (That is a judgment that can and should be debated, but it is not inherently racist.) Bellow's comment is racist insofar as he makes such a judgment without knowing much about the cultural achievements of the Zulus, thereby betraying his assumption that because they are Zulus the products of their culture are worth less than the products of his culture.[34] The difference between the versions of identity we see in Roth and in Bellow and the version we see in Taylor's work lies, then, in the range of people or things to which the notion of particularity extends. For Taylor, particularity in his revised liberalism is located at the level of the collective; for Bellow and Roth, particularity goes all the way down to the individual person. We are not all the same under the skin, but all different.

Though Bellow and Roth imagine an essentialist particularism at the core of identity, the kind of freedom these writers imagine may nevertheless be close, in some respects, to the sort described by Judith Butler and other theoreticians of performative identity who attempt to reject the notion of essentialism—whether an essentialist humanism or an essentialist particularism. I say this despite the fact that, as I argued earlier, Roth is not giving us in Coleman Silk a performative identity that succeeds in escaping essentialism.

Butler suggests, both in *Gender Trouble* and in *Bodies That Matter,* that identification, and the performative identities that follow from it, "is the assimilating passion by which an ego first emerges" rather than something an established ego—a preexisting and conscious "I"—chooses.[35] Likewise, she argues that the body itself "materializes" through repeated acts of discourse and identification, thus rendering both psyche and body the effects of discourse rather than preexisting conditions of it. Because, according to Butler, we cannot draw a line between the morphology of the body and our understanding of the body as gendered (between the part of sex that is biological and the part of sex that is cultural, for example—Butler wonders how it is that sex can have parts in the first place), we cannot even think the materiality of the body prior to the cultural notion of gender. Gender is thus a necessary condition for thinking of oneself as having or being a body at all.[36] Agency, according to Butler's account, lies in the repetition required to consolidate and (if only temporarily) stabilize the identities produced in this way; the need for such repetition means that the identities are inherently unstable and thus can be incrementally resisted even from within their own paradigms. Though her focus is primarily on gender identity rather than racial or ethnic identity (her chapter on Nella Larson notwithstanding), both the difficulty of agency and the possibility of resistance that Butler describes within the repetitive structure of identity formation recall the ways Bellow and Roth imagine their protagonists as being constituted by repeated interpellations to which they respond in evolving and often resistant ways, through repeated acts or uses of language that are figured as a kind of art. Where both Roth and Bellow diverge from Butler's version of identity is in their commitment to a core of the person that remains, if not outside representation, then outside the give and take of interpellation: Bellow's "actual" or Roth's secret. This endows the person with a kind of autonomy unavailable within Butler's paradigm, a kind of autonomy that, I have tried to show, is at the root of what it means for identity to be thought of as art rather than psychology.

That difference is important because psychoanalytic readings, as I argued in my analyses of Rose, Felman, and Caruth, conflate language and the psyche.

To put it another way, these critics collapse artistic production (or other kinds of representation) into the lived experience of unconscious processes like identification, over which we have little or no control. Diana Fuss, who in her *Identification Papers* is concerned more with the psyche and gender identity (and what Freud says about these things) than with literary art as such, acknowledges a distinction between identification and identity, between the unpredictable and unchosen psychic relations between ourselves and objects in the world on the one hand and the public representations of ourselves that we embrace (or refuse) in the form of identities, on the other. But Fuss quickly abandons the effort to maintain that distinction, going on to argue that the unconscious processes of identification figure so prominently in the choices we make about identity in the public realm that they cannot be separated out from an analysis of identity politics.[37] Stuart Hall, though he is making an argument not about gender identity but about cultural and political identity more broadly defined, makes a similar claim.[38] While Fuss and Hall are certainly right to note the complexity of the human psyche in such matters, I think Fuss is also right to note the distinction between the private psychic reality and the public embrace or construction of identity. This distinction seems more worthy of being maintained than Fuss or Hall think, as the examples of Roth and Bellow demonstrate. The art these two novelists invoke, imagined as taking place within a public realm and subject to the decisions of characters imagined in turn as conscious of themselves and their motives, presents us with a vision of the writer distinct from the writing he or she produces—and thus able as an agent to shape that writing. Again, an image from Roth is useful in encapsulating the point: in *The Ghost Writer* all four writers we see—Lonoff, the novelist Dencombe in the Henry James story-within-the-story, Nathan, and Anne Frank—are inveterate revisers. As we see Nathan tear up draft after draft of his letter to his father, we see how susceptible Nathan's efforts to define his identities as son, Jew, and writer are to his conscious efforts of mind and of writing. The fact that he cannot come to satisfaction with the letter that will help to define these things testifies to the very plasticity of the medium Nathan deploys. It can always be changed again, through an act of will.[39]

I have been focusing on agency in this discussion of identity in Bellow and Roth, the agency made possible by their resistance to the conflation of text and person. But in the context of the analysis that has driven this book from the start, it is not the agency of persons so much as the destruction of persons that is finally at stake in my readings of these two writers. Therefore, I want to conclude by asking what the visions of the person we see in Roth and Bellow have to tell us about genocide and our response to it.

Anthony Appiah, in reflecting upon the question of identity and survival, writes that while he prefers some given identity "life-scripts" to others (the life-script articulated by the Black Power movement, for example, to the one we find in *Uncle Tom's Cabin*), he wishes nevertheless "not to have to choose" such a life-script at all. "The politics of recognition requires that one's skin color, one's sexual body, should be acknowledged politically in ways that make it hard for those who want to treat their skin and their sexual body as personal dimensions of the self. And personal means not secret, but not too tightly scripted."[40] Roth and Bellow would certainly agree about not wanting to have to choose to live by—or to become—a script someone else has written, but Roth's vision of identity does indeed make the personal into the secret. And it is that difference, which we find in Roth's Coleman Silk and Faunia Farley, and find hinted at in Harry Trellman's failure to recognize Amy Wustrin in Bellow's *The Actual,* that makes these writers, to my mind, important. The secretness that constitutes Coleman Silk's essential self, and the sense of un-recoverable loss that is associated with Faunia's death when we realize—through the reference to her diary—that she, too, was ultimately a secret, model what to me is the most coherent way of thinking about what is lost in the mass destruction of persons. The loss of persons on a massive scale is finally, I think, not qualitatively different from the loss of one person. What is lost in either case is the unique being. The loss of culture—the loss of the things they do, of their beliefs and practices—is not separable from, is not a destruction distinct from, the loss of that being. Death makes clear the same fact that might be said to be the precondition of love among the living: the absolute otherness of the person one is not. It may be narrow of heart to suggest that this is a better way to think about the destruction of persons than those ways that imagine a recovery of the lost person in the recovery of their suffering—through the personification of texts, or the fantasy of trans-missible experience, or the repetition of the past within the present. But ulti-mately, I think it allows one to articulate more fully what massive loss of life entails—to articulate more fully what is at stake in an act of genocide. At the same time it allows the group or person who is left alive to leave that suffering where it occurs—in history—rather than carrying it forward into a new kind of unfreedom.

In the epilogue to *Renaissance Self-Fashioning*, Stephen Greenblatt tells the story of being asked, by a stranger on a plane, to mouth the words "I want to die." Greenblatt tells us that he refused to do it, despite the sad story the stranger had given him as an explanation for the request.[1] Greenblatt then offers, in reflecting upon this incident, a rationale for the study he has just completed. In refusing to mouth these words, he notes that he succumbed to an irrational fear that the man would then pull a knife and fulfill the mouthed desire and to a superstition that the words would stick to him somehow, "like a burr." But he says that he also defended and affirmed a belief, despite the contrary evidence of his preceding chapters, that autonomy in speech, however illusory or fictive that autonomy might be, was fundamental to his autonomy as a person. Greenblatt offers this last anecdote to suggest that the limits to autonomy his study revealed must be understood in the knowledge that, whatever may be true about the ways our historical moments shape us, we nevertheless, as living persons, believe that we actively make choices that define us; we believe, that is, that we are agents. Like Augie March, Artur Sammler, Coleman Silk, and Nathan Zuckerman, Greenblatt squirms when language recruits him to a fate he has not written himself.

Greenblatt's anecdote makes a well-chosen closure to what has come to be seen as a groundbreaking critical study. It not only offers the critic's reflections on the initial impulse and final product of his research, but also encapsulates the issues that came to be most striking about this critical approach for Greenblatt's detractors, issues that were held in common by those like Catherine Gallagher, Jonathan Goldberg, and Walter Benn Michaels, who like Greenblatt came to be known as New Historicists.[2] Debate about Greenblatt's work focused both on the limitations of personal autonomy that it had revealed and on its notion of the "social text," a view of the relation between language and the world that, in the power it accorded to signifying practices, demonstrated strong affinities with the deconstructive view of language that the return to history was in some sense meant to address. Lee Patterson, for example, sought to retrieve both agency and material history, arguing that "the skeptical self-cancellations of contemporary textuality should not subvert the category of the historically real," since "history is impelled by consequential and determinative acts of material production."[3]

The interest in subject-formation and the notion of the social text makes what we might call personification the "master trope" not only for de Man, then, but also for the criticism that displaced deconstruction. Personification in this sense—in the sense that what we think of as persons are the products of particular signifying systems—is so ubiquitous in New Historicism as to be empty of analytic interest when we think about it in the abstract.[4] It is worth noting this ubiquity, though, in order to understand in a philosophical and disciplinary context the specific cases of the personified text I have described in the foregoing chapters. In their discursive insistence on something beyond the textual—be it the life of Sylvia Plath, the bodies of Bradbury's Book People, the experiences of Bruno Dössekker, Art with his organic mouse head, Sammler who resists symbolhood, the actual Amy Wustrin or the secret Coleman Silk—these cases of personification seek to endow the text with a value that is visible only in the representation of a dialectic between texts and persons. To see personification as such, in other words, relies on seeing a difference between persons and texts, a difference that we know more about, but perhaps find harder to see, after the developments in literary criticism that have characterized the last three decades of the twentieth century.

The material difference between texts and persons comes down to embodiment, and embodiment (to oversimplify) comes down to the capacity for pain and the fact of mortality. Stephen Greenblatt's epilogue, and indeed, the notion of cultural genocide I have been discussing in one form or another throughout these chapters, points toward the inextricable materiality of the body and words and to the importance of the fear of death in our beliefs about how we might be made or unmade through language. The stranger sitting next to Stephen Greenblatt on the plane wanted to practice reading lips, after all, so that he could later read the body of his dying son. Elaine Scarry's *The Body in Pain* takes up this problem directly, showing how pain both erases the made world of culture—in the example of torture—and calls it forth— as, for example, in the chair, a bit of cultural furniture built to allay the pain of the tired body. Greenblatt and Catherine Gallagher, in *Practicing New Historicism*, acknowledge that body criticism is importantly tied to New Historicism; within that thread of contemporary criticism, Scarry's work, to my mind, is crucial to understanding the relation between persons and texts. For if the world is secular (and this is an important qualification), then it is difficult to say more about the relation between the body and culture's signifying systems than the philosopher Derek Parfit says in describing his Reductionist View about what persons are, which I discussed briefly in chapter 4 and that bears repeating here: the view that "the existence of a person, during any period, just consists in the existence of his brain and body, and the thinking of his thoughts, and the doing of his deeds, and the occurrence of many other physical and mental events."[5]

It becomes uninteresting and, indeed, impossible, to generalize for too long about the relation between persons and representations as that relation is imagined in the literature and criticism of the second half of the twentieth century, even though the subject itself is tantalizingly present throughout the period. It is only in specific instances of personification that we can see the implications of specific ways of imagining that relation, and it is those instances and their implications that constitute the heart of my work here. Generalization can in fact obscure the points I make in the preceding chapters. If one focuses, for example, on a disagreement about what persons are when reading the story of Binjamin Wilkomirski and trauma theory, one might well miss the point of the analysis. To put it another way, one does not have to agree with what some readers have called (usually critically) my "commonsense" view of persons in that chapter—the view that experience is a function not only of language but of embodiment, and that it is not reducible to either—in order to see that trauma theory and fake Holocaust memoirs advance a notion of persons that, among other things, requires a version of experience that, although it sees experience as a function of reading and writing, nevertheless brings to that notion of experience all the pathos and moral efficacy of the "commonsense" version. The question we are left with at the end of that chapter, then, is not What is experience? (a question about which the chapter has little to say) but rather, If we think of experience as the equivalent of reading, what importance do we wish to accord experience in our thoughts

about persons in the world? The story of Wilkomirski and trauma theory
does, I think, help us to think about *that* question. There is a difference,
then, between critique and analysis: my critique of trauma theory and its
implications may rely on one's agreeing with my understanding of persons
and experience in the terms Derek Parfit lays out; my analysis of trauma
theory and its implications does not rely on such agreement.

This is not, however, to disavow the critique or to claim that the critique
does not animate the analysis, for I hope to have shown that the implications
that follow from personifying the text are in many cases far from desirable.
By exalting—and, at the same time, reducing—the literary to the personal,
the text to the embodied person, we both constrict our freedom (to disagree,
to read, not to read) and expand our obligations (to agree, to read, not to
read). Memory (the knowledge of what we have experienced) is privileged
over learning; in much public discourse on the subject of the Holocaust, for
example, it has become more important to "remember" the Holocaust than
simply to learn about it. And the emerging discipline we are calling Holocaust
Studies has become beholden to statements of personal connection, to the
need to explain one's connection to one's subject in a way that is not required
by other kinds of scholarly work. Why should this be, when so few can now
remember the Holocaust and so many have the opportunity to learn about
it? Or as Geoffrey Hartman has put the question, in his discussion of public
discourse about the Holocaust, "can public memory still be called memory,
when it is increasingly alienated from personal and active recall?"[6] This notion
of memory comes to take precedence not only over learning but also over
imagination—over those thoughts we have about things we have not experienced or about things that might not exist in the actual world. Speaking to
college students recently at Yale, Cynthia Ozick discouraged them from reading her novella *The Shawl*, a beautifully crafted story about the Holocaust
that many find both emotionally powerful and morally compelling, because
she herself is not a survivor. She advised them that they should read all the
factual literature there is on the Holocaust before they look at her story. It
would be a shame if those students took her advice.

There are more practical reasons, too, why I think we should resist personifying texts or tying them in literal ways to the people who wrote them. One
of these reasons can be illustrated by a common argument about the disappearance of languages. The anthropologist Earl Shorris, for example, argues
for the preservation of small languages, citing the disappearance of words for
shades of blue, for spiritual aspects of wood, and for different understandings
of God that would follow if such languages were no longer spoken. But what

carries the weight of the argument, and, moreover, its political appeal, is the rhetoric of personification that makes cultural change the same as personal death. Shorris personifies languages throughout, suggesting that Noam Chomsky's linguistics are "murderous" and urging anthropologists not to "embalm" the "dead or dying languages" in file cabinets but to bring them back to life through his Clemente Courses in the Humanities.[7] (He makes this argument not in the pages of an academic book, but in *Harper's* magazine.) I am sympathetic to the desire to preserve the diversity of cultures, just as I am sympathetic to the desire to preserve the diversity of animals and plants; intuitively it seems like the right thing to do, and losses of this sort seem terrible. But why? Why is it better to have Yup'ik or Eyak spoken in the world than not to have it spoken? It is true that certain meanings are culture-bound, but can they be preserved in the language when the culture—the everyday beliefs and practices with which the language was entwined—no longer exists? Can we tell the people of such groups that they should not want running water or electricity because they should prefer the project of preserving their language and their culture? Is not the desire for this kind of preservation itself—or for the preservation of wilderness or spotted owls—the product, in some sense, of the fact we have electricity, running water, and the rest? Would we renounce our own acquisition and enjoyment of such things in order to preserve cultural or natural diversity?

I do not mean to take up these questions here or to suggest that they are unanswerable (all of these questions are addressed in different ways in anthropological, philosophical, environmental, and theological literature). I mean only to suggest all the kinds of thought that are foreclosed by the leap to conclusion that personification of language represents. If we believe language is the same thing as a person, of course we do not want it to die. End of discussion. The varied terms we have at our disposal to understand cultural shifts—as change, as progress, as genocide, as personal death—are too important to leave unexamined. If we are to resist the homogenization of the world's cultures or the destruction of natural habitats, then we need to develop arguments that are coherent, as well as ones that are emotionally powerful, for why we must do so. And we do not need to argue that the end of certain cultural practices or the destruction of certain habitats is the same as genocide in order to resist or, better yet, prevent genocide. It may be that the concept of genocide as imagined by Raphael Lemkin and developed in the United Nations Genocide Convention functions better as a description of the motivations of violence than it works as the description of what genocide destroys. Like domestic hate crimes legislation, it recognizes that violence and oppression committed against persons because of their race or ethnicity threatens society more, and differently, than random violence or violence motivated by specific personal animosity. Hate crimes or genocidal acts need to be punished more severely not because what they destroy is somehow different from what is destroyed by other kinds of large-scale violence and oppression but because the ideology motivating that destruction reduces an entire group of persons to the status of nonpersons. As Hannah Arendt put it, such crimes are a violation of the human status.

Finally, I want to resist the personification of texts and a literal understanding of the relation between a writer and her work because there is reason to believe that a just society requires imagination. We must be able to imagine, like those who stand in John Rawls's original position,[8] the position of the other whose life may or may not be like ours. Imagination is needed to bridge the yawning gap between persons—between one consciousness and another—a gap that exists as much within ethnically or racially defined groups as across these groups. Personal particularity, like the particularity of events or experiences, is particular all the way down. That said, we must find ways to connect and understand each other across that particularity. The fantasy of the personified text, the fantasy that we can really have another's experience, that we can be someone else, that we can somehow possess a culture we do not practice, elides the gap that imagination—preferable, in my mind, to identification—must fill. We must find not ourselves in the other (or the other in ourselves) but the other as we can know them without being them. The speaking voice of the other we hear in lyric poetry, the life of the other we observe in novels, can teach our imagination. Literature conceived of in these terms is, I think, the ally of justice.

Notes

Introduction

1. The text of the ad is reproduced in Lawrence Graver, *An Obsession with Anne Frank: Meyer Levin and the Diary* (Berkeley: University of California Press, 1995), 80–81.

2. The tension between these interpretations of the *Diary* came to light again in the late 1990s, when the play was revived on Broadway, though public opinion was certainly ready—not to say eager—for the true horror of Anne's death to have a presence in what had been an unflaggingly optimistic play. Reviewers noted that the revival differed little from the feel-good Goodrich and Hackett version, except that now it featured a more elaborate Hanukkah celebration (with a new song added), and ended, like Levin's adaptation, with the Nazi raid.

3. Letter from Meyer Levin to Otto Frank, October 8, 1953, quoted in Ralph Melnick, *The Stolen Legacy of Anne Frank: Meyer Levin, Lillian Hellman, and the Staging of the* Diary (New Haven, Conn.: Yale University Press, 1997), 88.

4. The two studies take significantly different views of Levin and the truth of his long-held belief that his play had been scuttled by Lillian Hellman, whom he saw as a Stalinist anti-Semite. Melnick argues that Levin was correct in thinking himself a victim of Hellman's politics, and while retreating at times from Levin's rhetoric—including the hyperbolic claims I cite above—he, like Levin, sees a parallel between the treatment of the play on Broadway and the events of the Holocaust. Graver gives a more balanced account that recognizes both the extent of Levin's obsession and the ways in which the Broadway establishment, and indeed, Otto Frank himself, manipulated Levin in their dealings with him over the *Diary*.

5. See, for example, Levin's November 17, 1968, letter to Martha Gellhorn quoted in Graver, *Obsession with Anne Frank,* 190.

6. See Meyer Levin, *The Obsession* (New York: Simon & Schuster, 1973).

7. Philip Roth, *The Ghost Writer* (New York: Farrar, Straus & Giroux, 1979; reprint, New York: Vintage, 1995), 159; also see "Femme Fatale" and following.

8. It is important to note, though, that the "Silence = Death" slogan has embedded in it a more concrete claim about the relation between blocked self-expression and death, for it is certainly the case that the failure to discuss the problem of AIDS openly, because of stigmas against homosexuality, caused the epidemic to take more lives than it might have. The slogan thus claims both a causal relation between the two terms and a relation of equivalence.

9. For those unfamiliar with these schools of criticism, it may be helpful to say a word about their basic characteristics. New Criticism, which arose in the 1930s and 1940s, emphasizes the reading of poems and other literary texts as works of art rather than as historical documents that are tied to the moment of their making. New Critics rejected the idea that the meaning of a text rested upon the intention of the author, seeing the meaning as independent of either the author's or the critic's will, embodied instead in ambiguity, paradox, and other characteristic features of literary language. Deconstruction, while it eschewed the idea of meaning as understood by New Critics, similarly focused on the text itself rather than on historical contingencies surrounding it. Rather than producing interpretations of texts, though, deconstruction sought to critique underlying assumptions about how language means, one of those assumptions being the necessary connection between language and human presence. For an excellent introductory account of these schools of criticism and others that have been important to literary studies in the twentieth century (an account to which my own is indebted), see Jonathan Culler, *Literary Theory: A Very Short Introduction* (Oxford: Oxford University Press, 1997).

10. Steven Knapp, *Literary Interest: The Limits of Anti-Formalism* (Cambridge, Mass.: Harvard University Press, 1993), 64; original emphasis.

11. W. K. Wimsatt and Monroe C. Beardsley, "The Intentional Fallacy" in W. K. Wimsatt, *The Verbal Icon* (Lexington: University Press of Kentucky, 1954), 5.

12. Knapp, *Literary Interest*, 78. For the full sense of Knapp's reading of New Criticism, see all of chapter 3, "The Concrete Universal."

13. See also J. Hillis Miller's discussion of "Narrative" in *Critical Terms for Literary Study*, ed. Frank Lentricchia and Thomas McLaughlin (Chicago: University of Chicago Press, 1990), 66–79. The essay, informed by de Manian theory, suggests that all narrative depends on "personification, or, more accurately and technically stated, *prosopopeia*, bringing protagonist, antagonist, and witness 'to life' " (75). Here Miller suggests that representations of persons (in literary "characters") are to be thought of not as representations but as personifications. This lays out a way of looking at the text which suggests (as Wimsatt— on Knapp's reading of him—does) that the character is imagined as itself a person in some significant way. For now, I want to suggest that this is made necessary by the resistance to the notion of representation and the desire to do without reference.

14. For identities as "life-scripts" see K. Anthony Appiah, "Identity, Authenticity, Survival," in *Multiculturalism: Examining the Politics of Recognition*, ed. Amy Gutmann (Princeton, N.J.: Princeton University Press, 1994), 162. Butler's argument about the inextricability of the body and the discourse of gender identity runs throughout *Bodies That Matter* (New York: Routledge, 1993) but is perhaps best summarized in her introduction.

15. For Rosenfeld's discussion of the relationship between the destruction of language

and the destruction of persons in the Holocaust, see chapter 7, "The Immolation of the Word," in *A Double Dying: Reflections on Holocaust Literature* (Bloomington: Indiana University Press, 1980), 129–53. He cites, among other instances, a passage in André Schwarz-Bart's *The Last of the Just* in which a Jewish family is encouraged to give over their books to a Nazi mob, to be burnt. The patriarch of the family insists that to do so is tantamount to giving themselves over to the same fate.

16. See, for example, Larry Kramer, *Reports from the Holocaust: The Story of an AIDS Activist* (New York: St. Martin's, 1994).

17. See Hannah Arendt, *Eichmann in Jerusalem: A Report on the Banality of Evil*, rev. and enl. ed. (New York: Viking, 1964).

18. Quoted in Lawrence J. LeBlanc, *The United States and the Genocide Convention* (Durham, N.C.: Duke University Press, 1991), 18. LeBlanc's history of the genocide convention and the approval process in the United States is balanced and thorough, and reproduces much of the important law and Senate testimony pertaining to the convention.

19. Quoted in LeBlanc, 22.

20. LeBlanc's account of the ratification process, stretching from the first Senate hearings in 1950 to the final ratification in 1989, shows clearly how the desire to protect America from charges of genocide for treatment of African-Americans shaped the debates on ratification. While LeBlanc argues that it would be going too far to blame American racism and anticommunism as the sole forces holding up ratification for nearly four decades, he shows that these were nevertheless prominent in the repeated Senate hearings on the convention throughout that period.

21. Alvin Rosenfeld used these descriptions for the Torah in his response to an earlier and much truncated version of this chapter, presented at a symposium entitled "The Holocaust: Literature and Representation," at the United States Holocaust Memorial Museum, sponsored by the Center for Advanced Holocaust Studies, May 24, 2001. This is not to say that Jewish tradition uniformly endorses the personification of even this most sacred text. In a short story by Shmuel Yosef Agnon, "The Tale of the Scribe" (in *Twenty-one Stories*, ed. Nahum N. Glatzer [New York: Schocken, 1970]), a scribe neglects his wife in his zeal for his religious calling, and we are left to wonder whether her barrenness might be the result of her husband's lack of attention. Finally, after her death, the scribe enacts a kind of marriage to the Torah scroll he is writing in her name. This Pygmalion-like story serves to teach a lesson: one must not replace actual persons—in need of our love and compassion—with a personified text, even the Torah. My thanks to Sidra Ezrahi for pointing this story out to me.

22. John Milton, "Areopagitica," in *Complete Poems and Major Prose*, ed. Merritt Y. Hughes (New York, Macmillan, 1957), 720.

23. Personification of a more formulaic kind is evident in writing from Spenser and Milton through the eighteenth century, where abstract concepts—like Milton's Sin and Death in *Paradise Lost*—are made into characters. Steven Knapp's analysis of this kind of personification in *Personification and the Sublime: Milton to Coleridge* (Cambridge, Mass.: Harvard University Press, 1985) has convinced me that this phenomenon, while it of course must be classified as personification, is not particularly relevant to the kind of personification—the personification of texts—with which I am concerned. According to Knapp's account, personification of abstractions has to do with the effort to impose form

on the formless, to negotiate the relationship between literary form and the sublime. This is not, except in the most general of terms, a problem central to the present analysis.

24. See Peter Novick, *The Holocaust in American Life* (Boston: Houghton Mifflin, 1999).

25. See Jerome Friedman, "Jewish Conversion, the Spanish Pure Blood Laws, and Reformation: A Revisionist View of Racial and Religious Antisemitism," *Sixteenth Century Journal* 18.1 (Spring 1987): 3–30.

26. See Kalí Tal, *Worlds of Hurt: Reading the Literatures of Trauma* (Cambridge: Cambridge University Press, 1996).

27. See Kirby Farrell, *Post-traumatic Culture: Injury and Interpretation in the Nineties* (Baltimore: Johns Hopkins University Press, 1998).

28. See Michael Rothberg, *Traumatic Realism: The Demands of Holocaust Representation* (Minneapolis: University of Minnesota Press, 2000); and Sara Horowitz, *Voicing the Void: Muteness and Memory in Holocaust Fiction* (Albany: State University of New York Press, 1997). Other major studies that have done, and continue to do, this important work include Sidra Ezrahi, *By Words Alone: The Holocaust in Literature* (Chicago: University of Chicago Press, 1980), and her later work; Shoshana Felman and Dori Laub, *Testimony: Crises of Witnessing in Literature, Psychoanalysis, and History* (New York: Routledge, 1992); Geoffrey Hartman, *The Longest Shadow: In the Aftermath of the Holocaust* (Bloomington: Indiana University Press, 1996); Marianne Hirsch, *Family Frames: Photography, Narrative, and Postmemory* (Cambridge, Mass.: Harvard University Press, 1997); Berel Lang, *Act and Idea in the Nazi Genocide* (Chicago: University of Chicago Press, 1990); Lawrence Langer, *The Holocaust and the Literary Imagination* (New Haven, Conn.: Yale University Press, 1975), as well as his later studies on the subject; James Young, *Writing and Rewriting the Holocaust: Narrative and the Consequences of Interpretation* (Bloomington: Indiana University Press, 1988), and his later work. For examples of how narrative theory is used in Holocaust Studies, see also the essays by Hayden White and Martin Jay in *Probing the Limits of Representation: Nazism and the "Final Solution,"* ed. Saul Friedlander (Cambridge, Mass.: Harvard University Press, 1992).

29. Wendy Steiner, "Postmodern Fictions, 1960–1990," in *Prose Writing, 1940–1990*, vol. 7 of *The Cambridge History of American Literature*, ed. Sacvan Bercovitch (Cambridge: Cambridge University Press, 1999), 434.

30. Wendy Steiner, 434.

31. Throughout this book I will use the terms *holocaust* and *genocide* interchangeably, and will use the conventionally capitalized *Holocaust* to refer to what Berel Lang has argued is more appropriately called the "Nazi genocide of the Jews." I acknowledge that there is considerable debate about these terms—in particular, about the use of a word meaning "burnt offering" to describe the crime of the Nazis. Giorgio Agamben and Berel Lang, to name just two, have taken issue with this usage, and, in general, I think their arguments have merit. I continue to use *Holocaust* because, despite these arguments, at the time of this writing "the Holocaust" is conventionally understood as referring to the murder of the Jews under the Third Reich; in keeping with my interest in talking not about the historical events themselves but about the way ideas about the Holocaust have played out in literature and criticism, I think it only accurate to use the term that has gained widest use and has come to stand for the idea of these events. I use lowercase *holocaust* and the

term *genocide* interchangeably for similar reasons: they have long been used this way in discourse about nuclear war.

32. For Lang's version of how current Jewish practice and Jewish identity relate to the Holocaust, see the introduction to his *Act and Idea in the Nazi Genocide*. Lang suggests there that Jews can have a special kind of connection to the Holocaust because their religious practice already allows one—in the traditions of midrash and the Haggadah—to enter as a participant into history through the reading of a text. Sara Horowitz (in *Voicing the Void*) notes that Lang's use of the term *literal* to describe the person's relation to the past in this discussion is "to use the term 'literal' in a way we do not usually understand it" (23). I agree with Horowitz but would suggest that Lang is not abandoning the usual meaning but expanding it to include what Horowitz characterizes as an "act of imaginative interpolation" (23). Horowitz does not allow for a religious special case that would legitimize Lang's usage, suggesting that "if, as midrash asks, we place ourselves at the Red Sea and at Sinai and speak out of a narrative of presence, we do so through an act of imaginative interpolation." I would suggest—and I think this is perhaps what Lang also wants to suggest—that one might legitimately make the claim of literality that Lang advances if one believes in a mystical process, underwritten by theology, in which telling the story does in some metaphysical way place the teller within the history being told. Horowitz does not posit a category of religious belief that is separate, in this particular case, from ordinary workings of imagination. To my mind, it is Lang's apparent religious belief that makes the personified text coherent in the introduction to *Act and Idea*, while the version of it applied to the secular writing of history—in his essay "The Representation of Limits" (in *Probing the Limits of Representation: Nazism and the "Final Solution,"* ed. Saul Friedlander [Cambridge, Mass.: Harvard University Press, 1992], 300–317), which I examine in chapter 3—is not coherent.

33. See, for example, Sidra Ezrahi's essay on the use of comic form and its relation to Purim traditions in *Life Is Beautiful* and *Jacob the Liar*, in "After Such Knowledge, What Laughter?" *Yale Journal of Criticism* 14.1 (Spring 2001).

Chapter One

1. Jacqueline Rose, *The Haunting of Sylvia Plath* (Cambridge, Mass.: Harvard University Press, 1991), 2. Rose's most important contributions in this regard are her discussion of misogyny in Plath criticism and her analysis of Anne Stevenson's biography of Plath.

2. George Steiner, "Dying Is an Art" (1965), in *Language and Silence: Essays on Language, Literature, and the Inhuman* (New York: Atheneum, 1967), 301. Al Strangeways quotes this passage as well and provides an excellent account of general critical response to Plath's Holocaust imagery ("'The Boot in the Face': The Problem of the Holocaust in the Poetry of Sylvia Plath," *Contemporary Literature* 37.3 [1996]: especially 382 n. 12).

3. George Steiner, "In Extremis," *Cambridge Review* 90.2187 (1969): 248.

4. In a BBC radio interview in 1962 Plath cites two different reasons for her interest in the Holocaust, first that "my background is . . . German and Austrian. . . . and so my concern with concentration camps and so on is uniquely intense" and second that "I'm rather a political person" (from "Sylvia Plath," in *The Poet Speaks: Interviews with Contem-*

porary Poets, ed. Peter Orr [London: Routledge, 1966], 167–72; quoted in Strangeways, "'The Boot in the Face,'" 375). As I discuss below, although Plath thus cites a personal connection to the Holocaust as the cause of her "intense" concern, she does not base her identification with Holocaust victims on either of these grounds; these may be reasons why she chooses the Holocaust in particular to figure suffering as opposed to some other image, but are not the grounds on which she will claim identification with the victims.

5. Steiner, "In Extremis," 248.

6. Ibid.

7. A. Alvarez, "The Literature of the Holocaust," *Commentary* 38.5 (1964): 65, 66.

8. Ibid., 67.

9. Edward Alexander, "Stealing the Holocaust," *Midstream* 26.9 (1980): 47.

10. By the late 1980s this critique was fairly well established among critics of Plath and began to be edged out by the psychoanalytic and poststructuralist criticism of which *The Haunting of Sylvia Plath* is the prime example. James Young in 1987 signals its decline by founding his analysis on a variation of its central question. Young suggests that we replace the moral question—"Should the Holocaust be used as a public image of reference?"—with a practical one: "How," Young instead asks, "has the Holocaust been used as a public image of reference?" Young stresses in the essay the figurative aspect of Plath's claims to identification, and eschews a literalization of the relation between Plath and the figure of the victim (*Writing and Rewriting the Holocaust,* 129; this chapter appeared as a separate essay in 1987).

11. Susan R. Van Dyne, *Revising Life: Sylvia Plath's Ariel Poems* (Chapel Hill: University of North Carolina Press, 1993), 5.

12. Ibid., 90.

13. Sylvia Plath, *Collected Poems,* ed. Ted Hughes (New York: Harper Perennial, 1992), 158. Each poem is hereafter cited parenthetically by page and the abbreviation *CP.* Quotations from within each poem will not carry separate citations.

14. Van Dyne, *Revising Life,* 52.

15. Other critics also focus on the images of transformation that recur in the *Ariel* poems, but none argue that the poetry actually transformed Plath, let alone the definition of woman. Rather, the images are read as figures for the transformation of Plath's poetic voice, which the *Ariel* poems immediately seem to reveal. This, for example, has been Ted Hughes's reading of the *Ariel* poems; he describes them as the writing of Plath's "real self, being the real poet"; "it was as if a dumb person suddenly spoke" (foreword to Sylvia Plath, *The Journals of Sylvia Plath,* ed. Ted Hughes and Frances McCullough [New York: Ballantine, 1982], xiv). Van Dyne imagines this process in reverse. The poems are not so much what happened when the "real poet" suddenly spoke—the product, that is, of a changed voice or a changed person—but poetic products that themselves changed the person.

16. This is not to say that Plath was uninterested in what it meant to be a woman. Both Susan Van Dyne and Jacqueline Rose show persuasively how questions about femininity and sexuality inform Plath's work. What I am arguing here is that her interest in becoming the famous Sylvia Plath encompassed, but also went beyond, her concern with gender.

17. Sylvia Plath, *The Journals of Sylvia Plath, 1950–1962,* ed. Karen V. Kukil (Lon-

don: Faber & Faber, 2000), 569. This edition of the journals is hereafter cited parenthetically as *J.*

18. Steiner, "In Extremis," 248.

19. Sylvia Plath, *Letters Home,* ed. Aurelia Schober Plath (New York: Harper & Row, 1975), 473. James Young also cites part of this passage, suggesting that "though she distinguishes one who has actually been through Belsen from one who was there only psychologically (i.e., imaginatively), the fact that one of them was literally in Belsen oppresses the other all the same. Through an imaginative association, she simultaneously reflects and creates a link between her private pain and a much more vast and overwhelming *Weltschmerz*" (*Writing and Rewriting the Holocaust,* 119). It is not clear to me what Young means here by "oppresses." In light of the rest of his argument, it most likely means that the general condition of suffering—the fact that the Holocaust happened—is suffered also by those who did not participate in the specific suffering of the camps. Young is right that Plath is trying to connect her condition and that of others, but he (like Strangeways) does not address *how* Plath imagines that connection to take place.

20. Young's claim that the camps became the type of extreme suffering explains, I think, Plath's choice of "Belsen" as the name of the extreme state. See Young, *Writing and Rewriting the Holocaust,* 140.

21. The editing provided by Frances McCullough and Ted Hughes in the abridged version of the journals regularizes Plath's sentence in such a way that the point I want to make is easy to miss. They change Plath's "though I sit on poems richer than any Adrienne Cecile Rich" to "though I sit on poems richer than any [from] Adrienne Cecile Rich," thus obscuring the striking equation Plath makes between the successful poem and the name of the author.

22. Letter of October 16, 1962, in *Letters Home,* 468.

23. The body's coverings are consistently for Plath a figure for representation, not only in the cycle of bee poems but also in her medical poems such as "Face Lift," where even the most intimate covering of the body, the skin, becomes a tailored and crafted representation.

24. The predicament of the speaker in this poem echoes the competing structures of desire and identification that Diana Fuss has found in Freud's work on identification. For Freud, one cannot both desire (or be the object of desire) and be identified with the desired or desiring person, since desire in Freud's formulation is predicated on an alterity that identification, in fantasy at least, erases. In this sense, Plath is reproducing what Fuss has shown is a Modernist (but enduring) understanding of the relationship between self and other. See Diana Fuss, *Identification Papers* (New York: Routledge, 1995), especially chapters 1 and 2.

25. David Holbrook's critique of "The Bee Meeting" registers this fact but uses it to support his thesis that Plath was mad: "that world [of ordinary village life in Devon] is coloured intensely by her strange subjective life, so that, for instance, in *The Bee Meeting,* a procedure for manipulating bees, a quite commonplace event in rural life, seems to her like a nightmare ritual, an atrocity." He goes on to argue that Plath's image of the hive "is an eminently schizoid-paranoid image." See Holbrook, *Sylvia Plath: Poetry and Existence* (London: Athlone, 1976), 212 and following.

26. For a brief and much more general account of Plath's desire for fame as the desire

for recognition by a special audience, see Leo Braudy, *The Frenzy of Renown: Fame and Its History*, 2d ed. (New York: Random House, 1997), especially 542. Braudy's excellent study allows us to see how Plath's desire for fame—and that of other writers of her generation—fits into a larger history of fame, reaching as far back as Homer and Alexander the Great.

27. This is, on a structural level, the same vision of identification that Berel Lang advocates for non-Jews thinking about the Holocaust, who through imaginative identification might "join" with those who experienced that Holocaust, rather than become one with those persons, as Lang suggests the Jewish person should. See Lang, *Act and Idea in the Nazi Genocide*, especially the introduction, "Writing between Past and Present," xiv–xv.

28. For this insight I am indebted to Oren Izenberg and Drayton Nabers, who together suggested this point through their questions and comments at a presentation of this material at Johns Hopkins University.

29. Jahan Ramazani, for example, finds in Plath's poetry a "remarkable anticipation of French theories of the feminine" (*Poetry of Mourning: The Modern Elegy from Hardy to Heaney* [Chicago: University of Chicago Press, 1994], 277).

30. Plath does give us a specific account in prose—in her journal—of how she imagined her psychic relation to the world, an account that may help us discern her own investment in what Rose refers to as shifts in subject position. In the February 20, 1956, entry, she writes, "I want to get back to my more normal intermediate path where the *substance* of the world is permeated by my being: eating food, reading, writing, talking, shopping: so all is good in itself, and not just a hectic activity to cover up the fear that must face itself and duel itself to death, saying: A Life Is Passing!" (*J*, 204: original emphasis). This passage suggests that Plath imagines a bounded self that nevertheless can both expand outward and, failing that, "face itself." The image here is of a self that can permeate the world—not, as Rose would have it, of a psyche so permeated by the world that it is no longer locatable in the person.

31. The phrase first appears in his case study of Fraulein Elisabeth von R.; he repeats it in the methodological essay he contributes at the end of the volume. Josef Breuer, Freud's collaborator on *Studies On Hysteria*, cites it in a note to his case study of Anna O. as if it were already an authoritative description of the phenomenon. While the phrase remains enclosed in quotation marks throughout *Studies On Hysteria*, suggesting that the symptom does not actually join the conversation in the same way a person joins conversation, Freud's early analysis nevertheless lays the foundation upon which Lacan can, half a century later, privilege language in his equally famous claim that the "unconscious is structured like a language." Freud's analysis of Elisabeth von R.'s specific physical symptoms suggests that the pains in her legs correspond to memories through a symbolic relation. See Breuer and Freud, *Studies On Hysteria*, vol. 2 of *Standard Edition of the Complete Psychological Works of Sigmund Freud*, ed. and tr. James Strachey (London: Hogarth, 1955; reprint, New York: Basic Books, 1957), 148–54, 296–98 (Freud), and 37 (Breuer).

32. Rose, *Haunting of Sylvia Plath*, 4.

33. Ibid., 8. Rose supports this claim by pointing out that it is difficult for anyone to determine what aspects of the world are projections of their own psychic reality and what aspects are independent of their psyche. While it is indeed difficult to make such determi-

nations, perhaps even impossible to do so with absolute certainty, Rose overlooks the fact that we live and think as if there were a distinction between what is inside and outside ourselves despite the fact that our determinations about such things will sometimes seem less than absolutely certain. That we can make—and revise—determinations about what is "me" in a human interaction and what is coming from someone else or from other material circumstances is an assumption central not only to psychotherapeutic practice but, more importantly, to our ideas of justice, for example. One need not be naive about the theoretical certainty of internal/external distinctions in order to make the claim that in practice—in human life—they exist. The evidence of Plath's journals and her poetry suggests that she herself was perhaps more than ordinarily aware of the distinction, or more precisely, of the divide, between herself and the world.

34. Ibid., 5. Jacqueline Rose is not the only critic to imagine "representation itself" as a psychic entity, or, to take a less extreme version of the position, to describe representation or language in general as sharing crucial attributes of the psyche. James Young, for example, in analyzing Plath's use of Holocaust imagery and the ethical questions critics have raised against it, suggests that the "actual crime" of using the image of the Holocaust to figure personal suffering "may be committed by the memory in public language itself." By attributing psychic phenomena—here, memory—to "language itself," Young effectively absolves Plath, or any other writer, of the "crime" he describes. Like Rose, Young takes established terms in the existing criticism—crime and guilt in this case—and relocates them to apply no longer to persons but to language (*Writing and Rewriting the Holocaust*, 130). More recently, Jahan Ramazani's analysis of what he calls Plath's "melancholic" elegies argues that "Plath directs the violence of melancholia at discourse itself, turning against the traditional elegiac use of the sign as restorer of the dead." While "discourse itself" looks at first like an object and not a subject here, Ramazani goes on to claim, via Julia Kristeva, that Plath is thus representing a kind of "primordial grief," the child's "loss—originally the loss of the mother when the child enters the father's symbolic order." Thus, according to Ramazani, when Plath expresses rage at her father in the "melancholic" elegies, she is actually expressing rage at language; in that "remarkable anticipation of French theories of the feminine," Plath recognizes that discourse itself is the father (*Poetry of Mourning*, 276–77).

35. What seems to me a better corrective to biographical criticism can be found in Langdon Hammer's essay "Plath's Lives: Poetry, Professionalism, and the Culture of the School" (*Representations* 75 [Summer 2001]: 61–88). Hammer uses biographical materials to understand the social and cultural conditions out of which Plath produced her poems, placing those poems' special attributes—what Hammer identifies as "self-consciousness" and "intensity" (66)—within the context of postwar poetic professionalism as it pertained especially to young women. Hammer's readings do not ignore the biographical in favor of an exclusive focus on the text of the poems, but neither do they reduce the poetry to being "about" Plath's life. He argues that Plath's "writing was a mode of self-construction that employed, but was not reducible to, autobiography: she didn't want to record a self, but to bring one into being" (67). Given this approach, perhaps it is not surprising that he also notes Rose's tendency to speak of the poems as if they were radically autonomous, and of Plath in such a way that "her agency as an author is rendered occult—that is, both hidden and mystified, assimilated to that of a ghost" (69).

36. Rose, *Haunting of Sylvia Plath*, 225.

37. It is certainly the case that in Kristeva's writing puns are intended to add layers of meaning to theoretical concepts in a way that circumvents ordinary logic and suggests just the kind of leap that Rose makes here, from *country* to that which is excluded from a country, *exile*, but Rose's reading in effect introduces a pun into Plath's text where none exists.

38. Rose, *Haunting of Sylvia Plath*, 225.

39. This may appear to simplify the way in which Rose understands this fact of Plath's biography to inform the poem "Daddy," since it is the psychological experience of Otto Plath's immigration, not just for him but for his family, rather than the mere fact of it that Rose suggests is relevant. But whether or not the fact is read for its psychological consequences or for any other kind of consequence in Plath's life—economic, social, political, religious—it is still that fact that is finally the referent of Rose's reading.

40. Rose, *Haunting of Sylvia Plath*, 226, 233.

41. Judith Butler goes even further in critiquing Kristeva's notion of the chora, calling it a "conflation of the *chora* and the feminine/maternal," and in particular, a conflation of the chora with the figure of the nursing mother (*Bodies That Matter*, 41).

42. See Toril Moi, *Sexual/Textual Politics* (New York: Methuen, 1985), concluding chapter; Kristeva, "Stabat Mater" and the other well-chosen selections in *The Kristeva Reader*, ed. Toril Moi (New York: Columbia University Press, 1986); and Cixous, "Castration or Decapitation?" *Signs* 7.1 (1981): 54. For the reference to Cixous, I am indebted to Gloria L. Cronin, who cites this passage in her essay "Fundamentalist Views and Feminist Dilemmas: Elizabeth Dewberry Vaughn's *Many Things Have Happened since He Died* and *Break the Heart of Me*," in *Traditions, Voices, and Dreams: The American Novel since the 1960's*, ed. Melvin J. Friedman and Ben Siegel (Newark, Del.: University of Delaware Press, 1995), 254–78.

43. Rose, *Haunting of Sylvia Plath*, 237–38.

Chapter Two

1. David Holbrook, *Sylvia Plath*, 3. Ted Hughes has suggested something similar about the relation between Plath's poetry and her death (most persistently, in his last collection of poems, *Birthday Letters*), arguing that by churning up the psychological material that made her late poems powerful, she also churned up the forces that would lead her to suicide. See my "Fatal Poetry and the Poetry of Fate," *Boulevard* (Fall 1998).

2. Holbrook's answer is psychological, as opposed to racial or ethnic, and imposes a slightly different normative criterion for poetry: he argues that the poetry should be read through the filter of Plath's psychology in order to correct what he calls her poetry's "falsities." Because Plath was, according to Holbrook, "schizoid," he supposes that we must understand Plath's imagery, too, as "schizoid," and in turn we must realize that the values expressed in her art—the idea for example, that death is desirable—are "inverted."

3. Holbrook, *Sylvia Plath*, 11.

4. George Steiner's analysis of Plath in "In Extremis" produces a similar notion of causality, though for Steiner the claim is only relevant insofar as it might—but does

not in the end—provide sufficient grounds for Plath's identification with Holocaust victims.

5. Raymond Aron, introduction to *Thinking about the Unthinkable*, by Herman Kahn (New York: Horizon, 1962), 10.

6. Kahn, *Thinking about the Unthinkable*, 19; hereafter cited parenthetically.

7. Ray Bradbury, *Fahrenheit 451* (New York: Ballantine, 1953), 51–52; hereafter cited parenthetically.

8. It is worth noting that Mailer also imagined the question of conformity as related to the idea of holocaust. Indeed, he begins his discussion of *Hip* and its effort to define the individual apart from the oppressive sameness of society with the speculation that conformity is an element of "the psychic havoc of the concentration camps and the atom bomb upon the unconscious mind of almost everyone alive in these years" (1). The "fear" of such destruction—and of the totalitarian structures that produce it—is what accounts, in Mailer's view, for the "collective failure of nerve" to which the Hipster responds (2). See Mailer, *The White Negro* (San Francisco: City Lights, 1957); reprint of the original essay published in *Dissent* the same year.

9. I am employing here, in a limited way, a notion of the literary text as something that has its own history, if not apart from, then nevertheless distinct from the history of social formations. Despite the fact that it is notoriously difficult to defend the category of literature as a set of texts defined by intrinsic properties, critics like Steven Knapp have shown that the category of the literary in fact exists and that we can define it, if only in what must be cultural terms—as what we call literature, or what, to employ Knapp's conclusions, elicits a certain kind of interest. I would argue that what we call literature is a possible object of historical study even though the act of interpretation—something that the New Critics would have confined to the literary text—is appropriate not just to what we call literature but to any text. For a brief and useful discussion of these issues and distinctions, see Lee Patterson, "Literary History," in *Critical Terms for Literary Study*, 2d ed., ed. Frank Lentricchia and Thomas McLaughlin (Chicago: University of Chicago Press, 1995), 250–62.

10. Jonathan Schell, *The Fate of the Earth* (New York: Knopf, 1982), 140. Hereafter cited parenthetically.

11. See Peter Singer, *Practical Ethics*, 2d ed. (Cambridge: Cambridge University Press, 1993); and Thomas Nagel, "Death" in *Mortal Questions* (Cambridge: Cambridge University Press, 1979) especially 4, 7, 10. Nagel writes that unless we assign good and ill to unconnected gametes, "it cannot be said that not to be born is a misfortune" (7). It is telling that Schell bases his moral argument about the value of the unborn and our obligations to them on the evocation of emotion rather than on a reasoned argument about our relation to them. Moral philosophy has consistently discounted emotion or affection as the basis for moral obligation, to the extent that Coleridge, to cite one example, discounts the moral value of charitable actions toward those we love: because we love them, we are in fact acting self-interestedly, not disinterestedly, when we are charitable toward them.

12. The significance of Schell's point is perhaps clearer when we compare it to Clarisse's view of abstract art in *Fahrenheit 451;* Clarisse sees such art as pure object rather

than pure process. Thus, both privilege what they take to be representational art, and in particular, art that represents persons: in Schell's case, because he confers upon the object an independent status analogous to a person's that enables it to enter into a "communion" with persons, and in Clarisse's case because it makes the object refer to something beyond itself and because it allows the viewer to imagine herself the same way, through identifying with the person in the painting just as Montag identifies with Clarisse or the library owner identifies with her books. Insofar as both Clarisse and Schell want the art object to have a relation to persons that looks like a person's relation to persons, their views are structurally similar.

13. Jacques Derrida, "No Apocalypse, Not Now (full speed ahead, seven missiles, seven missives)," *Diacritics* 14.2 (Summer 1984): 23, 26. Hereafter cited parenthetically.

14. Or, we might want to say, in deference to Peter Singer, an ability to experience that is particular to persons, which for Singer includes self-conscious animals like the higher primates. Derrida is in effect ascribing to the literary text precisely what Singer ascribes to certain animals in order to argue for their personhood.

15. J. Hillis Miller, *Versions of Pygmalion* (Cambridge, Mass.: Harvard University Press, 1990), 4.

16. Judith Butler, *Bodies That Matter*, 9.

17. See Jacques Derrida, *Demeure: Fiction and Testimony*, in *The Instant of My Death*, by Maurice Blanchot, and *Demeure: Fiction and Testimony*, by Jacques Derrida, tr. Elizabeth Rottenberg (Stanford: Stanford University Press, 2000). The description of literature given by Derrida in this essay (21) is similar to the one I quote from the earlier essay, as is the technique of following seven threads—in the earlier essay it is "seven missiles, seven missives," in the later it is "*seven* knotted trajectories" (25; original emphasis). More important, for my purposes, is the way the later essay repeats the description of textual loss as the loss of life. Referring to the "manuscript" that was taken from Blanchot during the war by a Russian army commander (the one who also orders that he be shot), Derrida asks, "What is a manuscript if it cannot be reconstituted?" His answer is that "it is a mortal text, a text insofar as it is exposed to a death without *survivance*" (100; original emphasis).

18. See Wlad Godzich, "The Domestication of Derrida," in *The Yale Critics: Deconstruction in America*, ed. Jonathan Arac, Wlad Godzich, and Wallace Martin (Minneapolis: University of Minnesota Press, 1983), especially 32–36.

19. Paul de Man, *Blindness and Insight: Essays in the Rhetoric of Contemporary Criticism*, 2d ed., revised (Minneapolis: University of Minnesota Press, 1983), 137.

20. Paul de Man, *The Resistance to Theory* (Minneapolis: University of Minnesota Press, 1986), 10.

21. Paul de Man, "Autobiography as De-Facement," in *The Rhetoric of Romanticism* (New York: Columbia University Press, 1984), 67–68. Interestingly, de Man's language here echoes John Barth's dismissal of women's writing as "secular news reports" two decades earlier.

22. Ibid., 70.

23. This essay, originally published in *Glyph* in 1977, is available as "Excuses (Confessions)" in Paul de Man, *Allegories of Reading: Figural Language in Rousseau, Nietzsche, Rilke, and Proust* (New Haven, Conn.: Yale University Press, 1979).

24. The text that is understood to be understandable because it is by someone recalls the argument made against de Man by Walter Benn Michaels and Stephen Knapp in "Against Theory." Michaels and Knapp's "wave poem" is assumed to be understandable precisely to the extent that the beachgoer believes that it has been written by someone, be that someone the suddenly intelligent wave or another beachgoer with a stick ("Against Theory," first published in *Critical Inquiry* [1982]; reprinted, together with rejoinders and their own counterresponse, in *Against Theory*, ed. W. J. T. Mitchell [Chicago: University of Chicago Press, 1985]).

25. De Man, "Autobiography as De-Facement," 79.

26. De Man, *Resistance to Theory*, 48.

27. Ibid., 10.

28. Walter M. Miller, Jr., *A Canticle for Leibowitz* (Philadelphia: Lippincott, 1960; reprint, New York: Bantam, 1997). "The Great Simplification," the movement the monks resist, was a simplification in two senses: it destroyed complex knowledge systems like mathematics and the sciences, and it simplified the problem of nuclear war, blaming it on scientific knowledge instead of on the people who decided what to do with that knowledge. Miller tempts the reader to make the same mistake, or rather, acknowledges a kind of connection between knowledge and weapons, by maintaining certain analogies between texts and weapons throughout the novel; those texts buried in casks in the Southwest, for example, recall missiles in their silos.

29. Or indeed, perhaps Benjamin, sometimes called Lazarus, is the resurrection of truth. Miller is thus revising the traditional story of the Wandering Jew, who, according to legend, was sentenced by Christ to live and wander forever, only to die at the Second Coming. In Miller's novel the Wandering Jew is not the victim of the Second Coming but the agent who brings it about.

30. See Novick, *Holocaust in American Life*, especially 28, 73, 116, 225.

31. We might also note here, as an example, that universalism was at this time imagined, at least by Meyer Levin, to be the destructive hallmark of Stalinism, the impetus both for Stalin's purges of Jews and for Lillian Hellman's desire to make Anne Frank seem less Jewish. Whatever Levin's fantasies may have been about Stalinism on Broadway, it is nevertheless the case that universalism was not a term that could be effectively opposed to communism.

32. Terrence Des Pres, *The Survivor: An Anatomy of Life in the Death Camps* (New York: Oxford University Press, 1976), 192, 193.

33. Des Pres does have an essay that engages the idea of nuclear holocaust, but it focuses more on the way poetry has developed in the shadow of that possibility. See Des Pres, "Self/Landscape/Grid," originally published in *New England Review and Breadloaf Quarterly* 5.4 (Summer 1983); reprinted in *Writing in a Nuclear Age*, ed. Jim Schley (Hanover, N.H.: University Press of New England, 1984), 3–12.

34. For Holbrook *(Sylvia Plath)*, the mother is the provider of such "care and concern," which may explain why Plath is the epitome of all that Holbrook opposes, since, through suicide, she abandoned her children. Indeed, the only poems Holbrook praises in his study are those like "Nick and the Candlestick" that show a glowing picture of motherly feelings, feelings that Holbrook claims are in fact those she had, some of the time, for her own children.

Chapter Three

1. Art Spiegelman, *Maus: A Survivor's Tale, Part 1: My Father Bleeds History* (New York: Pantheon, 1986), 159; hereafter cited parenthetically as *Maus I*.

2. Berel Lang, "The Representation of Limits," in *Probing the Limits of Representation: Nazism and the "Final Solution,"* ed. Saul Friedlander (Cambridge, Mass.: Harvard University Press, 1992), 316; original emphasis; hereafter cited parenthetically.

3. Eddy M. Zemach, "Custodians," in *Jewish Identity*, ed. David Theo Goldberg and Michael Krausz (Philadelphia: Temple University Press, 1993), 123.

4. Barbara Kingsolver, *Pigs in Heaven* (New York: HarperCollins, 1993).

5. Paul Ritterband, "Modern Times and Jewish Assimilation" in *The Americanization of the Jews*, ed. Robert M. Seltzer and Norman J. Cohen (New York: New York University Press, 1995), 378.

6. Charles S. Liebman, "Jewish Survival, Antisemitism, and Negotiation with the Tradition," in *The Americanization of the Jews*, ed. Robert M. Seltzer and Norman J. Cohen (New York: New York University Press, 1995), 436–37. The whole of "Part Seven: Surviving as Jews in Twenty-First-Century America," in Seltzer and Cohen, is of interest with regard to these issues.

7. See Arthur Hertzberg's conclusion, "The End of Immigrant Memory—What Can Replace It?" in *The Jews in America: Four Centuries of an Uneasy Encounter* (New York: Simon & Schuster, 1989), 377–88.

8. Zemach, "Custodians," 123.

9. See Zemach, "Custodians," 128. It is clear that Zemach is committed not only to the intrinsic value of perpetuation but also to the intrinsic value of diversity, though the rhetoric of cultural death cannot be said to be the same as the interest in diversity. It is the pathos of dying that motivates the effort to avoid cultural death, while the value of different kinds of life motivates the effort to ensure diversity.

10. Michael Goldberg, *Why Should Jews Survive? Looking Past the Holocaust toward a Jewish Future* (Oxford: Oxford University Press, 1995).

11. See Hertzberg, 382–83, for one brief account of how, and why, the Jewish community turned to the Holocaust as the ground for Jewish identity; see Novick, *The Holocaust in American Life*, for a more comprehensive account. One could argue that Jewish identity in Israel is different in this regard, since identification with the state constitutes another, sometimes secular, center for self-definition in addition to identification with the Holocaust.

12. Spielberg's taping project has since ended, though Yale's continues.

13. Lang summarizes his formula as follows: "The formula thus asserts that the risk or burden of evidence incurred in choosing among alternative historical representations increases—first—in proportion to the distance between the alternative chosen and those rejected; and secondly, with that distance multiplied by a moral weight assigned to the common issue at stake between them. In its mathematical form this would be $R = (A_1 - A_2) \times W$. How the 'weight' (of W) is determined is not itself part of the formula, although it emerges as a function of the moral community in which the judgment is made" (309).

14. To summarize the difference, the functionalist account takes the absence of a "Führer order" in the chronicle to mean that Hitler did not intend the entire trajectory of the Final Solution, that the killing of the Jews and others in camps was the result of

many individual actions and intentions. The intentionalist account asserts that Hitler and the top Nazi officials did conceive of and intend the entire shape and trajectory of violence against Jews during the war.

15. It is tempting, because of its title, to assimilate to Lang's point of view Pierre Vidal-Naquet's argument in *Assassins of Memory: Essays on the Denial of the Holocaust* (originally published in France in 1987, subsequently translated by Jeffrey Mehlman and published by Columbia University Press in 1992). But I believe that for Vidal-Naquet the rhetoric of murder signifies the intensity of his criticism of the revisionist historians rather than indicating a theoretical stance with regard to representations. Vidal-Naquet attacks the revisionists—albeit reluctantly—on the grounds of history and on the grounds of their clear anti-Semitic intentions, not on the grounds that the facts they distort are morally present and by right should be treated like persons. It is worth noting, however, that the French have indeed embraced a definition of revisionism that appears to be grounded on the conflation I have described in Lang's philosophy: Holocaust denial—or the denial of genocide—is now a crime in France, which suggests that the Holocaust itself (as it exists in nonrevisionist representations of history, that is) merits protection in the same way that persons (in libel laws, for example) merit protection.

16. Lang has emphasized to me, in private correspondence, that the moral difficulties he sees in Holocaust denial, a version of which he finds in all Holocaust representation, do "not necessarily, and in my view should not, lead to censorship or other forms of legislative action" (letter to the author, November 26, 2000; my thanks to Professor Lang for permission to quote this). In the essay I consider here, Lang cites an attempt made by a group of French historians to curb such revisionism in which the historians claim "a moral *presence* for matters of fact" (313; original emphasis). Again, I note that only persons have moral *presence;* such presence is not, in our practical experience, attributed to inanimate objects. The extent to which an inanimate object—a chair, for instance— is at issue in moral dilemmas is the extent to which it is attached to other human beings: I do not take that chair because it belongs to someone else; if I do take it, I violate the *person's* rights, not the chair's.

17. The relative weight of each part of this dual mission has been the subject of controversy throughout the museum's history. For an account of the effort to define the museum's mission, see Jeshajahu Weinberg and Rina Elieli, *The Holocaust Museum in Washington* (New York: Rizzoli, 1995).

18. My thanks to Raye Farr, director of the film and video collection at the United States Holocaust Memorial Museum, for volunteering this anecdote after hearing me present part of this analysis at the museum.

19. Marianne Hirsch, *Family Frames,* 254. The I.D. cards and the "Tower of Faces" are just two elements of the complete identificatory experience the museum design seeks to produce over the course of any individual's visit. Museum designer Ralph Applebaum describes how the entire interior of the museum seeks to replicate the journey of the victims "as they moved from their normal lives into ghettos, out of ghettos onto trains, from trains to camps, within the pathways of the camps, until finally to the end . . . if visitors could take that same journey," Applebaum claims, "they would understand the story because they will have experienced the story" (*For the Living,* WETA-TV [PBS] transcript, roll 128, tape-27, 3–4; quoted in Edward T. Linenthal, *Preserving Memory:*

The Struggle to Create America's Holocaust Museum [New York: Viking, 1995], 170; ellipsis in Linenthal.)

20. Steven Spielberg, director, *Schindler's List* (Universal Pictures, 1993).

21. Geoffrey Hartman notes that Spielberg may not be successful in merging history and fiction, the real and the representational because "so much in the movie is structured like a fiction, so much is like other action films, though based on documented history, that the blurring between history and fiction never leaves us free from an interior voice that murmurs: 'It is (only) a film'" (*The Longest Shadow*, 88). Nevertheless, this merging is clearly what Spielberg is attempting to accomplish. See chapter 6 of *The Longest Shadow*, "The Cinema Animal," for a full discussion of the questions and problems attendant upon Spielberg's mode of representation in *Schindler's List*.

22. See, among other articles about the director and the film, Edward Guthman, "Spielberg's 'List': Director Rediscovers His Jewishness While Filming Nazi Story," *San Francisco Chronicle*, December 12, 1993; reprinted in *Oskar Schindler and His List: The Man, the Book, the Film, the Holocaust and its Survivors*, ed. Thomas Fensch (Forest Dale, VT: Paul S. Eriksson, 1995), 50–55.

23. Art Spiegelman, *Maus: A Survivor's Tale, Part 2: And Here My Troubles Began* (New York: Pantheon, 1991), 11; hereafter cited parenthetically as *Maus II*.

24. Spiegelman subsequently produced an ironic twist on this use of Nazi discourse to define identities in the present. "Mein Kampf, My Struggle," a two-page cartoon spread appearing in the *New York Times Magazine*'s special issue on confessional writing (May 11, 1996, 36–37), shows the (human-headed) cartoonist walking the underground terrain of his mind, stalked by an enormous mouse. In this version of *Mein Kampf*, Hitler's paranoia about the Jews becomes Art's paranoia about the success of his Jewish mice. He complains that "remembering those who remembered the death camps is a tough act to follow." But it seems that the camps will define Jews forever, even against the discontinuity of generations which Spiegelman points out here ("My parents died," he writes in a box over the frame showing his crying son Dashiell, "before I had any kids"): the cartoon ends as Art begins the story of the next generation, "Dash is four years old, and his sister is almost nine. (Two of their grandparents survived Auschwitz.)" Here Spiegelman appears to recognize the tyranny of *employing* the Nazi definition, casting himself in Hitler's role—as the author of something called *Mein Kampf*—as he bequeaths that definition to the next generation. When speaking of *Maus*, on the other hand, Spiegelman is clear that employing the Nazi definition was felicitous: he claims that *Maus* "was made in *collaboration* with Hitler" (original emphasis; Art Spiegelman, "Drawing Pens and Politics: Mightier Than the Sore-head," *Nation* [January 17, 1994], 46; quoted in Thomas Doherty, "Art Spiegelman's *Maus*: Graphic Art and the Holocaust," *American Literature* 68.1 [1996]: 74. Doherty examines how Spiegelman's cartoon constructs its relation to the history of certain visual media, including that of Third Reich political cartooning and cinema—which is why he is interested in this "collaboration." Doherty's essay, along with Joseph Witek's *Comic Books as History: The Narrative Art of Jack Jackson, Art Spiegelman, and Harvey Pekar* [Jackson: University Press of Mississippi, 1989], provides a historical and generic context in which to understand *Maus*, making it distinct both from the main body of existing *Maus* criticism and from the present essay).

25. See Marianne Hirsch, "Family Pictures: *Maus*, Mourning, and Post-Memory,"

Discourse 15.2 (Winter 1992–93): 3–29; the essay was later included as chapter 1 in her *Family Frames*. Hirsch writes that the "really shocking and disturbing breaks in the visual narrative—the points that fail to blend in—are the actual photographs and the one moment in which the drawing style and convention changes [in "Prisoner on the Hell Planet" and the two photographs in *Maus II*]" (16). I argue just the opposite, that these are precisely not breaks in narrative but rather the endpoint of the narrative's work, which is to make the mouse head *real*.

26. The question of why Spiegelman uses mouse-persons is of course taken up—in passing at least, if not as a central concern—by every critic who writes about these books. Short reviews have tended to read the animal heads as a way of defamiliarizing what has become a commercialized story; Michael Rothberg, in a critical essay, pushes this thesis to its limit with his claim that the animal heads give the reader a "shock of obscenity" that will, for Rothberg, be Spiegelman's strategy for representing a particularly American version of Jewish identity. (See "'We Were Talking Jewish': Art Spiegelman's *Maus* as 'Holocaust' Production," *Contemporary Literature* 35.4 [1994]: 661–87; quotation on 666; the essay was later included in his *Traumatic Realism*). Joshua Brown reads the heads as an allegory for "the social relations of Eastern Europe"; he argues that Spiegelman's use of Hitler's racist paradigm undermines that paradigm because the animal heads bring it to "its fullest, tense realization" ("Of Mice and Memory," *Oral History Review* 16.1 [1988]: 105–8). While the allegory might hold for Vladek's story, it does not explain why Americans like Art still wear the marks of the "social relations of Eastern Europe"; accounting for this fact would require Brown to make a distinction—which he does not in fact make— between the mouse head and the mouse mask. Miles Orvell, on the other hand, recognizes the distinction between the mouse mask and the mouse head and reads in it a distinction between Art—who, Orvell argues, feels inauthentic once his father has died—and his father—whose identity is "more authentic." Art's "inauthenticity" is the sign of what Orvell calls the "sense of living posthistorically" ("Writing Posthistorically: *Krazy Kat, Maus,* and the Contemporary Fiction Cartoon," *American Literary History* 4.1 [1992]: 110– 28; quotation on 125. The essay has been included in chapter 8 of *After the Machine: Visual Arts and the Erasing of Cultural Boundaries* [Jackson: University Press of Mississippi, 1995]). While Orvell is undoubtedly correct that the mask indicates inauthenticity, he leaves unexamined the way in which Art becomes inauthentic and the way in which he returns to authenticity; these transitions, rather than the fact of the mask itself, reveal the character of the identity Spiegelman creates with the mouse head. Marianne Hirsch has explained the change from head to mask as progress from duplication of "the Nazi's racist refusal of the possibility of assimilation or cultural integration" to a moment when "in *Maus II* these dichotomous attitudes blur" ("Family Pictures," 13). For Hirsch, then, the heads extend the divisions of history into the present, but the changes from mask to head and back indicate only that Spiegelman's "access to mouse identity [has become] more mediated" (13). In the CD-ROM edition of the books, Spiegelman himself explains the distinction between the heads and the masks as marking a different time period in the chronology of the story.

27. Spiegelman has claimed that in fact it is his lack of specific information about his father's and mother's experience that makes the "blank" mouse faces appropriate and that makes them attach more closely with real persons. He explains that "it would be counterfeit

to try to pretend that the drawings are representations of something that's actually happening. I don't know what a German looked like who was in a specific small town doing a specific thing. . . . To use these ciphers, the cats and mice, is actually a way to allow you past the cipher at the people who are experiencing it. So it's really a much more direct way of dealing with the material" (Spiegelman and Françoise Mouly, "Jewish Mice, Bubblegum Cards, Comics Art, and Raw Possibilities," interview by Joey Cavalieri, *Comics Journal* 65 [1981]: 105–6; quoted in Witek, *Comic Books as History,* 102).

28. Art conflates himself with his mother, as well, in part 1 of *Maus.* In the short comic "Prisoner on the Hell Planet: A Case History" included in *Maus I,* Art accuses his mother of having *"murdered"* him when in fact she has killed herself (*Maus I,* 103; original emphasis). Outside the covers of *Maus,* Spiegelman has described his breakdown at the age of twenty—just before his mother's suicide—in terms of conflation with his parents: in the hospital, apparently, he actually hoarded string as his father had at Auschwitz (see David Gerber, "Of Mice and Jews: Cartoons, Metaphors, and Children of Holocaust Survivors in Recent Jewish Experience: A Review Essay," *American Jewish History* 77.1 [1987]: 168). Michael Staub has claimed that both Art's accusation of his mother and his accusation of Vladek at the end of *Maus I* "work to undercut . . . any impulse readers might have to see survivors—or their children—as either saints or heroes" ("The Shoah Goes On and On: Remembrance and Representation in Art Spiegelman's *Maus,*" *MELUS* 20.3 [1995]: 41). While the behavior we see in these scenes may indeed make it difficult to categorize characters as "saint" or "hero," what is more important is that the scenes *do* produce other categories—"murderer," "victim," and, by extension, "survivor"—which can be occupied in turn by Art, Vladek, and Anja. In contrast, Marianne Hirsch's reading of *Maus*'s photographs, while both registering and describing the conflation, in fact relies on it. She argues that "these family photographs are documents both of memory (the survivor's) and of what I would like to call post-memory (that of the child of the survivor whose life is dominated by memories of what preceded his/her birth)" ("Family Pictures," 8). Hirsch's sentence does not make clear whose memories dominate the child's life; as written, they appear to belong to the child in spite of the fact that the memories are of things that "preceded his/her birth."

29. See Wardi's contextualization of her study in her introduction for a brief description of this debate as well as her place within it (*Memorial Candles: Children of the Holocaust,* tr. Naomi Goldblum [New York: Routledge, 1992], 5–6). For another version of the "second generation" debate—one that does not share Wardi's assumptions—see Gerber, "Of Mice and Jews," 164–65. Gerber also provides a list of the key texts in this debate.

30. Wardi, *Memorial Candles,* 2, 5.

31. The members of the group frequently share each other's memories and imagined scenarios. The conversations between members of the group often focus on comparing dreams and the feelings that go with them; moreover, the members often seem to agree that their dreams mean similar things. On some occasions group members take the images of another's dream and play them out in their own imagination of their parents' traumas. It is clear from Wardi's commentary on these conversations that the "work" of therapy is done through the production of emotion; in the effort to produce emotion—or, to put it in the language of popular psychology, to *access* emotion that is already there in the

unconscious—any kind of imaginative work, including making up stories or focusing on someone else's dream images, is helpful if it produces the desired response. Wardi would not claim that these constructions constitute memory or that their truth is either available or important, and she reminds herself and her readers more than once that these young people did not in fact experience the Holocaust; nevertheless, the identification with the survivor figure that the therapists encourage relies on these images and on the transferability of memory and emotion between persons.

32. Freud admits that he needs a biological transmission of guilt and trauma in order to produce the kinds of behavior he thinks make up the Jewish character; cultural or face-to-face transmission alone is not enough to produce the powerful influence of the primal murder that he sees in the history of the Jewish people. Notoriously, Lamarckianism provided that biological account, but Freud knew that Lamarck's theories had been discredited by modern genetics. Freud's history is, of course, speculative (he originally called it a "historical novel"); he does not presume to have solved the problem of transmission even if he does think that *Moses and Monotheism* tells the truth about Jewish character.

33. The notion of absorption is the most striking of these because it relies on physical transmission rather than on cultural or psychological transmission, while nevertheless avoiding the claim of biological transmission: Wardi suggests that she, as a baby, "absorbed" some of the "thoughts and anxieties running through her father's head" when he came home and held her in his arms after doing relief work for Jews in prewar Italy (*Memorial Candles*, 2).

34. The process of therapy itself aims to produce Jewish identity, or, to use Wardi's terms, the late stages of therapy are often signaled by an interest in seeing oneself as part of the Jewish nation. Wardi describes this as a sign of health, as the marker of "mature" identification with the traumas the parents experienced.

35. In 1997 Spiegelman published a children's book entitled *Open Me . . . I'm a Dog!* (New York: HarperCollins). A black fabric leash dangles from the top of the book's spine, the front and back flyleaves are cut from fuzzy paper, and the blurb on the back cover reads, "Through the magic of words and pictures leaps a book that's not only playful as a puppy—it IS a puppy! Honest." It seems clear that the point I am making here about *Maus* brings to light Spiegelman's continuing interest in imagining representation as if it were the equivalent of a person—or in this case, a talking dog.

36. Art Spiegelman, "A Problem of Taxonomy," *New York Times Book Review*, December 29, 1991, 4.

37. Sarah Horowitz discusses Spiegelman's letter in the opening chapter of *Voicing the Void;* for her, it underscores the discomfort of many—and epitomized by Spiegelman—with fiction as a genre. She argues that the letter draws a sharp (and for Horowitz, false) distinction between fiction and truth, even while *Maus*'s own fictional artifices allow Spiegelman to communicate truths that could not be communicated without fictional devices.

38. This is not the first time that the *Book Review*'s categorizing has given rise to this argument: the editors placed Forrest Carter's *The Education of Little Tree*, a "memoir" about growing up with Cherokee grandparents, on the nonfiction list, but critics soon revealed that Carter was in fact a Ku Klux Klan member and segregationist speechwriter, a.k.a. Asa Carter. Despite the claim on the front cover, "A True Story by Forrest Carter,"

the story of Little Tree was entirely fabricated. The *Book Review* duly moved the title to the fiction list. It is no coincidence that this other case of "taxonomic difficulty" (as Spiegelman puts it in his letter to the editor) also arose with regard to racial or cultural identity. As Henry Louis Gates, Jr., has pointed out, fake testimonials and memoirs attributed to minority authors have been used for over a century for purposes ranging from the effort to abolish slavery to the effort to sell books. While Gates goes on to reflect about the importance of literal truth value in only the vaguest of ways—reminding the reader, for example, that "a book is a cultural event; authorial identity, mystified or not, can be part of that event" and that "fact and fiction have always exerted a reciprocal effect on each other" ("'Authenticity,' or The Lesson of Little Tree," *New York Times Book Review*, November 24, 1991, 29)—*Maus* makes it quite clear why literal truth value is powerful, and why it is powerful in the 1980s and 1990s in a way it is not in the examples of slave narrative Gates points to. Narratives of cultural identity—and in particular minority cultural identity—assume the status of personhood (as I have shown) in a way that slave narratives in the nineteenth century did not. Thus, the classification of these representations as fiction or nonfiction has come to imply a classification of people.

39. See Mark Crispin Miller's polemical readings of television in *Boxed In* (Evanston, Ill.: Northwestern University Press, 1988); on irony, see the introduction (14–15) and especially his discussion of Orwell's *1984* as it bears on contemporary media and Enlightenment philosophy (321 and following).

40. My reading is thus distinct from readings like James Young's, which make mediation and irony the very center of *Maus*'s meditation on the relationship between past and present. It is certainly clear why one might read *Maus* this way, since mediation and irony saturate the structure of the storytelling represented. My contention is that the mediation only masks, as it were, Spiegelman's conflation of past and present and the literalism that underlies that conflation. See James E. Young, "Art Spiegelman's *Maus* and the After-Images of History," chapter 1 of *At Memory's Edge: After-Images of the Holocaust in Contemporary Art and Architecture* (New Haven, Conn.: Yale University Press, 2000).

Chapter Four

1. Binjamin Wilkomirski, afterword of *Fragments: Memories of a Wartime Childhood*, tr. Carol Brown Janeway (New York: Schocken, 1996). For their invaluable comments on an earlier version of this chapter, I would like to thank the members of the New York Americanists group, the editors at the *Yale Journal of Criticism*, and the members of the Holocaust Working Group at the Whitney Humanities Center, Yale University.

2. André Aciman, "Innocence and Experience" (a review of several books on the persecution of Jewish children), *New Republic* 218.3 (January 19, 1998): 30.

3. See, for example, Harvey Peskin, "Holocaust Denial: A Sequel," *Nation* 268.14 (April 19, 1999): 34–38. Peskin argues that the controversy may be causing other child survivors who could corroborate Wilkomirski's story to keep silent, because "to be disbelieved is to be hunted again" (38). This belief also played itself out in the way the press, especially in Europe, initially treated with great discretion the doubts about Wilkomirski's identity. Many reporters have been careful to insert into the story of those doubts a warning that Wilkomirski's errors might be used to bolster the claims of Holocaust deniers who

seek to discredit all testimonial evidence. The American coverage, by contrast, is rather more strident in tone.

4. Wilkomirski was awarded, for example, France's prestigious Prix de Memoire de la Shoah, and he was featured as a speaker during a fund-raising tour for the National Holocaust Memorial Museum in Washington, D.C.

5. Robert Hanks, "Where Naughty Children Get Murdered," review of *Fragments*, by Binjamin Wilkomirski, *Independent* (London), December 8, 1996, 31.

6. See Philip Gourevitch, "The Memory Thief," *New Yorker* 75.15 (June 14, 1999): 56.

7. His publisher recounts how Wilkomirski wept almost continuously through the book tour and fund-raising activities that followed *Fragments*'s publication and the prizes awarded to it, and this evident misery is cited by just about everyone who has written about or interviewed Wilkomirski, both before and after the questions about his identity intensified. Cited in Gourevitch, "Memory Thief," 51.

8. Wilkomirski has argued that he never actually claimed that he remembered the death of his father and the disappearance of his brothers, and indeed, these figures are identified hesitantly in the memoir: "maybe my father," "maybe my brothers." But this local hesitation is eclipsed by a narrative that goes on to assume, in myriad ways, that these were in fact memories of a father and brothers.

9. This account of Wilkomirski's comments comes from an article by Dan Perry, published in *Sueddeutsche Zeitung*, April 22, 1995; then cited (and translated by Martin Ostwald) in Aciman, "Innocence and Experience," 32. Aciman's essay, it should be pointed out, was written before the more damning discoveries about Wilkomirski, which came to light in Daniel Ganzfried's article later the same year.

10. Gourevitch, "Memory Thief," 65.

11. See Elena Lappin, "The Man with Two Heads," *Granta* 66 (Summer 1999): 43. Gourevitch gives a slightly different version of this episode, where Bernstein recounts what must have been his answer to Wilkomirski's question: "I told him it would be terrible if—" Bernstein recalls, "*if* those papers contained something that he had gone through" ("Memory Thief," 59; original emphasis).

12. It is interesting to note the claim that Blake Eskin makes about his own relation to the European past in the context of his discussion of Binjamin Wilkomirski. "I was born in America," he writes, "but Wilkomirski [the surname] represented who I was before I became an American. This heritage was unknown and perhaps unknowable, but seemed essential and was something I still carried with me" (*A Life in Pieces* [New York: Norton, 2002], 20). Eskin seems to be identifying himself not simply *with*, but *as* the relatives— by the name of Wilkomirski—whom his family had left in Riga when they emigrated to the United States in the early twentieth century. This is the only way to make sense of the claim that he "was" someone before he "became" an American at birth. The logic Eskin uses here is thus not substantially different from Binjamin's, though Eskin asserts what he clearly imagines as a more authentic claim to identity because he—unlike Bruno Dössekker—really is genetically related to the Wilkomirskis of Riga.

13. Gourevitch, "Memory Thief," 57.

14. Felman and Laub, *Testimony*, 47, 48; hereafter cited parenthetically.

15. On this point I am indebted to Johanna Bodenstab. Her comments on an early

version of this essay, as well as her own work on survivor testimony from the Fortunoff Archive, have helped me to think through these issues.

16. Hartman, *Longest Shadow*, 152 ("secondary trauma"). Hartman suggests that, from the media's transmission of images of atrocity, "a 'secondary trauma' could arise" that would produce, finally, feelings of both fascination and indifference (152). The alternative is what Hartman calls "the testimony-encounter," the encounter with the survivor telling her story in a videotaped testimony. In such an encounter, "the narrative that emerges through the alliance of witness and interviewer does not present, however grim its contents, either a series of fixed images that assault the eyes or an impersonal historical digest. The narrative resembles that most natural and flexible of human communications, a story— a story, moreover, that, even if it describes a universe of death, is communicated by a living person who answers, recalls, thinks, cries, carries on. The hope is, then, that second-ary trauma, insofar as it is linked to violent yet routinized images, will not injure either the witnesses recalling the events, or young adults and other long-distance viewers to whom extracts of the testimonies are shown" (154). He reflects that "it would be ironic and sad if all that education could achieve were to transmit a trauma to later generations in a secondary form" (154) and expresses reservations about "Laub's positive view of . . . secondary trauma" in which the listener becomes "'a participant and co-owner of the traumatic event'" (165, n. 10; second quotation is Laub, cited by Hartman).

17. Ruth Leys has pointed out, in response to an earlier version of this analysis, that identification on the Freudian model has little to do with choosing whom or what one identifies with, that identification is largely an unconscious and unwilled process. Leys is certainly right about Freud's version of identification (for a useful synopsis of Freud's ideas about identification, see J. LaPlanche and J.-B. Pontalis, "Identification," in *The Language of Psycho-analysis,* tr. Donald Nicholson-Smith [London: Hogarth, 1973; re-print, New York: Norton, 1974], 205–8); my analysis describes what I take to be the literary-critical use of the structure Freud describes. And so, while there may be uncon-scious reasons behind the Yale students' identification with the Holocaust survivors whose testimony they listen to, my concern here is not the facts of their psyches (which may or may not have accorded with the psychic states Felman imputes to them) but with Felman's representation of them. There are ways, of course, to read the kind of identifications that Felman describes in relation to her own psyche; indeed, this is what Dominick LaCapra has done (see my discussion below of his essay "The Personal, the Political, and the Tex-tual"). But rather than trying, like LaCapra, to psychoanalyze the persons who are repre-sented in and through her writing, I want to read the representation itself as a literary artifact, in order to show how the text works as such and how it fits into a history of late-twentieth-century literature.

18. For accounts of these discoveries and responses, see Alan B. Spitzer, *Historical Truth and Lies about the Past: Reflections on Dewey, Dreyfus, de Man, and Reagan* (Chapel Hill: University of North Carolina Press, 1996); Werner Hamacher, Neil Hertz, and Thomas Keenan, eds., *Responses: On Paul de Man's Wartime Journalism* (Lincoln: Univer-sity of Nebraska Press, 1989); and Paul de Man, *Wartime Journalism, 1939–1943*, ed. Werner Hamacher, Neil Hertz, and Thomas Keenan (Lincoln: University of Nebraska Press, 1988).

19. We might note, once again, the similarity between Wilkomirski's account of himself

at the opening of his memoir—his alienation from his "mother tongue"—and Felman's account of the traumatized person, in this case de Man.

20. Indeed, suicide has become part of the form of the authentic survivor story, a fact borne out in the Wilkomirski story. Wilkomirski's writing and his personal fragility have been compared with the writing and suicide of Primo Levi, and critics of Wilkomirski are sometimes warned by his supporters that their skepticism may cause Wilkomirski's suicide. Daniel Ganzfried suggests—perhaps outrageously—that some of those supporters would be secretly pleased if he did commit suicide, since that would become a kind of proof that he was telling the truth (Gourevitch, "Memory Thief," 65–66). Here, Felman provides de Man with a comparable suicide.

21. For a detailed account of de Man's precise relation to the publication of this journal, see "Paul de Man: A Chronology," in *Responses,* ed. Hamacher, Hertz, and Keenan, xviii (the entry for December 10, 1942).

22. Dominick LaCapra, "The Personal, the Political, and the Textual: Paul de Man as Object of Transference," *History and Memory* 4.1 (Spring/Summer 1992): 12.

23. In May 1985 President Reagan visited the military cemetery at Bitburg (in what was then West Germany), home to forty-nine graves of Waffen SS troopers, Hitler's elite guard. He and Chancellor Helmut Kohl laid a memorial wreath at the graves. As one might imagine, the incident outraged many in Germany and around the world.

24. In *Representing the Holocaust: History, Theory, Trauma* (Ithaca, N.Y.: Cornell University Press, 1994), LaCapra argues that the historian must "work through," in the Freudian sense of that phrase, the material he writes about and that doing so is particularly important for those writing Holocaust history because of the traumatic nature of the materials the historian must engage. LaCapra thus sees the psychoanalytic session—with its dynamics of transference and counter-transference—as the model for scholarly work.

25. Tal, *Worlds of Hurt,* 59.

26. It should be said, however, that LaCapra read the essay singly, not as part of *Testimony,* though I think it unlikely that his critique would be substantially different even if he had seen it in this context, or that, even if different, it would come to coincide with mine.

27. Her logic, in brief, runs as follows: The camps traumatized their survivors so deeply that some committed suicide; the suicide silenced their testimony to the trauma; the historian by his or her testimony to the trauma can restore what was lost in the suicide; therefore, the historian can reverse suicide.

28. Geoffrey Hartman has noted, and criticized, the way Lanzmann himself announces his film as bringing back the dead (*Longest Shadow,* 52). Felman seems to be following the filmmaker's lead in her analysis. Unfortunately—pointing up the risks of relying on such conflations—Srebnik is "killed" later by Polish villagers who give their (often ignorant) interpretations of the event that Srebnik describes among them: "the Polish villagers are . . . unaware of the precise ways in which they themselves are actually *enacting* both the Crucifixion and the Holocaust *in annihilating Srebnik,* in *killing once again the witness* whom they totally dispose of, and *forget*" (*Testimony,* 267; original emphasis). This "killing once again the witness" is, Felman tells us, a "second Holocaust." Felman thus turns effortlessly from Srebnik's resurrection to his murder.

29. See Des Pres, *The Survivor;* and Robert Jay Lifton and Eric Markusen, *The Geno-*

cidal Mentality: Nazi Holocaust and Nuclear Threat (New York: Basic Books, 1990). Both of these studies, in their most general claims, argue that the significance of the Nazi genocide lies in its relation to the ongoing, and potentially more lethal, problem of nuclear war.

30. By contrast, Des Pres gives, as his best example of the "talent for life," a survivor's story about enjoying a bowl of soup in the camps; he argues that this ability to take pleasure simply in attending to the needs of the body is characteristic of those who survived and of the larger biological-cultural phenomenon he is describing. For an encapsulated version of Levi's opposite notion of the physical as the end of culture and personhood, we can look to the opening poem in *Survival in Auschwitz* (tr. Stuart Woolf [New York: Macmillan, 1961]; originally published as *If This Is a Man*). It asks the reader, who returns home in the evening to "hot food and friendly faces" to

> Consider if this is a man
> Who works in the mud
> Who does not know peace
> Who fights for a scrap of bread
> Who dies because of a yes or a no.
> Consider if this is a woman,
> Without hair and without name
> With no more strength to remember,
> Her eyes empty and her womb cold
> Like a frog in winter. (8)

The implication, of course, is that this is not a man, not a woman, who lives this way. Levi thus suggests that what constitutes the person can be destroyed by such things as working in the mud, fighting for food, living only in the terrible present. For Des Pres, continuing simply to live—in the biological, literal sense—in the face of such things is precisely what marks the "talent for life" he finds central to personhood.

31. Walter Benn Michaels has argued (in "'You Who Never Was There': Slavery and the New Historicism, Deconstruction and the Holocaust," *Narrative* 4.1 [January 1996]) that, by making it possible for people who could not experience the Holocaust historically to experience it through performative testimony, Felman allows Jewish identity to float free from race and religion to become entirely cultural (12–13). Though the "deconstructive performative" does indeed provide a technology that can connect the present person to a past she did not experience, it does not in *Testimony* enable the "complete triumph of the notion of culture," as Michaels suggests (13). Insofar as performative utterance performs trauma rather than performing the historical event we call the Holocaust, it strips race, religion, *and* culture from the notion of identity.

32. Cathy Caruth, *Unclaimed Experience: Trauma, Narrative, and History* (Baltimore: Johns Hopkins University Press, 1996), 115 n. 5 to the introduction; hereafter cited parenthetically.

33. As Freud and the psychoanalytic profession—and Caruth—conceive it, trauma is epitomized by the survivor of the accident who only later learns he almost died and who then becomes ill. Given this conception of the structure of trauma, one might argue that it is the ability to categorize the accident—in this case, as a near-death experience— that appears to bring on the symptoms of trauma. This is the sort of scenario that the

film *Life Is Beautiful* leads one to imagine, in which categorizing a terrible experience as something else (in the film, as a children's game) prevents it from being experienced as trauma at all. Less fantastically, we might call to mind the way people become angry or upset at their parents' behavior toward them as children because, as adults, they under-stand—and can categorize—inappropriate behavior that, as children, they simply accepted as normal. These instances are simplistic, of course; most of us assume that Freud was accurate at least in the notion that we have what he called an unconscious, which registers things like our childhood experiences in a way that perhaps our conscious mind—the mind responsible for assigning experiences to categories—does not, opening the door for a conscious response to experiences after the fact. Here I want only to suggest that the mental action of categorizing appears not to preclude the experience of something as trau-matic, but rather to enable it.

34. "De Man's critical theory of reference," Caruth explains, "ultimately becomes a narrative, and a narrative inextricably bound up with the problem of what it means to fall (which is, perhaps, de Man's own translation of the concept—of the experience—of trauma)" (*Unclaimed Experience*, 7).

35. See Ruth Leys's far more detailed account and critique of Caruth's use of *Moses and Monotheism* and implicit reliance on Lamarckianism, in chapter 8 of *Trauma: A Genealogy* (Chicago: University of Chicago Press, 2000), especially 285 and following.

36. Take, for instance, a sentence in the chapter "Literature and the Enactment of Memory": "It [the question of the difference between life and death] opens it [the woman's history] up, however, not by asking for a knowledge she owns and can thus simply state within her story, but by calling upon the movement of her not knowing within the very language of her telling" (37). Here, "not knowing" has something called "movement" within "her telling." It is not at all clear to me what it would mean for "not knowing" to move, but it is clear that such an ability is required in order for what is not known to be transmitted—that is, to move—from one person to another.

37. See Leys, *Trauma*, especially chapter 8.

38. Another way of describing this difference would be to say that both Caruth and Felman depart from de Man in taking his theories about language and extending them beyond the purview of the literary, into the realm of psychoanalysis. Where de Manian deconstruction is often accused of insulation from the historical, trauma theory's reading of de Man argues that rather than being divorced from history, de Man's ideas in fact give an account of the most significant and painful essence of history, its most infamous instances of violence, betrayal, and conflict. Trauma theory is a departure from de Manian deconstruction, then, because it significantly extends the categories of object to which deconstruction applies.

39. Though Caruth mentions this as an instance of memorization more than once, it is clear that the businessman's attempts to speak English are distinct from Okada's memorization not only because the businessman memorizes English as opposed to French, but also because he memorizes phrases in order to use them as communication; he uses the language, that is, to intend meaning. By contrast, Okada, according to Caruth's account, memorizes only to perform, not to intend meaning.

40. This claim is worked out largely in Caruth's discussion of the French woman's story about her German lover. It is clear that in the film the French woman sees the act

of telling the story of their love and his death as a betrayal, as a sign that the first love is replaceable by another love. Caruth, following Freud's analysis of mourning, generalizes this notion that representation is replacement, the turning of particular into universal; in its generalized formulation, the particular retains the pathos it gains as the object of mourning both in the film and in Freud's analysis (see chapter 2 of *Unclaimed Experience,* especially 27–33).

41. Don DeLillo, *Underworld* (New York: Scribner, 1997), 537. Hereafter cited parenthetically.

42. Derek Parfit, *Reasons and Persons,* corrected ed. (Oxford: Clarendon Press, 1987), 275.

Chapter Five

1. See Paul Gilroy, *Against Race: Imagining Political Culture beyond the Color Line* (Cambridge, Mass.: Harvard University Press, 2000). The term *camps* for Gilroy connotes both politicized (and usually racial) identity groups and what Gilroy sees as the exemplary historical instance of the politics of race, the Nazi concentration camps.

2. Appiah, "Identity, Authenticity, Survival," 162.

3. Saul Bellow, the Jefferson Lectures (1977); reprinted in *It All Adds Up* (New York: Viking, 1994), 127.

4. For an interesting analysis of conformity, masculinity, and the suburb in novels of this period, see Catherine Jurca, *White Diaspora: The Suburb and the Twentieth-Century American Novel* (Princeton, N.J.: Princeton University Press, 2001).

5. Bellow's work has often been read as transcendental, in the nineteenth-century sense of that term; see, for example, R. W. B. Lewis, *The American Adam: Innocence, Tragedy, and Tradition in the Nineteenth Century* (Chicago: University of Chicago Press, 1955), where he argues that Augie March is an American Adam, modeled on the Adams of Emerson, Thoreau, and Whitman; Steven Gerson works to revise and extend Lewis's interpretation in his "The New American Adam in *The Adventures of Augie March,*" *Modern Fiction Studies* 25.1 (1979): 117–28.

6. As Kurt Dittmar has pointed out, *Mr. Sammler's Planet* is not "a novel about the Holocaust" and it does little, beyond the level of basic content, to satisfy critics who have seen Bellow, as the great Jewish-American novelist, as neglectful of the Holocaust. See his "The End of Enlightenment: Bellow's Universal View of the Holocaust in *Mr. Sammler's Planet,*" in *Saul Bellow at Seventy-Five,* ed. Gerhard Bach (Tübingen: Gunter Narr Verlag, 1991), 79.

7. Saul Bellow, *Mr. Sammler's Planet* (New York: Penguin, 1996), 137; hereafter cited parenthetically. (For readers who wish to refer to the 1970 Viking edition, add about four to the page numbers from the Penguin edition cited here.) On Bellow and religious Jewish identity, see David H. Hirsch, "Jewish Identity and Jewish Suffering in Bellow, Malamud, and Philip Roth," *Saul Bellow Journal* 8.2 (Summer 1989): 47–58; for an overview of Bellow's responses to being labeled a "Jewish-American writer" see Ben Siegel, "Simply Not a Mandarin: Saul Bellow as Jew and Jewish Writer," in *Traditions, Voices, and Dreams,* 62–88. Both Siegel and L. H. Goldman (in "The Jewish Perspective of Saul Bellow," in *Saul Bellow, A Mosaic,* ed. L. H. Goldman, Gloria L. Cronin, and Ada Aharoni [New

York: Peter Lang, 1992], 3–20) use Bellow's own acknowledgments of the importance of his Jewish background to qualify and even dismiss other statements in which Bellow resists the critical focus on this aspect (or indeed, any aspect) of his life. There is plenty of criticism that seeks to locate Bellow's fiction in a culturally, if not religiously, Jewish context; for an example of this criticism, see Goldman, "'Shuffling Out of My Vulgar Origins': The Masculinist-Elitist Language of Saul Bellow's Fiction," *MELUS* 16 (1989–90): 33–42, which argues that Bellow's style and his characters' prejudices are distinctly Yiddish.

8. It is revealing that S. Lillian Kremer, in her chapter on Bellow in *Witness through the Imagination: Jewish American Holocaust Literature* (Detroit: Wayne State University Press, 1989), constructs a distinction between the Holocaust and the Apache's accident, noting (quite rightly, if we are doing comparative history) that the "hypothetical accident" is quite unlike the "calculated government program of genocide" (48). Pointing out the difference, however, does not help us understand why Sammler describes them as in some sense the same thing. The question, then, is how the novel presents these things in such a way that we are asked to imagine them as equivalent.

9. The reading I offer here may shed some light on the criticism of Bellow made by Toni Morrison in *Playing in the Dark: Whiteness and the Literary Imagination* ([New York: Vintage, 1992], 59), to the effect that the figure of the African becomes a symbolic one in service to the definition of Bellow's protagonist's whiteness. While Morrison is specifically referring to *Henderson the Rain King*, it is not hard to see how her criticism might be shaped to fit the figure of the black pickpocket in *Mr. Sammler's Planet*. What Morrison does not take into account, however, is how the very act of making persons into symbols becomes part of what Bellow's fiction thematizes and critiques. Morrison also fails to note, in the case of Henderson, that he is an ironic figure whose search for an effective identity through his travels in Africa is bound up with the distasteful aspects of his Gentile origins (Henderson is the only Bellow protagonist who is not Jewish). Morrison is right, then, that the African serves the definition of whiteness in *Henderson*, but she does not register the critique of Gentile whiteness that is mobilized at the same time, in and through Henderson's encounter with the African tribe.

10. Saul Bellow, "There Is Simply Too Much to Think About," in *It All Adds Up*, 173; hereafter cited parenthetically.

11. The representation of the particular individual entails, for Bellow, the representation of contradiction. In a novel like *Herzog*, and even within the novels I have discussed at length, Bellow provides more than a whiff of the deterministic view of history I have argued he rejects—and, especially in *Herzog*, of Jewish history in particular. In *Mr. Sammler's Planet*, for example, Artur Sammler reflects that the sexually liberated Angela must be somehow mistaken in thinking that she can obtain a "release" (72) from the Orthodox Jewish lives that her ancestors lived, suggesting, in that moment of reflection, that the past must have a determining force over the individual. Bellow has said that he works always to contain within his novels contradictory points of view because he aims, in the tradition of writers like Dostoyevsky and Thomas Mann, to represent the thinking person. Like the denizens of Mann's Magic Mountain, Bellow's narrators constantly debate with themselves and with others. One cannot write the philosophical novel, as Bellow aims to do, without representing contradictions and inconsistencies in logic and contrasting

arguments about whatever subject is at hand. This very commitment to the structure of the philosophical novel, evident not only in Bellow's novels but also in the constantly shifting arguments about the Palestinian-Israeli conflict that we find in his memoir, *To Jerusalem and Back*, may well raise a question about whether the resistance to categorization is thus also a resistance to any final intellectual position; at the same time, that commitment does not call into question the centrality of the person who is free to thus vacillate.

12. Saul Bellow, *The Actual* (New York: Viking, 1997), 3, 16; hereafter cited parenthetically.

13. Philip Roth, *Ghost Writer*, 103-4, 102; hereafter cited parenthetically.

14. Philip Roth, *The Facts: A Novelist's Autobiography* (New York: Farrar, Straus & Giroux, 1988), 162; hereafter cited parenthetically.

15. Philip Roth, "This Butcher, Imagination," *New York Times Book Review*, February 14, 1988, 3; quoted in Alan Cooper, *Philip Roth and the Jews* (Albany: State University of New York Press, 1996), 53. I am indebted to Cooper's extensive research on all of Roth's writing—from the smallest article to all the novels published at the time of the book's publication—for alerting me to this passage.

16. Philip Roth, *Goodbye, Columbus and Five Short Stories* (Boston: Houghton Mifflin, 1959; reprint, New York: Vintage, 1993), 135; hereafter cited parenthetically.

17. I think this is true despite the fact that Roth takes up the question of the Holocaust again in *Operation Shylock*. This novel may seem to be central to the issues I am raising here because in it Roth doubles identities, blurs fiction and nonfiction, and has Moishe Pipik (as the *character* Philip Roth calls his double) insist that any Jew today can only think he is singular because of the Holocaust (his logic being that, had not six million Jews died, there would, for example, be more than one or even two Philip Roths today). While Michael Rothberg, in his *Traumatic Realism*, gives a useful reading of the novel, especially of how and why it blurs fact and fiction, for the purposes of the present argument I find *Operation Shylock* finally more clever than profound. It is not clear to me, in the end, what it has to say about identity and the Holocaust, even though these two things dominate the plot; in this novel, Roth seems just to enjoy the act of saying itself. Perhaps another reader will be able to make more of these issues in the novel than I can.

18. In *The Facts* Roth describes his view of Jewish identity in terms that make this connection very clear. He writes that "to me, being a Jew had to do with a real historical predicament into which you were born and not with some identity you chose to don after reading a dozen books" (126). You enter into the "historical predicament" of Jewishness by virtue of birth, by the fact of who your parents are; thus, family history inserts you into the larger history of the world. This view is the opposite of the one I have described in Bellow's *Augie March*, where Augie must leave his family of origin in order to enter history. I will have more to say about this understanding of Jewish identity in the context of the discussion below of *The Human Stain*.

19. For those unfamiliar with the novel, I refer here to the final line, "So [*said the doctor*]. Now vee may perhaps to begin. Yes?" After the entire novel has given us only the ranting voice of Alex Portnoy detailing the sexual, scatological, and sentimental details of his family and himself, this concluding line gives us a new voice, that of Alex's psychiatrist, who, on my reading, has listened patiently with us all along. (One might also argue

that the preceding is all said in Alex's head, not aloud to the doctor. I am indebted to Pericles Lewis for pointing out this possible reading.) See Roth, *Portnoy's Complaint* (New York: Random House, 1969; reprint, New York: Vintage, 1994), 274.

20. Philip Roth, *The Human Stain* (Boston: Houghton Mifflin, 2000), 321.

21. Coleman describes his children, earlier in the novel, as those "who carried his origins in their genes and who would pass those origins on to their own children" (177).

22. See Michaels, "Autobiography of an Ex-White Man: Why Race Is Not a Social Construction," *Transition* 7.1 (Fall 1998). This argument is related to the one Michaels makes in *Our America*, where he shows how notions of cultural identity collapse into traditional, and discredited, structures of racial identity.

23. The story of Roth's conflict with the Jewish community is detailed in part in *The Facts*, in the chapter entitled "All in the Family," which includes an account of his hostile reception at Yeshiva University in the early 1960s, after the publication of *Goodbye, Columbus*. The outcry against Roth has returned on and off throughout his career, often enough to prompt the critic Alan Cooper to devote an entire book to a well-researched account of that opposition and a reading of Roth's work that defends against it. See Cooper, *Philip Roth and the Jews*. Bellow has always resisted categorization along ethnic, racial, or political lines. While he is willing to assign others' work to the category of "Jewish" fiction, for example—as we can see in the collection *Great Jewish Short Stories* which he introduced and which included stories by Bernard Malamud and Roth, as well as traditional stories from Jewish legend and religious tradition—he has always argued that his own fiction should not be understood in those terms. For more examples and a good overall discussion of Bellow's thoughts on his relation to Jewishness, see James Atlas, *Bellow* (New York: Random House, 2000), especially 128–29, 247, 291–92, 546–47.

24. See Kremer, "Scars of Outrage: The Holocaust in *The Victim* and *Mr. Sammler's Planet*," chapter 1 in *Witness through the Imagination;* L. H. Goldman, "The Holocaust in the Novels of Saul Bellow"; and Alan Berger, "Holocaust Survivors and Children in *Anya* and *Mr. Sammler's Planet*," both in *Modern Language Studies* 16.1 (Winter 1986), a special issue on the Holocaust and literature. James Atlas also reads *The Victim* as imbued with Bellow's sense of the Holocaust (*Bellow*, 127–28).

25. See Budick, "*Yizkor* for Six Million: Mourning the Death of Civilization in Saul Bellow's *Seize the Day*," in *New Essays on* Seize the Day, ed. Michael P. Kramer (Cambridge: Cambridge University Press, 1998). For other readings of the novella that seek to categorize Bellow's work as specifically Jewish, though not through reference to the Holocaust, see Michael P. Kramer, "The Vanishing Jew: On Teaching Bellow's *Seize the Day* as Ethnic Fiction"; and Hana Wirth-Nesher, "'Who's He When He's at Home?': Saul Bellow's Translations," both in *New Essays on* Seize the Day.

26. Ethan Goffman, *Imagining Each Other: Blacks and Jews in Contemporary American Literature* (Albany: State University of New York Press, 2000), 140.

27. The identification between Jews and blacks that Goffman constructs reproduces, in the context of contemporary literary-critical discourse, a peculiar tradition that Michael Rogin has described in relation to early twentieth-century American film. In "Blackface, White Noise: The Jewish Jazz Singer Finds His Voice," Rogin shows how *The Jazz Singer*

features an identification between Jews and blacks that bolsters a particular version of Jewish identity. In the film, Al Jolson puts on blackface in order to reimagine himself, and first generation American Jews in general, as white and thus, American. Under the blackface, the Jew makes a provisional identification with the black, which, Rogin argues, both liberates him from his Jewish immigrant roots (in *The Jazz Singer,* from his cantor father) and makes him white, since to put on blackface implies a white face underneath, a white face that will be revealed as such when the blacking is wiped away. This structure of racial identity emerges at a time (in the 1920s) when anti-Semitism in America made identification between Jews and blacks not only plausible—both were racially persecuted groups, with blacks more and more concentrated in northern cities alongside the immigrant Jews—but pragmatic, since by combining their efforts to counteract racism both groups could benefit. But Rogin reveals that in *The Jazz Singer* this identification serves not to benefit both groups but rather to make Jews white at the cost of reinforcing the racist stereotypes, so evident in blackface minstrelsy, that set blacks apart. See Michael Rogin, *Blackface, White Noise: Jewish Immigrants in the Hollywood Melting Pot* (Berkeley: University of California Press, 1996). I am summarizing the argument in chapter 4 of the book (73–120).

28. Steven Milowitz, *Philip Roth Considered: The Concentrationary Universe of the American Writer* (New York: Garland, 2000), ix.

29. I would speculate that this strain of Bellow criticism has been appealing in part because it works against the dismissal of Bellow as a neoconservative or, worse, as a racist. By reminding readers that Bellow is a member of a minority group that has suffered persecution and by making that fact central to the interpretation of his work, he comes to seem sympathetic to, rather than critical of, popular identity politics. This is certainly the effect of Ethan Goffman's argument.

30. Marianne Hirsch gives an excellent analysis of universalism as it functions in this exhibit in her *Family Frames,* chapter 2, "Reframing the Human Family Romance."

31. Amy Gutmann, ed., *Multiculturalism: Examining the Politics of Recognition* (Princeton, N.J.: Princeton University Press, 1994). The volume consists of a central essay on liberalism and multiculturalism by Charles Taylor, followed by short commentaries on his arguments by several scholars and longer essays by Jürgen Habermas and K. Anthony Appiah. The collection as a whole acknowledges the problem of coerciveness in the collective identities promoted by what Taylor calls "the politics of recognition" in contemporary multicultural societies, even though the contributors differ on whether that coerciveness is better or worse than a liberalism that is procedural and does not seek to promote or protect any particular identity group.

Other collections of essays that are useful in placing Bellow's and Roth's versions of identity and recruitment in the context of arguments about liberalism and multiculturalism would include Avery Gordon and Christopher Newfield, eds., *Mapping Multiculturalism* (Minneapolis: University of Minnesota Press, 1996); Stuart Hall and Paul du Gay, eds., *Questions of Cultural Identity* (London: Sage, 1996); and David Theo Goldberg, ed., *Multiculturalism: A Critical Reader* (Oxford: Blackwell, 1994). Hall's perspective on identity, multiculturalism, and their politics accords much greater importance to the psychoanalytic understanding of identification, unlike the essays in the Gutmann and Taylor volume, which presuppose that the subject within liberalism is an autonomous, conscious subject who deliberates and decides (or should be allowed to deliberate and decide) about the groups with which he or she will identify. The Gordon and Newfield volume takes a more Marxist approach, attempting to add considerations of class to the kinds of difference to which multiculturalism should attend. The last collection, which is large and contains a wide range of critical perspectives, is particularly helpful for the way many contributors take up the question of the practical politics—the national, world, and academic politics—of multiculturalism.

32. Taylor confesses that he does not know whether or not Bellow actually made this remark; James Atlas's biography has since given an account of the incident and Bellow's explanation of it (Bellow claims he was misunderstood in a telephone interview). See Taylor, "The Politics of Recognition," in *Multiculturalism*, 42; and Atlas, *Bellow*, 573–75. Atlas suggests in the context of describing this incident that Bellow, despite being cast as a neoconservative, always saw himself as a liberal and held political positions that did not accord with neoconservative ideals. As my reading here demonstrates, I think Bellow's work supports Bellow's view of himself.

33. Taylor, "Politics of Recognition," 71.

34. Susan Wolf, in her response to Taylor's essay, makes a version of this point (Comment on "The Politics of Recognition," by Charles Taylor, in *Multiculturalism*, ed. Gutmann, 79–80).

35. Butler, *Bodies That Matter*, 13.

36. I am not entirely convinced that Butler has succeeded in integrating an account of the body into performative identity in *Bodies That Matter*, even though she is directly responding to the criticism, leveled against *Gender Trouble*, that performative identity requires both a preexisting "I" who is doing the performing and a material bodily reality that (by virtue of opposition) marks gender as culturally defined. I am not convinced because I am not sure, in the end, what Butler means by the body "materializing" only through our notions of gender. The term *materializing* seems to account for the physical fact of the body, but in the end does not, since it continues to place the body as not co-created but postdated in relation to discourse, and in this sense not material in and of itself as a thing distinct from discourse. This seems important, for even if the body cannot be thought without gender discourse, it can still exist without it, and that capacity marks the body as something that cannot simply be conflated with discourse.

37. See Fuss, *Identification Papers*, especially the introduction.

38. Hall describes his effort as one of bringing together, in his discussion of identification, the Foucauldian emphasis on discourse and the psychoanalytic understanding of the subject. He thus sees a distinction between these two approaches to identification but is attempting, precisely, to integrate them into one theoretical conception. See Stuart Hall, "Who Needs 'Identity'," introduction to *Questions of Cultural Identity*, 1–17.

39. Roth invokes this same idea in his autobiography, when describing the pain of writing *My Life as a Man*, after the break-up of his first marriage. "The only experience worse than writing it," he explains, "would have been for me to have endured that marriage without afterward having been able to find ways of reimagining it into a fiction with a persuasive existence independent of myself" (*The Facts*, 152).

40. Appiah, "Identity, Authenticity, Survival," 162 ("life-scripts") and 163.

Conclusion

1. The man explained that he had a son, whom he was going to visit, who had lost his ability to enunciate, and who was depressed and wanted to die. The father, afraid he would not be able to understand his son's mouthed words, wanted to practice reading lips for the phrase he most feared his son would try to utter: the phrase "I want to die." See Greenblatt, *Renaissance Self-Fashioning: From More to Shakespeare* (Chicago: University of Chicago Press, 1980), epilogue; quotations on 255, 256.

2. See Stephen Greenblatt and Catherine Gallagher, *Practicing New Historicism* (Chicago: University of Chicago Press, 2000).

3. Lee Patterson, *Negotiating the Past: The Historical Understanding of Medieval Literature* (Madison: University of Wisconsin Press, 1987), 63, 62.

4. The preoccupation with the person and with autonomy, and moreover, with threats to the person and autonomy that Greenblatt's final anecdote reflects, characterized the work of many New Historicists. Catherine Gallagher, for example, in *Nobody's Story,* sought to recover a history of women's writing by examining authorial and fictional personas "in the act of dematerializing" (see the introduction to *Nobody's Story* [Berkeley: University of California Press, 1994], xviii). New Historicist and feminist critics began a process of recovery not only of historical material and texts by excluded categories of persons, but also of the "subjectivities" of these excluded persons as revealed in the signifying practices of various historical moments. This is perhaps best epitomized by Jonathan Goldberg's work on Renaissance sexualities in *Sodometries: Renaissance Texts, Modern Sexualities* (Stanford, Calif.: Stanford University Press, 1992).

5. Parfit, *Reasons and Persons,* 275.

6. "Public Memory and Its Discontents," chapter 7 of *The Longest Shadow;* quotation on 99. Hartman suggests that literature is an antidote to this kind of memory and to coercive versions of identity such as I have examined in these chapters. He writes that "one reason literature remains important is that it counteracts the impersonality and instability of public memory, on the one hand, and on the other the determinism and fundamentalism of a collective memory based on identity politics. Literature creates an institution of its own, more personal and focused than public memory yet less monologic than the memorializing fables common to ethnic or nationalist affirmation" (107).

7. See Earl Shorris, "The Last Word: Can the World's Small Languages Be Saved?" *Harper's* 301.1803 (August 2000): 38, 35.

8. For those unfamiliar with Rawls's "original position," see John Rawls, *A Theory of Justice,* rev. ed. (Cambridge, Mass.: Belknap Press of Harvard University Press, 1999).

Works Cited

Aciman, André. "Innocence and Experience." *New Republic* 218 (January 19, 1998): 26–28.

Agnon, Shmuel Yosef. *Twenty-one Stories*. Edited by Nahum N. Glatzer. New York: Schocken, 1970.

Alexander, Edward. "Stealing the Holocaust." *Midstream* 26.9 (1980): 47–51.

Alvarez, A. "The Literature of the Holocaust." *Commentary* 38.5 (1964): 65–66.

Appiah, K. Anthony. "Identity, Authenticity, Survival." In *Multiculturalism: Examining the Politics of Recognition*, edited by Amy Gutmann. Princeton, N.J.: Princeton University Press, 1994.

Arendt, Hannah. *Eichmann in Jerusalem: A Report on the Banality of Evil*. Rev. and enl. ed. New York: Viking, 1964.

Aron, Raymond. Introduction to *Thinking about the Unthinkable*, by Herman Kahn. New York: Horizon Press, 1962.

Atlas, James. *Bellow*. New York: Random House, 2000.

Bellow, Saul. *The Actual*. New York: Viking, 1997.

———. *The Adventures of Augie March*. New York: Viking, 1953.

———. *Herzog*. New York: Viking, 1964.

———. *It All Adds Up*. New York: Viking, 1994.

———. *Mr. Sammler's Planet*. New York: Viking, 1970. Reprint, New York: Penguin, 1996.

———. *Seize the Day*. New York: Viking, 1956.

———. *To Jerusalem and Back: A Personal Account*. New York: Viking, 1976.

———. *The Victim*. New York: Vanguard, 1947.

Berger, Alan. "Holocaust Survivors and Children in *Anya* and *Mr. Sammler's Planet*." *Modern Language Studies* 16.1 (1986): 81–87.

Bradbury, Ray. *Fahrenheit 451*. New York: Ballantine, 1953.

Braudy, Leo. *The Frenzy of Renown: Fame and Its History.* 2d ed. New York: Random House, 1997.

Breuer, Josef, and Sigmund Freud. *Studies on Hysteria.* Edited and translated by James Strachey. Originally published as vol. 2 of *Standard Edition of the Complete Psychological Works of Sigmund Freud,* ed. James Strachey. London: Hogarth Press, 1955. Reprint, New York: Basic Books, 1957.

Brown, Joshua. "Of Mice and Memory." *Oral History Review* 16 (1988): 105–8.

Budick, Emily Miller. "*Yizkor* for Six Million: Mourning the Death of Civilization in Saul Bellow's *Seize the Day.*" In *New Essays on* Seize the Day, edited by Michael P. Kramer. Cambridge: Cambridge University Press, 1998.

Butler, Judith. *Bodies That Matter.* New York: Routledge, 1993.

Carter, Forrest. *The Education of Little Tree.* New York: Delacorte, 1976.

Caruth, Cathy. *Unclaimed Experience: Trauma, Narrative, and History.* Baltimore: Johns Hopkins University Press, 1996.

Cixous, Hélène. "Castration and Decapitation." Translated by Annette Kuhn. *Signs* (1981): 41–55.

Cooper, Alan. *Philip Roth and the Jews.* Albany: State University of New York Press, 1996.

Cronin, Gloria L. "Fundamentalist Views and Feminist Dilemmas: Elizabeth Dewberry Vaughn's *Many Things Have Happened since He Died* and *Break the Heart of Me.*" In *Traditions, Voices, and Dreams: The American Novel since the 1960's,* edited by Melvin J. Friedman and Ben Siegel, 254–78. Newark, Del.: University of Delaware Press, 1995.

Culler, Jonathan. *Literary Theory: A Very Short Introduction.* Oxford: Oxford University Press, 1997.

DeLillo, Don. *Libra.* New York: Penguin, 1988.

———. *Ratner's Star.* New York: Knopf, 1976.

———. *Underworld.* New York: Scribner, 1997.

———. *White Noise.* New York: Penguin, 1984.

De Man, Paul. "Autobiography as De-Facement." In *The Rhetoric of Romanticism.* New York: Columbia University Press, 1984.

———. *Blindness and Insight: Essays in the Rhetoric of Contemporary Criticism.* Rev. 2d ed. Minneapolis: University of Minnesota Press, 1983.

———. "Excuses (Confessions)." *Allegories of Reading: Figural Language in Rousseau, Nietzsche, Rilke, and Proust.* New Haven, Conn.: Yale University Press, 1979.

———. *The Resistance to Theory.* Minneapolis: University of Minnesota Press, 1986.

———. *Wartime Journalism, 1939–1943.* Edited by Werner Hamacher, Neil Hertz, and Thomas Keenan. Lincoln: University of Nebraska Press, 1988.

Derrida, Jacques. *Demeure: Fiction and Testimony.* In *The Instant of My Death,* by Maurice Blanchot, and *Demeure: Fiction and Testimony,* by Jacques Derrida. Translated by Elizabeth Rottenberg. Stanford: Stanford University Press, 2000.

———. "No Apocalypse, Not Now (full speed ahead, seven missiles, seven missives)." *Diacritics* 14.2 (Summer 1984): 20–31.

Des Pres, Terrence. "Self/Landscape/Grid." In *Writing in a Nuclear Age,* edited by Jim Schley, 3–12. Hanover, N.H.: University Press of New England, 1984.

————. *The Survivor: An Anatomy of Life in the Death Camps*. New York: Oxford University Press, 1976.

Dittmar, Kurt. "The End of Enlightenment: Bellow's Universal View of the Holocaust in *Mr. Sammler's Planet*." In *Saul Bellow at Seventy-Five: A Collection of Critical Essays*, edited by Gerhard Bach. Tübingen: Gunter Narr Verlag, 1991.

Doherty, Thomas. "Art Spiegelman's *Maus*: Graphic Art and the Holocaust." *American Literature* 68 (1996): 69–84.

Eskin, Blake. *A Life in Pieces*. New York: Norton, 2002.

Ezrahi, Sidra. "After Such Knowledge, What Laughter?" *Yale Journal of Criticism* 14.1 (Spring 2001): 287–313.

————. *By Words Alone: The Holocaust in Literature*. Chicago: University of Chicago Press, 1980.

Farrell, Kirby. *Post-traumatic Culture: Injury and Interpretation in the Nineties*. Baltimore: Johns Hopkins University Press, 1998.

Felman, Shoshana, and Dori Laub. *Testimony: The Crisis of Witnessing in Literature, Psychoanalysis, and History*. New York: Routledge, 1992.

Freud, Sigmund. *Moses and Monotheism*. Translated by Katherine Jones. New York: Random House, 1939.

Friedlander, Saul, ed. *Probing the Limits of Representation: Nazism and the "Final Solution."* Cambridge, Mass.: Harvard University Press, 1992.

Friedman, Jerome. "Jewish Conversion, the Spanish Pure Blood Laws, and Reformation: A Revisionist View of Racial and Religious Antisemitism." *Sixteenth Century Journal* 18.1 (Spring 1987): 3–30.

Fuss, Diana. *Identification Papers*. New York: Routledge, 1995.

Gallagher, Catherine. *Nobody's Story*. Berkeley: University of California Press, 1994.

Gates, Henry Louis, Jr. " 'Authenticity,' or The Lesson of Little Tree." *New York Times Book Review*, November 24, 1991, 29.

Gerber, David. "Of Mice and Jews: Cartoons, Metaphors, and Children of Holocaust Survivors in Recent Jewish Experience: A Review Essay." *American Jewish History* 77 (1987): 159–75.

Gerson, Steven. "The New American Adam in *Augie March*." *Modern Fiction Studies* 25.1 (1979): 117–28.

Gilroy, Paul. *Against Race: Imagining Political Culture beyond the Color Line*. Cambridge, Mass.: Harvard University Press, 2000.

Godzich, Wlad. "The Domestication of Derrida." In *The Yale Critics: Deconstruction in America*, edited by Jonathan Arac, Wlad Godzich, and Wallace Martin. Minneapolis: University of Minnesota Press, 1983.

Goffman, Ethan. *Imagining Each Other: Blacks and Jews in Contemporary American Literature*. Albany: State University of New York Press, 2000.

Goldberg, David Theo, ed. *Multiculturalism: A Critical Reader*. Oxford: Blackwell, 1994.

Goldberg, Jonathan. *Sodometries: Renaissance Texts, Modern Sexualities*. Stanford, Calif.: Stanford University Press, 1992.

Goldberg, Michael. *Why Should Jews Survive? Looking Past the Holocaust toward a Jewish Future*. Oxford: Oxford University Press, 1995.

Goldman, L. H. "The Holocaust in the Novels of Saul Bellow." *Modern Language Studies* 16.1 (1986): 71–80.

———. "The Jewish Perspective of Saul Bellow." In *Saul Bellow, A Mosaic*, edited by L. H. Goldman, Gloria L. Cronin, and Ada Aharoni, 3–20. New York: Peter Lang, 1992.

———. "'Shuffling Out of My Vulgar Origins': The Masculinist-Elitist Language of Saul Bellow's Fiction." *MELUS* 16 (1989–90): 33–42.

Gordon, Avery, and Christopher Newfield, eds. *Mapping Multiculturalism*. Minneapolis: University of Minnesota Press, 1996.

Gourevitch, Philip. "The Memory Thief." *New Yorker* 75.15 (June 14, 1999): 48–62, 64–68.

Graver, Lawrence. *An Obsession with Anne Frank: Meyer Levin and the Diary*. Berkeley: University of California Press, 1995.

Greenblatt, Stephen. *Renaissance Self-Fashioning: From More to Shakespeare*. Chicago: University of Chicago Press, 1980.

Greenblatt, Stephen, and Catherine Gallagher, *Practicing New Historicism*. Chicago: University of Chicago Press, 2000.

Guthman, Edward. "Spielberg's 'List': Director Rediscovers His Jewishness While Filming Nazi Story." In *Oskar Schindler and His List: The Man, the Book, the Film, the Holocaust and Its Survivors*, edited by Thomas Fensch, 50–55. Forest Dale, Vt.: Paul S. Eriksson, 1995.

Gutmann, Amy, ed. *Multiculturalism: Examining the Politics of Recognition*. Princeton, N.J.: Princeton University Press, 1994.

Hall, Stuart. "Who Needs 'Identity'?" Introduction to *Questions of Cultural Identity*, edited by Stuart Hall and Paul du Gay, 1–17. London: Sage, 1996.

Hall, Stuart, and Paul du Gay, eds. *Questions of Cultural Identity*. London: Sage, 1996.

Hamacher, Werner, Neil Hertz, and Thomas Keenan, eds. *Responses: On Paul de Man's Wartime Journalism*. Lincoln: University of Nebraska Press, 1989.

Hammer, Langdon. "Plath's Lives: Poetry, Professionalism, and the Culture of the School." *Representations* 75 (Summer 2001): 61–88.

Hanks, Robert. "Where Naughty Children Get Murdered." Review of *Fragments*, by Binjamin Wilkomirski. *Independent* (London), December 8, 1996, 31.

Hartman, Geoffrey. *The Longest Shadow: In the Aftermath of the Holocaust*. Bloomington: Indiana University Press, 1996.

Hertzberg, Arthur. *The Jews in America: Four Centuries of an Uneasy Encounter*. New York: Simon & Schuster, 1989.

Hirsch, David H. "Jewish Identity and Jewish Suffering in Bellow, Malamud, and Philip Roth." *Saul Bellow Journal* 8.2 (1989): 47–58.

Hirsch, Marianne. *Family Frames: Photography, Narrative, and Postmemory*. Cambridge, Mass.: Harvard University Press, 1997.

Holbrook, David. *Sylvia Plath: Poetry and Existence*. London: Athlone, 1976.

Horowitz, Sara. *Voicing the Void: Muteness and Memory in Holocaust Fiction*. Albany: State University of New York Press, 1997.

Hungerford, Amy. "Fatal Poetry and the Poetry of Fate." *Boulevard* (Fall 1998): 94–100.

Jurca, Catherine. *White Diaspora: The Suburb and the Twentieth-Century American Novel.* Princeton, N.J.: Princeton University Press, 2001.

Kahn, Herman. *Thinking about the Unthinkable.* New York: Horizon, 1962.

Kingsolver, Barbara. *Pigs in Heaven.* New York: HarperCollins, 1993.

Knapp, Steven. *Literary Interest: The Limits of Anti-formalism.* Cambridge, Mass.: Harvard University Press, 1993.

———. *Personification and the Sublime: Milton to Coleridge.* Cambridge, Mass.: Harvard University Press, 1985.

Kramer, Larry. *Reports from the Holocaust: The Story of an AIDS Activist.* New York: St. Martin's, 1994.

Kramer, Michael P. "The Vanishing Jew: On Teaching Bellow's *Seize the Day* as Ethnic Fiction." In *New Essays on* Seize the Day, edited by Michael P. Kramer. Cambridge: Cambridge University Press, 1998.

Kremer, S. Lillian. *Witness through the Imagination: Jewish American Holocaust Literature.* Detroit: Wayne State University Press, 1989.

Kristeva, Julia. *The Kristeva Reader.* Edited by Toril Moi. New York: Columbia University Press, 1986.

LaCapra, Dominick. "The Personal, the Political, and the Textual: Paul de Man as Object of Transference." *History and Memory* 4.1 (Spring/Summer 1992): 5–38.

———. *Representing the Holocaust: History, Theory, Trauma.* Ithaca, N.Y.: Cornell University Press, 1994.

Lang, Berel. *Act and Idea in the Nazi Genocide.* Chicago: University of Chicago Press, 1990.

———. "The Representation of Limits." In *Probing the Limits of Representation: Nazism and the "Final Solution,"* edited by Saul Friedlander, 300–317. Cambridge, Mass.: Harvard University Press, 1992.

Langer, Lawrence. *The Holocaust and the Literary Imagination.* New Haven, Conn.: Yale University Press, 1975.

LaPlanche, J., and J.-B. Pontalis. *The Language of Psycho-analysis.* Translated by Donald Nicholson-Smith. London: Hogarth, 1973. Reprint, New York: Norton, 1974.

Lappin, Elena. "The Man with Two Heads." *Granta* 66 (Summer 1999): 7–65.

LeBlanc, Lawrence J. *The United States and the Genocide Convention.* Durham, N.C.: Duke University Press, 1991.

Levi, Primo. *Survival in Auschwitz.* Translated by Stuart Woolf. New York: Macmillan, 1961.

Levin, Meyer. *The Obsession.* New York: Simon & Schuster, 1973.

Leys, Ruth. *Trauma: A Genealogy.* Chicago: University of Chicago Press, 2000.

Liebman, Charles S. "Jewish Survival, Antisemitism, and Negotiation with the Tradition." In *The Americanization of the Jews,* edited by Robert M. Seltzer and Norman J. Cohen. New York: New York University Press, 1995.

Lifton, Robert Jay, and Eric Markusen. *The Genocidal Mentality: Nazi Holocaust and Nuclear Threat.* New York: Basic Books, 1990.

Linenthal, Edward T. "The Boundaries of Memory: The United States Holocaust Memorial Museum." *American Quarterly* 46 (1994): 406–33.

———. *Preserving Memory: The Struggle to Create America's Holocaust Museum.* New York: Viking, 1995.

Mailer, Norman. *The White Negro.* San Francisco: City Lights, 1957.

Melnick, Ralph. *The Stolen Legacy of Anne Frank: Meyer Levin, Lillian Hellman, and the Staging of the Diary.* New Haven, Conn.: Yale University Press, 1997.

Michaels, Walter Benn. "Autobiography of an Ex-White Man: Why Race Is Not a Social Construction." *Transition* 7.1 (Fall 1998): 122–43.

———. *Our America: Nativism, Modernism, and Pluralism.* Durham, N.C.: Duke University Press, 1995.

———. "'You Who Never Was There': Slavery and the New Historicism, Deconstruction and the Holocaust." *Narrative* 4.1 (January 1996): 1–16.

Michaels, Walter Benn, and Stephen Knapp. "Against Theory." In *Against Theory,* edited by W. J. T. Mitchell. Chicago: University of Chicago Press, 1985.

Miller, J. Hillis. "Narrative." In *Critical Terms for Literary Study,* edited by Frank Lentricchia and Thomas McLaughlin, 66–79. Chicago: University of Chicago Press, 1990.

———. *Versions of Pygmalion.* Cambridge, Mass.: Harvard University Press, 1990.

Miller, Mark Crispin. *Boxed In.* Evanston, Ill.: Northwestern University Press, 1988.

Miller, Walter M., Jr. *A Canticle for Leibowitz.* Philadelphia: Lippincott, 1960. New York: Bantam, 1987.

Milowitz, Steven. *Philip Roth Considered: The Concentrationary Universe of the American Writer.* New York: Garland, 2000.

Milton, John. "Areopagitica." In *Complete Poems and Major Prose.* Edited by Merritt Y. Hughes. New York, Macmillan, 1957.

Moi, Toril. *Sexual/Textual Politics.* New York: Methuen, 1985.

Morrison, Toni. *Playing in the Dark: Whiteness and the Literary Imagination.* New York: Vintage, 1992.

Nagel, Thomas. *Mortal Questions.* Cambridge: Cambridge University Press, 1979.

Novick, Peter. *The Holocaust in American Life.* Boston: Houghton Mifflin, 1999.

Orvell, Miles. *After the Machine: Visual Arts and the Erasing of Cultural Boundaries.* Jackson: University Press of Mississippi, 1995.

Parfit, Derek. *Reasons and Persons.* Corrected ed. Oxford: Clarendon, 1987.

Patterson, Lee. "Literary History." In *Critical Terms for Literary Study.* 2d ed. Edited by Frank Lentricchia and Thomas McLaughlin, 250–62. Chicago: University of Chicago Press, 1995.

———. *Negotiating the Past: The Historical Understanding of Medieval Literature.* Madison: University of Wisconsin Press, 1987.

Peskin, Harvey. "Holocaust Denial: A Sequel." *Nation* 268.14 (April 19, 1999): 34–38.

Plath, Sylvia. *Collected Poems.* Edited by Ted Hughes. New York: Harper Perennial, 1992.

———. *The Journals of Sylvia Plath.* Edited by Ted Hughes and Frances McCullough. New York: Ballantine, 1982.

———. *The Journals of Sylvia Plath, 1950–1962.* Edited by Karen V. Kukil. London: Faber & Faber, 2000.

———. *Sylvia Plath's Letters Home.* Edited by Aurelia Plath. New York: Harper & Row, 1975.

Ramazani, Jahan. *Poetry of Mourning: The Modern Elegy from Hardy to Heaney.* Chicago: University of Chicago Press, 1994.

Rawls, John. *A Theory of Justice.* Rev. ed. Cambridge, Mass.: Belknap Press of Harvard University Press, 1999.

Ritterband, Paul. "Modern Times and Jewish Assimilation." In *The Americanization of the Jews,* edited by Robert M. Seltzer and Norman J. Cohen. New York: New York University Press, 1995.

Rogin, Michael. *Blackface, White Noise: Jewish Immigrants in the Hollywood Melting Pot.* Berkeley: University of California Press, 1996.

Rose, Jacqueline. *The Haunting of Sylvia Plath.* Cambridge, Mass.: Harvard University Press, 1991.

Rosenfeld, Alvin. *A Double Dying: Reflections on Holocaust Literature.* Bloomington: Indiana University Press, 1980.

Roth, Philip. *The Facts: A Novelist's Autobiography.* New York: Farrar, Straus & Giroux, 1988.

———. *The Ghost Writer.* New York: Farrar, Straus & Giroux, 1979. Reprint, New York: Vintage, 1995.

———. *Goodbye, Columbus and Five Short Stories.* Boston: Houghton Mifflin, 1959. Reprint, New York: Vintage, 1993.

———. *The Human Stain.* Boston: Houghton Mifflin, 2000.

———. *Operation Shylock.* New York: Simon & Schuster, 1993.

———. *Portnoy's Complaint.* New York: Random House, 1969. Reprint, New York: Vintage, 1994.

Rothberg, Michael. *Traumatic Realism: The Demands of Holocaust Representation.* Minneapolis: University of Minnesota Press, 2000.

Schell, Jonathan. *The Fate of the Earth.* New York: Knopf, 1982.

Shorris, Earl. "The Last Word: Can the World's Small Languages Be Saved?" *Harper's* 301.1803 (August 2000): 35–43.

Siegel, Ben. "Simply Not a Mandarin: Saul Bellow as Jew and Jewish Writer." In *Traditions, Voices, and Dreams: The American Novel since the 1960's,* edited by Melvin J. Friedman and Ben Siegel, 62–88. Newark, Del.: University of Delaware Press, 1995.

Singer, Peter. *Practical Ethics.* 2d ed. Cambridge: Cambridge University Press, 1993.

Spiegelman, Art. *Maus: A Survivor's Tale. Part 1: My Father Bleeds History.* New York: Pantheon, 1986.

———. *Maus: A Survivor's Tale. Part 2: And Here My Troubles Began.* New York: Pantheon, 1991.

———. "Mein Kampf, My Struggle." *New York Times Magazine,* May 11, 1996, 36–37.

———. *Open Me . . . I'm a Dog!* New York: HarperCollins, 1997.

———. "A Problem of Taxonomy." *New York Times Book Review,* December 29, 1991, 4.

Spielberg, Steven, director. *Schindler's List.* Universal Pictures, 1993.

Spitzer, Alan B. *Historical Truth and Lies about the Past: Reflections on Dewey, Dreyfus, de Man, and Reagan.* Chapel Hill: University of North Carolina Press, 1996.

Staub, Michael. "The Shoah Goes On and On: Remembrance and Representation in Art Spiegelman's *Maus.*" *MELUS* 20.3 (1995): 32–46.

Steiner, George. "In Extremis." *Cambridge Review* 90.2187 (1969): 247–49.

―――. "Dying Is an Art." In *Language and Silence: Essays on Language, Literature, and the Inhuman*. New York: Atheneum, 1967.

Steiner, Wendy. "Postmodern Fictions, 1960–1990." In *Prose Writing 1940–1990*, vol. 7 of *The Cambridge History of American Literature*, edited by Sacvan Bercovitch. Cambridge: Cambridge University Press, 1999.

Strangeways, Al. " 'The Boot in the Face': The Problem of the Holocaust in the Poetry of Sylvia Plath." *Contemporary Literature* 37 (1996): 370–90.

Tal, Kalí. *Worlds of Hurt: Reading the Literatures of Trauma*. Cambridge: Cambridge University Press, 1996.

Taylor, Charles. "The Politics of Recognition." In *Multiculturalism: Examining the Politics of Recognition*, edited by Amy Gutmann. Princeton, N.J.: Princeton University Press, 1994.

Van Dyne, Susan R. *Revising Life: Sylvia Plath's Ariel Poems*. Chapel Hill: University of North Carolina Press, 1993.

Vidal-Naquet, Pierre. *Assassins of Memory: Essays on the Denial of the Holocaust*. Translated by Jeffrey Mehlman. New York: Columbia University Press, 1992.

Wardi, Dina. *Memorial Candles: Children of the Holocaust*. Translated by Naomi Goldblum. New York: Routledge, 1992.

Weinberg, Jeshajahu, and Rina Elieli. *The Holocaust Museum in Washington*. New York: Rizzoli, 1995.

Wilkomirski, Binjamin. *Fragments: Memories of a Wartime Childhood*. Translated by Carol Brown Janeway. New York: Schocken, 1996.

Wimsatt, W. K., and Monroe C. Beardsley. "The Intentional Fallacy." In *The Verbal Icon*, by W. K. Wimsatt. Lexington: University Press of Kentucky, 1954.

Wirth-Nesher, Hana. " 'Who's He When He's at Home?': Saul Bellow's Translations." In *New Essays on* Seize the Day, edited by Michael P. Kramer. Cambridge: Cambridge University Press, 1998.

Witek, Joseph. *Comic Books as History: The Narrative Art of Jack Jackson, Art Spiegelman, and Harvey Pekar*. Jackson: University Press of Mississippi, 1989.

Wolf, Susan. Comment on "The Politics of Recognition," by Charles Taylor. In *Multiculturalism: Examining the Politics of Recognition*, edited by Amy Gutmann. Princeton, N.J.: Princeton University Press, 1994.

Young, James E. *At Memory's Edge: After-Images of the Holocaust in Contemporary Art and Architecture*. New Haven, Conn.: Yale University Press, 2000.

―――. *Writing and Rewriting the Holocaust: Narrative and the Consequences of Interpretation*. Bloomington: Indiana University Press, 1988.

Zemach, Eddy M. "Custodians." In *Jewish Identity*, edited by David Theo Goldberg and Michael Krausz, 119–29. Philadelphia: Temple University Press, 1993.

Index